ENGLISH NOBLEWOMEN IN THE
LATER MIDDLE AGES

THE MEDIEVAL WORLD

Editor: David Bates

Already published

CHARLES THE BALD

Janet L. Nelson

WILLIAM MARSHAL: COURT, CAREER AND CHIVALRY IN
THE ANGEVIN EMPIRE 1147–1219

David Crouch

ENGLISH NOBLEWOMEN IN THE LATER MIDDLE AGES

Jennifer C. Ward

ENGLISH NOBLEWOMEN IN THE LATER MIDDLE AGES

Jennifer C. Ward

LONGMAN
London and New York

Longman Group UK Limited
Longman House, Burnt Mill,
Harlow, Essex CM20 2JE, England
and Associated Companies throughout the world.

Published in the United States of America
by Longman Publishing, New York

First published 1992

ISBN 0 582 05966 6 CSD
ISBN 0 582 05965 8 PPR

British Library Cataloguing in Publication Data
A catalogue record for this book is
available from the British Library

Library of Congress Cataloguing in Publication Data
Ward, Jennifer C.
English noblewomen in the later Middle Ages / Jennifer C. Ward.
p.   cm. – (The Medieval world)
Includes bibliographical references and index.
ISBN 0–582–05966–6 (CSD) – ISBN 0–582–05965–8 (PPR)
1. Women – England – Social conditions.   2. Nobility – England–
–History.   3. England – Social conditions – Medieval period,
1066–1485.   I. Title.   II. Series.
HQ1599.E5W37   1992
305.48'9621 – dc20   91–46369
CIP

SET IN 10.5/12 Baskerville by 9
Produced by Longman Singapore Publishers (Pte) Ltd.
Printed in Singapore

CONTENTS

LIST OF TABLES

EDITOR'S PREFACE

Our understanding of women's place in medieval society has developed enormously during the last few years, and, in this book, Dr Jennifer Ward makes a further significant contribution. Women emerge from this study as powerful figures within English aristocratic society, able to exert influence not just because of their personalities, but because there were many areas in which society expected them to be active and to exercise power of various kinds. Although English society in the later Middle Ages was unquestionably a male-dominated one, the role of women was crucial in a multitude of ways, all of which Dr Ward explores thoroughly and concisely.

Jennifer Ward's extensive personal researches are deployed to great effect in this book; in particular, her work on the life of Elizabeth de Burgh, for which the unusually extensive records frequently illuminate many central themes. Her own work is expanded by copious references to the accumulated results of others' research. The book's strength is in its wide-ranging treatment of the practicalities of the woman's place in late medieval English society. It begins with the key subject of marriage, which is seen as a crucial mechanism in the formation of alliances between families and as a means to social advancement. Although women rarely chose their partners, affection and loyalty clearly played a significant part in marriages. In the same way, the apparently impersonal process of medieval child-rearing is shown as one in which strong bonds were formed, which were often the basis of long-lasting relationships between mothers and their sons and daughters. The chapters which deal with the household, estate management and patronage show women to have been deeply involved in the business side of medieval life as a matter of course, and to have acted very effectively and efficiently. Their efforts often had to complement those of their husbands and, on occasion, replace them. Dr Ward covers a remarkably diverse set of subjects in a short space and the reader will eventually find himself or herself well informed on matters such as dress, education, tombs, widowhood and religious patronage. She also places women's efforts carefully within a wider social context, and the book is therefore a valuable contribution to discussion of late medieval politics, estate management, the family, and the Church. This third volume in the Medieval World series carries out splendidly the series' aim of combining scholarship with an accessible approach to a subject of central importance.

David Bates

PREFACE

This book has developed out of the growing interest in women's history, and aims to provide a synthesis on English noblewomen in the later Middle Ages, between *c.*1250 and *c.*1450. The term noblewoman has been taken in a broad sense to cover the daughters, wives and widows of the higher and lesser nobility and of the knights and gentry. In spite of the growing stratification of the nobility in the later Middle Ages, their ambitions and aspirations remained broadly similar; all hoped and worked for greater estates and aimed at a noble lifestyle. In an age when land was the key to social position noblewomen had an important place in society. As heiresses they transmitted estates to their husbands' families, and as wives and more especially as widows they defended their inheritances and exercised local power through their households and their patronage, showing an ability to attract and retain their affinities. In their management of their estates and in their religious patronage they complemented the work of their husbands and families.

In the course of the text imperial measurements have been used, and towns and villages placed in the counties to which they belonged before the local government changes of 1974. Sums of money are given in the old form, as used before decimalisation. One pound consisted of twenty shillngs and each shilling of twelve pence; the penny was divided into two halfpennies or four farthings. The mark, a unit of account, was worth thirteen shillings and four pence.

While working on the book I have incurred a number of debts, and I would like especially to thank David Bates, the general editor of the series, and the Academic Department at Longmans for their help, suggestions and corrections. Any remaining mistakes are mine. I would also like to thank the friends and colleagues with whom I have discussed parts of the book and who have accompanied me to many of the sites associated with medieval noblewomen.

Goldsmiths' College, London
November 1991

IN MEMORY OF MY PARENTS

. . . . .

INTRODUCTION

The English noblewoman of the later Middle Ages, living in the period between the mid-thirteenth and mid-fifteenth century, is more elusive than her male counterpart. The sources have far less to say about her than about her father, husband, sons and brothers. Until recently historians have paid most attention to the heiress who brought lands and sometimes titles to her husband's family, and to the dowager who through her longevity might permanently damage her son's prospects through diminishing his wealth. With the growth of interest in women's history, it has been increasingly realised that this approach has led to overmuch reliance being placed on certain types of evidence and therefore a failure to appreciate all the roles which a noblewoman could play in late medieval society, both within the family and outside it.

Noblewomen undoubtedly derived their status from their fathers and husbands, and enjoyed a position at the top of the social hierarchy. There was, however, considerable variety within the nobility as to lands and wealth. At the top of the scale were to be found younger sons and daughters of the king, at the bottom members of the gentry whose importance was confined to their own locality. This range within the nobility is to be found throughout the later Middle Ages, but at the same time there is no doubt that the nobility was becoming more rigidly hierarchical. In the mid-thirteenth century the title of earl was the only one to distinguish the greatest nobles from the rest; by 1450 the use of the titles of duke and marquis increased this differentiation, and the failure of male heirs and the transfer of inheritances through marriage had concentrated power in the hands of relatively few nobles. The establishment of the parliamentary peerage in the fourteenth century also heightened the

I

exclusiveness of the leading nobility. Further down the noble scale, the sense of hierarchy was emphasised by the use of the terms of knight and esquire and also by the emergence of the term gentleman by the end of the fourteenth century. Although the hierarchy was increasingly defined, the nobility was by no means a closed caste, and there were plenty of opportunities for movement within it, and for new families to gain noble status.

In spite of the differences of title, wealth and influence, certain common factors stand out. The English nobility derived its wealth primarily from land, over which it exercised varying degrees and kinds of lordship. The bonds of knighthood and chivalry gave the nobility a common outlook and lifestyle, an interest in warfare and tournaments, and a love of splendour and display. All nobles faced common problems in the administration of their lands and the enhancement of their incomes, whether it was a matter of running a small group of manors, or a vast inheritance. All exercised political and judicial power to a greater or lesser degree, whether in the king's council, in parliament, or in the county. They shared common religious beliefs, and were ultimately concerned with the fate of their souls.

Both contemporaries and later historians have had far more to say about lords, knights and gentry than about their mothers, sisters, wives and daughters. This is partly due to the emphasis put on war, politics and government in which men played the dominant roles. The Church's teaching about women, particularly with reference to Eve, the expulsion from the Garden of Eden, and the Fall of mankind, stressed their inferiority and subordination. This emphasis was reflected in late medieval law which probably had the greatest influence on contemporary and later attitudes to women. The law allowed women to hold and inherit land, and they were responsible for the services due from the land some of which would be performed by a deputy. According to feudal custom a father's inheritance was divided equally among his daughters in the event of there being no sons, and such a partition of a noble estate affected many of the greatest families in the later Middle Ages. However, women did not have independent standing in the eyes of the law unless they were widowed. The law made the father responsible for both his sons and daughters while they were children, but once the son was of age the father's responsibility for him ceased. His responsibility for his daughter passed to her husband, and the married woman was unable on her own to bring litigation or plead in the courts. Once she was widowed and termed a *femme sole* she was allowed this right, but it would again cease if she remarried.

The law's emphasis on the subordination of women for much of their lives must have limited their freedom of action to some extent. Yet when the sources are assessed and examined, there proves to be a wide range of evidence to show that noblewomen could and did play a vital role in late medieval society. Late medieval chroniclers were primarily interested in action and great events, whether in England or abroad, and this means that their references to noblewomen tend to be few and far between. On the whole the top noblewomen get more mention than the wives or widows of knights or gentry. Although there are occasional signs of misogyny, there is no reason to suppose that the chroniclers were deliberately biased against women; many noblemen were only referred to occasionally, if at all. The chroniclers reflected what was regarded as important at the time. In his obituary on Roger Damory in 1322, the author of the *Vita Edwardi Secundi* described him as a poor knight who had risen high in the king's favour, been married to the king's niece and received her share of the earldom of Gloucester; however he had rebelled against the king and was considered by many as lacking in gratitude. There was no reason to say more about the king's niece, Elizabeth de Burgh, who proved to be one of the most formidable dowagers of the fourteenth century.[1]

Occasionally, a particular episode is treated in detail, and violence, scandal and gossip may well be involved. Several of the chroniclers of Edward II's reign gave an account of the abduction of the countess of Lancaster by John, earl Warenne in 1317, an event which had political rather than personal undertones. *The Westminster Chronicle* referred to the shotgun marriage of John of Gaunt's daughter Elizabeth to John Holland, Richard II's half-brother, and commented with disapproval on Robert de Vere's divorce of the king's cousin, Philippa de Coucy, and remarriage to one of the queen's chamber women, Agnes Lancecron.[2] Very occasionally, noblewomen's political involvements were mentioned, as when early in Henry IV's reign Robert de Vere's

1 *Vita Edwardi Secundi* ed. N. Denholm-Young London 1957 123.

2 *The Westminster Chronicle, 1381–94* eds. L.C. Hector and B.F. Harvey Oxford 1982 188–90, 192–4.

mother, the countess of Oxford, spread the report through Essex that Richard II was alive.[3]

It was, however, far more usual for references to noblewomen to be given in the context of their families, and for details to be given principally of marriages but also to a lesser degree of births and deaths. Where the chronicle was being kept in a monastery under the patronage of a noble family more information was given, partly because it was available and partly to enhance the prestige of the house; the annals kept at Tewkesbury Abbey give detailed information as to the family of Richard de Clare, earl of Gloucester (d.1262).[4] Similarly, a chronicler working in the same locality as the great family was likely to be well informed on the family's affairs. *The Chronicle of Bury St Edmunds* entered many of the marriages and deaths of the top nobility in the later thirteenth century, but proved particularly well-informed on the second marriage of Edward I's daughter Joan of Acre. Joan's first husband was Gilbert de Clare, earl of Gloucester, who had extensive estates in Suffolk and one of whose main centres lay at Clare, and it is likely that the chronicler used local information in his detailed coverage of Joan's second marriage to Ralph de Monthermer, which took place in secret and aroused the anger of the king.[5] Chroniclers with knowledge of what was going on in London and at the royal court were also in a position to provide extra detail and comment. In writing of Piers Gaveston's marriage to Margaret de Clare, the daughter of Gilbert and Joan, the author of the *Vita Edwardi Secundi* pointed out that it strengthened his position by increasing the support of his friends and restraining the barons' dislike of him.[6]

It was very rare for any chronicler to describe character and personality, whether of men or women, except in very general terms. Adam of Usk's description of Joan Beauchamp, lady of Abergavenny, as a second Jezebel is highly unusual and was related to her order for three thieves to be hanged on the feast of

3 *Thomae Walsingham quondam monachi Sancti Albani Historia Anglicana* ed. H.T. Riley (2 vols) London 1863–4 II 262. *The Chronicle of England by John Capgrave* ed. F.C. Hingeston London 1858 285–6.

4 *Annales de Theokesberia* in *Annales Monastici* ed. H.R. Luard (5 vols) London 1864–9 *passim*.

5 *The Chronicle of Bury St Edmunds, 1212–1301* ed. A. Gransden London 1964 134.

6 *Vita Edwardi Secundi* 2.

the Ascension.[7] Where some description is given by the chronicler there is little sign of individuality. 'The history of the foundation and founders of the abbey of Wigmore', in *Monasticon Anglicanum*, gives a detailed account of the Mortimer family, especially of the exploits of its male members, and reference is made to marriage alliances and to the birth of children. The personal descriptions come over as standardised models. In writing of Philippa, the wife of Edmund, earl of March (d.1381), the writer selected what he regarded as the important things about her from the viewpoint of the Mortimer family and the abbey. He therefore stressed her relationship with the royal family; she was the daughter of Lionel, duke of Clarence and the granddaughter of Edward III and thus provided the Mortimers with a claim to the throne. She was a great heiress, bringing the Mortimers estates in England, Wales and Ireland. Although her father had been buried at Clare priory, Philippa herself was buried at Wigmore. Last, but by no means least, she was the mother of a son and heir to the earldom.[8]

Chronicles throw valuable light on particular families and give the impression that women's main importance was in connection with marriage, children and inheritance. When the chronicles are compared with the royal and legal records, the emphasis is still seen to rest on the family, but the importance of land and lordship is substantiated, and it is possible to obtain more information on the lower ranks of the nobility. Marriage contracts, claims to inheritances and property settlements all emphasise the link between the noblewoman and land, a link which was vital because of the way in which land conferred power in the later Middle Ages. The transfer of land between families as a result of the marriage of heiresses resulted in accumulations of power in the hands of the existing nobility and in the rise of new families to wealth and influence. All this material portrays the noblewoman as she was seen in the eyes of the law, and a clear distinction was drawn between the daughter, the wife and the widow.

The marriage contract was drawn up between the respective fathers or guardians, and provided for the marriage between their children, the money or land to be handed over by the

7 *Chronicon Adae de Usk, 1377–1421* ed. E.M. Thompson London 1904 63, 228.

8 Sir William Dugdale *Monasticon Anglicanum* eds. J. Caley H. Ellis and B. Bandinel (6 vols) London 1817–30 VI part 1 353.

bride's father, and the land to be settled on the couple by the father of the bridegroom. When claims to an inheritance were brought after the marriage, it was the husband who officially prosecuted the case, although there are instances of wives taking an active part in the proceedings. Daughters and wives were not seen as having an independent existence in the eyes of the law; their fathers or husbands acted for them. However, once a noblewoman was widowed, she was herself responsible for her lands until she remarried, and many outstanding late medieval noblewomen chose to remain widows. Many women outlived their husbands, and widows therefore constituted an influential social group.

Assignments and quarrels over dower, as described in the records of chancery and the royal courts, make clear how important widowed landowners could be, both in relation to their own families and the local and national community. This impression is reinforced by the private estate material which has survived, the accounts, valors and court rolls of widows' estates. Some of these women were not only rich but remarkably long-lived. Elizabeth de Burgh, the youngest daughter of Earl Gilbert de Clare and Joan of Acre, and born in 1295, inherited in 1317 one-third of the Clare lands, worth about £2,000 a year, and also held lands settled jointly on her and her first and third husbands, and dower from her second husband. She lived as a widow from 1322 until her death in 1360, and both royal and private records show her energetically pursuing her rights. Even longer-lived was Margaret de Brotherton, born about 1320, who was married first to John, Lord Segrave and subsequently to Walter, Lord Mauny, but who chose to live as a widow from 1372 until she died in 1399. She eventually held the whole inheritance of her father Thomas de Brotherton, earl of Norfolk, and also the Segrave lands which had mostly been settled jointly on her and her first husband. Again the records show her as an active landowner, and with an income of £3,000 a year she could sustain the title of duchess of Norfolk which was conferred on her by Richard II in 1397.

The impression given by documents emanating from the royal government and the royal courts and material relating directly to the estates is that noblewomen, especially widows, played a more active and multi-faceted role than the chroniclers suggest. This impression is reinforced by the evidence from household accounts, a term which covers a wide variety of documents, although all relate in differing ways to the running of the household. They survive from the early thirteenth century and their value to the historian depends on the purpose for which they were drawn up and the concern for detail of the individual clerk. Accounts were drawn up on a yearly as well as a daily basis, the yearly accounts giving details of provisioning the household for the full financial year from Michaelmas to Michaelmas (29 September), and the daily ones giving details of consumption day by day. These can sometimes be checked against counter-rolls, which contained on one side daily and weekly totals of expenditure and on the other a shortened version of the annual account. Individual departments of the household produced their own accounts for incorporation in the yearly roll, particular members of the household, such as the children, were accounted for separately, and separate accounting is also found for journeys. Livery rolls can also be found among the household accounts, and these are invaluable for reconstructing the noble-woman's affinity. Occasionally the accounts include details of personal expenditure, whether on almsgiving, purchases of clothes and jewels, or building activities.

Taken altogether, the household accounts provide consider-able detail on the life of noblewomen in the later Middle Ages, especially on their style of living, social contacts and place within the community. They have certain drawbacks. Sometimes the whole system of accounting proved too elaborate for the clerks, and entries were left blank and totals not entered. The accounts give too rigid an impression of departmentalisation within the household. As far as provisioning was concerned, it cannot be assumed that the account is complete, as garden supplies were not included, and sometimes the same applies to items which did not have to be purchased. Clerical error can only be checked where a large number of accounts survive for the same year. In spite of these problems, however, without household accounts far less would be known about noblewomen.

One point made abundantly clear by the accounts is that it was not only the widow who had an active role to play in society. Among the wealthier members of the nobility the wife had her own household and catered for her own needs during her husband's absences. Eleanor de Montfort was running her household mainly on her own during the spring and summer of 1265.[9] Elizabeth,

9 *Manners and household expenses of England in the thirteenth and fifteenth centuries* ed. T.H. Turner London 1841 1–79.

countess of Hereford and daughter of Edward I, was living with her own household while her husband was fighting in Scotland. Elizabeth Berkeley, the wife of Richard Beauchamp, earl of Warwick, was responsible for her household and lands while her husband was engaged in Henry v's French campaigns. In the case of Anne, duchess of Buckingham in the mid-fifteenth century, the household was being run in her name and supervised by her after she had made her second marriage to Lord Mountjoy.[10]

Most of the other household accounts which survive were drawn up for widows, and the households range from the widows of knights to those of women of the highest standing. Katherine de Norwich, whose roll of household expenses survives for 1336–7, was the widow of Sir Walter de Norwich, chief baron of the exchequer and acting treasurer at various times under Edward II. Alice de Bryene's household book for 1412–13 has been published; she was the widow of Sir Guy de Bryene (d.1386), son of one of Edward III's captains in the Hundred Years War.[11] The largest collection of noblewomen's accounts to survive is from the household of Elizabeth de Burgh, dating from the end of Edward II's reign until her death in 1360.

These sources give plenty of information on life and activities, but the historian also wants to know about the noblewoman's own attitudes. Two sources throw some light on these, namely wills and letters, but both have to be used carefully, as they were usually dictated, and it is impossible to know whether the clerk altered or embellished what the woman wanted to say. Although many noblewomen could read in the later Middle Ages, it was less usual for them to be able to write, and in any case it was rare for wills to be drawn up until the testator was on her deathbed. It is, however, possible to gain an insight into attitudes by treating collections of wills and letters comparatively. The analysis of different types of bequest in a number of wills shows where the testator's main interests lay, whether in religion, in her family, in her household, or elsewhere. With reference to the letters of a particular correspondent, it is likely that the woman's

10 PRO E101/365/20; 366/30. C.D. Ross, 'The household accounts of Elizabeth Berkeley, countess of Warwick, 1420–1' *Transactions of the Bristol and Gloucestershire Archaeological Society* LXX (1951) 81–105. BL Additional MS 34213; Egerton Roll 2210.

11 BL Additional Roll, 63207. *Household Book of Dame Alice de Bryene, 1412–13* ed. V.B. Redstone trans. M.K. Dale Ipswich 1931.

real views were being expressed if the tone and subject-matter were consistent in a number of letters penned by different clerks.

The wills of a wide range of noblewomen survive for the fourteenth and fifteenth centuries. Most are the wills of widows, as a wife who predeceased her husband needed his consent before she could make a will. It is unusual to find references to land in the wills, as the succession to the estates was covered by the law of inheritance and by the terms of existing entails and settlements over jointure. The wills were mainly concerned with religious provision for the salvation of souls, and with families, servants and friends. They thus provided ample information on religious beliefs and practice and on personal relationships, and through the bequests throw considerable light on personal possessions, such as clothing, jewels, furnishings, plate and books.

The letters surviving for the thirteenth and fourteenth centuries are sparse, although Elizabeth de Burgh's household accounts show that numerous letters were received and dispatched. It was not until the fifteenth century, with the survival of such collections as the Stonor and Paston correspondence, that an impression of women's interests and activities can be gained from their letters. The letters, like the wills, give an insight into the nature of family and other relationships which cannot be gleaned from other sources. The letters also show the important role played by women on their estates during their husbands' absences and after they were widowed, and throw light on personal possessions and taste.

Noblewomen enjoyed the romantic literature of the later Middle Ages, which reflected the fantasy rather than the actuality of noble life. One work of literature stands out as concentrating on women's role in society, Christine de Pisan's *Treasure of the city of ladies or the book of the three virtues*, and this reinforces the evidence of the documentary sources.[12] Christine was highly unusual in being a prolific woman writer, an occupation which she took up after she was widowed in order to support her family. She was patronised by the French court, and *The book of the three virtues* was written in Paris in 1405. What she had to say was as applicable in England as it was in France. Christine

12 The work has been published in translation. Christine de Pisan *The treasure of the city of ladies or the book of the three virtues* trans. S. Lawson Harmondsworth 1985.

accepted the social hierarchy and values of her own time as the guarantee of stability, and she realised that women, especially widows, could suffer from insecurity and needed to safeguard their reputations and have the support of husbands and families. At the same time she stressed women's abilities and the serious role they had to play in society. The book discussed women in all social groups but much of it is concerned with princesses and great ladies, and Christine brought out the varied responsibilities they exercised in practice. Some of these functions were laid down by the religious teaching of the time; emphasis was placed on the noblewoman's love of God and obedience to her husband, and she was seen as a peacemaker, as maintaining her husband's honour and reputation, and giving charity to the poor. Much of her activity centred on running the household, bringing up her children and caring for her women companions and servants. During her husband's absence, however, she was expected to take over his responsibilities, manage his estates or even run the kingdom, and take his place in the council. She had to be adaptable to be able to pick up or shed duties according to whether her husband was there or not, and Christine was in no doubt that women had the ability to do this. As she herself knew from personal experience, women needed to be especially self-reliant when widowed.

The buildings and artefacts used by medieval noblewomen have mostly disappeared. The sites and ruins of their castles can still be seen, together with some of the churches which they patronised, but the building work which they ordered and financed is hard to identify. Plate has been melted down and refashioned, jewels have been reset, and furnishings have decayed. Only the occasional piece survives to give some idea of former magnificence. In just a few cases, books owned by noblewomen have survived. It is fortunate that household accounts and wills often provide a vivid picture of the splendour and display which noblewomen and noblemen undoubtedly enjoyed.

Taken altogether, there is a wide range of available source material for studying late medieval English noblewomen. Most of the records are formal and impersonal, and in the personal records which survive, such as letters, it is only occasionally that emotional commitment comes through. All these sources have long been used by historians who have not necessarily questioned them for the light they shed on women's history. The denigration of women in many works of medieval literature and their lack of legal identity for much of their lives have been taken to mean that the noblewoman's role was subordinate and shadowy. Clearly women could not participate in warfare and formal politics, but this does not mean that their role in medieval society was invariably insignificant. What that role was will be examined in the following chapters.

Chapter 1

MARRIAGE

It was taken for granted in the later Middle Ages that the sons
and daughters of noble families would marry unless they entered
the Church, and marriage was arranged at an early age. It
usually took place publicly with the couple pledging their consent
in the presence of witnesses and this was often done in the
presence of a priest and in the context of a religious ceremony,
although this was not in fact obligatory until after the Council of
Trent (1545–63). According to the chroniclers, the marriage was
accompanied by celebration and festivity which could be lavish
and expensive. In addition to the two families concerned, other
members of the nobility were invited and entertainments were
provided. In the summer of 1328 Edward III and his mother
attended the weddings of two of Roger Mortimer's daughters at
Hereford, when solemn jousts were staged. At the wedding
ceremony at Arundel castle in July 1384, when Thomas Mowbray, earl of Nottingham married Elizabeth, the daughter of
Richard, earl of Arundel and widow of Sir William de Montague,
the festivities lasted for over a week and all who wanted to were
free to come and go. The wedding was attended by Richard II
and his queen, and the earl gave a present to all the members of
their household. Very occasionally politics spoilt the celebrations, as when some nobles' fears of treachery brought to
nothing the Round Table which had been planned for Gilbert,
earl of Gloucester's marriage to Matilda de Burgh in 1308.[1]
Sometimes supplementary celebrations were staged later on, as

---

1 *Chronica Adae Murimuth et Roberti de Avesbury* ed. E.M. Thompson Rolls Series
London 1889 57. *The Westminster Chronicle 1381–94* eds. L.C. Hector and B.F.
Harvey Oxford Medieval Texts Oxford 1982 88. *Vita Edwardi Secundi* ed. N.
Denholm-Young Nelson Medieval Classics London 1957 6.

when the earls and barons welcomed Marie de St Pol to London in 1321 after her marriage to Aymer de Valence, earl of Pembroke.[2]

The Church defined marriage as a sacrament and from the time of Pope Alexander III (1159–81) consent was regarded as the basis of marriage. This consent had to be given by the two parties concerned in the present tense; they had to promise to marry at the present time, not at some point in the future. Peter Lombard considered that both consent and consummation were essential to marriage and many later churchmen agreed with him, emphasis being put on sexual relations for the purpose of procreating children. The Church set the age for marriage at puberty when girls had reached the age of twelve and boys the age of fourteen. Children could be betrothed at seven years old, the age of reason, although this would not be binding for another five or seven years. If any marriage took place before the age of seven, the partners had to confirm their consent when they reached maturity. The Church's doctrine on marriage was accepted by the lay authorities, but betrothals and marriages did occasionally take place before the parties were seven years old. Richard Neville was aged six when he married Anne Beauchamp, the daughter of Richard, earl of Warwick, a marriage which resulted in him succeeding to the Warwick earldom in 1449. There are a number of instances where children were married at the age of nine or ten, but in most cases marriages took place when they were in their teens.

The Church was concerned to limit the marriage of close kinsmen and in the later Middle Ages marriage was forbidden within four degrees of kindred and affinity (affinity covering relationships created by marriage); spiritual relationships as between godparents and godchildren also fell within the prohibited degrees. Fortunately for the nobility, which was highly interrelated, the Church took it upon itself to give dispensations where necessary, and the securing of a dispensation was often an essential part of the marriage preparations. Thus in 1323, at the king's request, a dispensation to marry was issued to John, the son of the earl of Kildare, and Joan, the daughter of Hugh le Despenser the younger, who were related in the fourth degree. John of Gaunt needed a dispensation before he could marry

2 *Annales Paulini* in *Chronicles of the reigns of Edward I and Edward II* ed. W. Stubbs (2 vols) Rolls Series London 1882–3 I 264, 292.

Blanche, daughter of Henry, duke of Lancaster. In many cases the dispensation was obtained after the marriage and was essential in order to ensure that the children were regarded as legitimate; this occurred in 1297 in the case of Guy Beauchamp, son of the earl of Warwick, and Isabella, daughter of Gilbert de Clare, earl of Gloucester. Sometimes it was only discovered after the marriage that the relationship existed. This was alleged for John Mowbray and Elizabeth de Vere who asserted that the relationship was discovered by men more skilled in the law than those they had consulted earlier. Punishment was meted out by the Church when the marriage was entered into in full knowledge that the parties were within the prohibited degrees; in 1390 the Bishop of Ely was ordered to separate Thomas, Lord Morley and his wife for a time before granting them a dispensation to contract their marriage again, and it was laid down that which-ever party survived was not to remarry.[3]

During the later Middle Ages the Church's right to regulate marriage was accepted. The Church focussed attention on the couple by placing its emphasis on consent. It preferred that the marriage should take place in public, the system of banns being applied throughout Christendom by the Fourth Lateran Council of 1215, but it accepted clandestine marriages provided that both parties had given their consent. The nobility, however, saw marriage in the context of the family and the inheritance, and attention was likely to focus on these issues. The arranged marriage was accepted as the norm and parents and guardians took a practical and hard-headed approach. Whatever the personal feelings involved, marriage necessitated careful nego-tiations concerning money and property, the right settlement being considered essential for the establishment of the new household. Political as well as landed considerations had to be taken into account, especially with the highest nobility, and in cases of wardship the king or lord as well as the family was involved. In view of these conditions, the question arises as to how free the consent of the parties to a noble marriage actually was and how much pressure was brought to bear by parents.

The extent of the differences between the ideas of the Church and those of landed society comes out strongly in the case of

3 *Calendar of Entries in the Papal Registers relating to Great Britain and Ireland. Papal letters 1198–1304* 570; ibid. *1305–42* 231; ibid. *1342–62* 385, 605; ibid. *1362–1404* 385.

Joan, known as the fair maid of Kent; her father was Edmund, earl of Kent, the youngest son of Edward I. In 1340, at the age of twelve, Joan made a clandestine marriage to Sir Thomas Holland. Unfortunately while he was fighting in Prussia she was persuaded to marry William de Montague, son of the earl of Salisbury, who refused to give her up on Holland's return. It was only in 1349 that the papal Curia decided that the Montague marriage was invalid and that Joan was really Holland's wife. What mattered in the eyes of the Church was the consent that Joan had expressed, although secretly, to Holland; from the point of view of her family and the Montagues the clandestine marriage simply did not count. Joan alleged that she was afraid of the consequences if she refused to obey family and friends. Interestingly enough, she made another clandestine marriage to the Black Prince after Holland's death.[4]

Clandestine marriages and abductions attracted attention often through the subsequent legal proceedings, but they were the exception rather than the rule among the late medieval nobility for both first and later marriages. Only occasionally is it known why they occurred. Margery Paston's marriage to Richard Calle, discussed later in the chapter, was the result of mutual love, and it is likely that personal attraction combined with parental disapproval was the reason for other clandestine marriages. In many cases, however, it is probable that the attraction of an heiress's or widow's land was more powerful than the personal factors. The girls and widows who were abducted mostly held widespread estates or had the prospect of inheriting considerable landed wealth. This was as true of Ralph Stafford's abduction of Hugh Audley's daughter Margaret in 1334 as it was of the abduction of her aunt, Elizabeth de Burgh, by Theobald de Verdun eighteen years before.

In the majority of cases it proved possible to accommodate both the nobility's ideas on the arranged marriage and the Church's concern with consent. Marriage was seen by noble families as a way of augmenting and consolidating their lands and rising in political power and social influence. It was essential to try to ensure that there would be heirs to whom the inheritance would pass and who would safeguard it for future generations. In an age when expectation of life was comparatively short, there

---

4 K.P. Wentersdorf 'The clandestine marriages of the Fair Maid of Kent' *Journal of Medieval History* v (1979) 203–31.

was every reason for noble families to embark on marriage negotiations when their children were young. There is little sign that the children themselves, whether daughters or sons, were consulted. Daughters especially had a passive role to play, both in forging alliances with other members of the nobility, and as heiresses bringing their family's estates into new hands. According to feudal law, if a noble had no sons, his daughters received equal shares of the inheritance, and the failure of male heirs in many noble families in the later Middle Ages meant that the heiress was of vital importance. The use of the entail in this period enabled a nobleman to leave his lands to his nearest male relative rather than to daughters, but this only happened in a minority of cases.

The rise of noble families in the Middle Ages was usually the result of royal service and favour and advantageous marriages. Often the two factors were combined, royal patronage including the bestowal of heiresses. Families such as the Nevilles, Percies and Staffords all rose to power in this way, the marriages usually becoming more spectacular as they grew more powerful. The Staffords, for instance, were building up their position through marriage in the thirteenth century, notably through Robert Stafford's marriage to Alice Corbet of Caus which strengthened their position in Shropshire. It was, however, in the fourteenth century with Ralph Stafford's second marriage and his service in the Hundred Years War that the family really rose to prominence. In 1334 Ralph abducted and married Margaret Audley, heiress to one-third of the inheritance of the Clare earls of Gloucester, which had been worth over £2,000 when the lands had been partitioned in 1317. Margaret's lands gave Ralph the standing and wealth he needed when Edward III granted him the title of earl in 1351. Ralph hoped for even greater things for his family by betrothing his eldest son to Matilda, the elder daughter and heiress of Henry of Grosmont, but his son died in 1347, long before Henry. More successful was the marriage of Anne, daughter and eventually heiress of Thomas of Woodstock, duke of Gloucester, to Thomas, earl of Stafford, in 1389 and subsequently to his brother Earl Edmund. Anne's lands enabled her son to maintain the title of duke of Buckingham which he was granted in 1444.[5]

---

5 C. Rawcliffe *The Staffords, earls of Stafford and dukes of Buckingham, 1394–1521* Cambridge 1978 8–18.

Marriage to an heiress was a means by which new men, sometimes aliens, could, with the king's support, become prominent among the English nobility. William Marshal acquired lands and wealth in 1189 through his marriage to Isabella, daughter and heiress of Richard Strongbow. Simon de Montfort established himself in England not only by the royal grant of the earldom of Leicester, but also through his marriage to Henry III's sister Eleanor, the widow of William Marshal the younger. William Marshal's granddaughter Joan was married to Henry III's half-brother William de Valence in 1247, and was awarded Pembroke and Wexford in the partition of the Marshal lands.

In all these cases the king was able to use his powers of patronage to reward relatives and favourites. Although it became increasingly usual in the fourteenth century for nobles to use the enfeoffment to use to prevent their lands from falling into royal hands when a minor succeeded, the king still had custody of the person of the heir and the right to dispose of his or her marriage. These rights could be sold, the price being determined by the status of the heir and the degree of royal favour enjoyed by the recipient. Ralph Neville paid 3,000 marks each for the wardship and marriage of John de Mowbray, earl of Norfolk and Richard, duke of York.[6] These men became the husbands of his daughters Katherine and Cicely.

Kings were anxious to snap up heiresses for their younger sons and nephews, and this contributed to the accumulation of power and titles at the top of the noble hierarchy. Edward I's nephew Thomas, earl of Lancaster, was betrothed to Alice de Lacy in 1292 when he was about fourteen years old and she was eleven. Alice was the daughter and heiress of Henry de Lacy, earl of Lincoln, and Edward I ensured in the marriage settlement that the whole Lacy inheritance would come to Thomas and Alice. On the death of his father-in-law in 1311, Thomas added the title of earl of Lincoln to the titles of Lancaster and Leicester which he had inherited from his father. On the death of Thomas's nephew, Henry of Grosmont, duke of Lancaster, in 1361 the estates were divided between his two daughters, but the death of the elder daughter brought all the lands into the hands of John of Gaunt, who had married Henry's younger daughter Blanche. Edward III secured an heiress for his second son, Lionel,

---

6 J.R. Lander 'Marriage and politics in the fifteenth century: the Nevilles and the Wydevilles' *Bulletin of the Institute of Historical Research* XXXVI (1963) 121.

duke of Clarence, by marrying him to Elizabeth de Burgh, countess of Ulster, who also inherited her grandmother's share of the Clare inheritance. His youngest son, Thomas of Woodstock, married the elder daughter and co-heiress of Humphrey de Bohun, earl of Hereford. In all these cases the beneficiaries were men who already enjoyed high status but who added greatly to their landed wealth through marriage.

Among the lower nobility and gentry marriage to an heiress was just as highly prized and proved to be of major significance in the rise of families. Most of the heiresses came from landed families, although London heiresses were also in demand. County studies have shown that it was often the most powerful local families who secured the richest prizes.[7] The changing status of the family is to some degree reflected in its marriages. The Bourchier family, who became earls of Essex under Edward IV, built up their power in the fourteenth century as lawyers and royal servants and as Essex gentry, accumulating land as a result of careful marriages; John Bourchier married the daughter and heiress of Walter de Colchester of Stansted in Halstead, which became the family centre, while his son Robert married the heiress of Sir Thomas Prayers of Sible Hedingham. Royal service and marriage were similarly both important for the family of Ferrers of Groby; Henry de Ferrers married Isabella, fourth daughter and co-heiress of Theobald de Verdun, in about 1331, and his son William married the sister and eventual co-heiress of William Ufford, earl of Suffolk. The Paston fortunes were based on marriage as well as on the law; William Paston I married the heiress Agnes Berry, who brought him manors in Norfolk, Suffolk and Hertfordshire, while John Paston I's marriage to Margaret Mautby secured further estates in Norfolk and his connection with Sir John Fastolf.

Heiresses had a vital role to play in the transmission of estates and power and in the changing fortunes of noble and gentry families, and there is no doubt of the very careful planning which went into their marriages. Sometimes, however, the plans went awry because of abduction and a clandestine marriage. It was all very well for Hugh Audley to secure a commission of oyer

7 S.M. Wright *The Derbyshire gentry in the fifteenth century* Derbyshire Record Society VIII (1983) 42–3. C. Carpenter 'The fifteenth-century English gentry and their estates' *Gentry and lesser nobility in late medieval Europe* ed. M. Jones Gloucester 1986 38–9.

and terminer against Ralph Stafford for abducting his daughter, but he had to accept the fact of their marriage.[8] Deaths and entails meant that the marriage was very much a gamble, since it did not always work out as planned. This has already been seen in the case of the Lancaster inheritance; the death of Ralph Stafford's eldest son prevented a share from coming into the hands of the Stafford family, while the death of Henry of Grosmont's elder daughter meant that the whole inheritance came into the hands of John of Gaunt. An earlier entail could result in an apparent heiress not being entitled to inherit. Elizabeth was the only child of Thomas, Lord Berkeley (d. 1417) and succeeded to the Lisle lands through her mother. She and her husband Richard, earl of Warwick, also expected to succeed to the Berkeley inheritance but as a result of an entail made in 1349 the heir was adjudged to be her cousin James, in spite of vigorous attempts by Elizabeth, her daughters and their respective husbands to secure what they regarded as their rights. Finally, the husband of an heiress might find himself outmanoeuvred. According to Froissart, Thomas of Woodstock planned to secure the whole Bohun inheritance by putting his wife's sister in a convent. While Thomas was away from home on campaign, John of Gaunt succeeded in securing Mary de Bohun as the wife of his eldest son Henry Bolingbroke, and the inheritance had to be divided.[9]

A woman might well find as a result of family deaths that she became an heiress after her marriage, and her husband and family gained far more than they had ever anticipated. Such a change of fortune is found with the Clare family in the early fourteenth century. When Gilbert de Clare, earl of Gloucester married Joan of Acre in 1290, Edward I limited the succession to the estates to the children of the marriage, thus excluding Gilbert's two daughters by his first marriage. However, with the birth of a son, Gilbert, and his marriage in 1308 to Matilda de Burgh, the succession must have seemed secure, and the marriages of his three sisters offered alliance with the most powerful non-royal noble family in England but not the prospect of wide estates. Eleanor married Hugh le Despenser the younger in 1306, Margaret married Piers Gaveston, and Elizabeth John de Burgh,

8 *Calendar of Patent Rolls 1334–8* 298.

9 *Chronicles of England, France and Spain by Sir John Froissart* ed. T. Johnes (2 vols) London 1857 I 623–4.

the eldest son of the earl of Ulster. The whole situation was radically altered with Gilbert's death at the battle of Bannockburn, and although his widow declared that she was pregnant no heir was born. Although Edward II postponed partitioning the inheritance for nearly three years, the three sisters were certainly the heiresses. By 1314 Margaret and Elizabeth had been widowed and their remarriage was a matter of major political significance, given the difficulties of Edward II's reign. As for Hugh le Despenser the younger, his power at the end of the reign was essentially based on his wife's inheritance.

Although noble families preferred heiresses for their sons if they could afford them and secure them, there were never enough heiresses to go round. Property was therefore not the only factor taken into consideration by parents planning marriages for their children. The prospect of useful political alliances, whether at court or in the locality, and of connections with other nobles and gentry was regarded as of major importance in the interests of the family, and the alliances served a variety of purposes.

Occasionally the alliance came about as a result of civil war and family considerations were more marked than usual. One marriage with emergency political overtones dates from the period of the Barons' Wars in the mid-thirteenth century.[10] Robert de Vere, earl of Oxford, was one of the Disinherited who made his peace with the king after the Dictum of Kenilworth of 1266. His agreement with Roger Mortimer of Wigmore for the restoration of his lands is dated 11 March 1268, and the marriage contract for his son Robert, then aged ten, to marry Mortimer's daughter Margaret when the children reached puberty dates from about the same time. The earl paid Roger a fine of 4,000 marks to recover his lands, and Roger remitted 1,000 marks of this in order to have the marriage. Margaret was to be dowered with 100 librates of land for life when the wedding took place, and if Robert succeeded to the earldom, as he did in 1296, Margaret was to have her dower according to the law of England. It was laid down that if Robert died before the marriage took place Margaret was to marry his next brother Hugh.

This was an extreme case of using marriage to make peace between families, but instances are also found of using marriage to settle disputes over land. About 1319 Roger Mortimer,

10 G.W. Watson 'Marriage settlements' *Genealogist* XXXIII (1917) 134–6. BL Harley MS 1240 fo. 37v.

grandson of the Roger of the mid-thirteenth century, arranged
the marriage of his daughter Katherine to Thomas Beauchamp,
with the king's consent, in order to put an end to the quarrel
between the families over the lordship of Elfael; Mortimer
probably granted it to the Beauchamps as Katherine's marriage-
portion. Marriages were also planned to put an end to family
feuds, and again the Mortimers can be used as an example.
William de Bohun was closely involved with the seizure of
Roger Mortimer in 1330, and his marriage to Roger's widowed
daughter-in-law, Elizabeth de Badelesmere, was arranged to put
an end to the enmity between the families. In 1341 a dispensation
was issued to allow Hugh le Despenser, son of the younger
Despenser, and Elizabeth, daughter of William de Montague,
earl of Salisbury, to remain married in order to lessen the strife
between their families. The reason for hatred in this case
presumably lay in Hugh le Despenser the younger being the
favourite of Edward II, while William de Montague was a very
close friend and supporter of Edward III.[11]

Rather more mundane but also more usual were the marriages
designed to build up local connections. During the later Middle
Ages the knights and gentry of the counties became strongly
interrelated, just like the top nobility. Such marriages not only
conferred status on a family, but could bring immediate advantages. When Thomas Ferrers married the daughter of Leonard
Hastings in 1448, he secured a connection with the council of the
duke of York whose support he needed to defend his lands in
Essex.[12] Families in border areas used marriage to acquire lands
and to strengthen their relations with local families. Several of
the children of Roger Mortimer, first earl of March, made
marriage connections with families in the Welsh Marches and
the West of England. The build-up of the Percies' power in
Northumberland in the fourteenth century was achieved partly
through marriage.

It was always seen as advantageous for members of the
nobility to strengthen their links with each other. This has
already been seen with the connections forged between the Clares
and the de Burghs in the double marriage in 1308 between

11 G.A. Holmes *The estates of the higher nobility in fourteenth-century England*
Cambridge 1957 13. *Calendar of entries in the papal registers relating to Great
Britain and Ireland. Papal letters 1305–42* 186, 527–8, 553.

12 Carpenter 'The fifteenth-century English gentry and their estates' 39.

Gilbert, earl of Gloucester and Matilda de Burgh and between John de Burgh and Gilbert's youngest sister, Elizabeth. This policy was to be found in all noble families, and those with large numbers of daughters and the money for their dowries extended their connections markedly. The relationships were taken further with the remarriage of widows, to be considered later. The most successful and possibly the most ambitious practitioner in making these alliances was Ralph Neville, created first earl of Westmorland in 1397, who had twenty-two children by his two marriages, first to Margaret, daughter of Hugh, earl of Stafford, and secondly to Joan Beaufort, daughter of John of Gaunt. The children of the first marriage made less spectacular marriages than those of the second, but the advantages of local alliances were seized with the marriages of three of Margaret's daughters to the northern lords, de Mauley, Dacre of Gillesland and Scrope of Bolton. The marriages of Joan's daughters forged links with the Despenser, Percy, Mowbray, York and Stafford families, and her sons secured the heiresses of the Montagues, Beauchamps and Fauconbergs. It appears that Ralph put his emphasis on land and connection, Joan Fauconberg having been an idiot from birth.[13]

Alliances for reasons of politics, connection and prestige were not limited to England, especially in the thirteenth and early fourteenth centuries, but were forged with families in mainland Europe. Richard de Clare, earl of Gloucester, a man with high ambitions for his family, arranged for the marriage of his eldest daughter Isabella to the marquis of Montferrat in 1258, a marriage which cost him 4,000 marks.[14] This type of marriage highlighted the standing and power of the bride's family. Marriages also reinforced existing links between a family and the Continent. Aymer de Valence, earl of Pembroke, inherited four castellanies in western France, and both his wives were daughters of French lords; Beatrice was the daughter of Ralph de Clermont, Constable of France, and Marie the daughter of Guy de Châtillon, count of St Pol and Butler of France.[15]

For families eager to gain the highest prestige an alliance with

13 Lander 'Marriage and politics in the fifteenth century' 119–22.

14 *Calendar of Charter Rolls 1257–1300* 4–5.

15 J.R.S. Phillips *Aymer de Valence, earl of Pembroke 1307–24* Oxford 1972 2–8. H. Jenkinson 'Mary de Sancto Paulo, foundress of Pembroke College, Cambridge' *Archaeologia* LXXXVI (1915) 405.

the royal family was the ultimate goal. Such alliances had advantages on both sides: the noble family increased its reputation among the nobility while the Crown was able to provide for younger sons and daughters at relatively little cost. Such alliances are found throughout the later Middle Ages. Richard de Clare, earl of Gloucester, wanted a royal marriage for his eldest son Gilbert and satisfied his ambition in 1253 with his marriage to Henry III's niece, Alice de la Marche, daughter of Hugh XI, count of La Marche and Angoulême. A much closer alliance was made in 1290 with Gilbert's second marriage to Edward I's daughter, Joan of Acre. Edward I was in fact anxious to use such marriages to provide for his family and to tie the top nobility more closely to the Crown. His daughter Elizabeth married Humphrey de Bohun, earl of Hereford, his nephew Thomas, earl of Lancaster married Alice de Lacy, and his granddaughter Joan, daughter of Henry, count of Bar, married John de Warenne.[16] These alliances can be compared with Edward III's policy of securing heiresses for his younger sons.

All noble families planning marriages for their children had twin considerations in mind, the desire to secure an heiress if at all possible, and the need to make an advantageous alliance. Negotiations were sometimes prolonged and did not necessarily result in success. Preliminary inquiries had to be followed up by solid bargaining which might well prove abortive either because satisfactory terms could not be reached, or, occasionally, because one of the parties took matters into his or her own hands. Early negotiations for Elizabeth Paston's marriage broke down and she was not married until she was nearly thirty years old. Margaret Paston, writing to her husband John, probably in 1463, told him that his mother was making inquiries about a good marriage for their daughter Margery; there was universal family condemnation when Margery insisted on marrying the bailiff, Richard Calle.[17] Over two hundred years earlier, in 1237, there was similar careful consideration by Henry III and his council as to possible wives for the minor Richard de Clare, earl of Gloucester, and it was agreed that the earl of Lincoln could have the marriage for 5,000 marks, the king remitting 2,000

16 K.B. McFarlane 'Had Edward I a "policy" towards the earls?' *The nobility of later medieval England* Oxford 1973 248–267.

17 *Paston letters and papers of the fifteenth century* ed. N. Davis (2 vols) Oxford 1971–6 I 30–2, 40–1, 206–7, 286–7, 336–8, 341–4, 350–1, 408–10, 541–3.

marks, provided that the count of La Marche did not take up the offer for one of his daughters. Richard had already been secretly married to Margaret de Burgh, but she died in November 1237 and within two months Richard was married to Matilda de Lacy.[18]

Marriage settlements were drawn up by the men of the family, although king and council might well be involved in the marriages of the top nobility. Women were only occasionally mentioned, as in the agreement of 1315 for the marriage of Hugh de Courtenay and Margaret de Bohun, which was made between Queen Margaret, Earl Humphrey de Bohun and Elizabeth, his wife, on the one side and Hugh's father on the other.[19] It is, however, likely that mothers had a say in marriage alliances and possibly encouraged the ambitions of their husbands. Collections such as the Paston Letters make it clear that all members of the family, women as well as men, became involved in the negotiations. The Paston mothers were anxious to get their children married well. Margaret Paston took a hand in the arrangements for her son John III's marriage to Margery Brews, which took place in 1477. Finding that Margery's father was holding out for a good settlement for his daughter, she suggested to Margery's mother that the two women should sort out the difficulty between them, and she transferred her own manor of Sparham to the couple.[20]

The marriage settlement itself was primarily concerned with monetary and property matters, and it was on these issues that many projected marriages foundered. The main obligations on each side are brought out in the 1315 agreement for the Courtenay-Bohun marriage. Earl Humphrey was to pay 1,000 marks for the marriage. Hugh's father agreed to enfeoff his son and Margaret jointly with land worth 400 marks which Margaret was to continue to hold if she outlived Hugh. If Hugh succeeded his father, Margaret was to have dower in all his lands. In fact Hugh inherited his father's estates in 1341; he died in 1377 and his widow survived him by about fourteen years. The three main elements in the contract comprised the dowry, jointure and dower, and all underwent development in the later Middle Ages

---

18 F.M. Powicke *Henry III and the Lord Edward* (2 vols) Oxford 1947 II 760–8.

19 Watson 'Marriage settlements' *Genealogist* XXXIV (1918) 29–30. PRO DL27/13.

20 *Paston letters* I 378, 500–1, 605–7, 662–3.

with the result that women gained greater landed security. In addition to their interests in family and patrimony, parents were concerned to look after their daughters' long-term economic interests.

In every case the bride's father was expected to provide a dowry and in the thirteenth century this took the form of money or land. The *maritagium*, the gift of land to a daughter on marriage, reverted to the grantor or his family if the grantees left no children. Practice varied even within the same family as to whether money or land was given. Richard de Clare, earl of Gloucester, gave a dowry of 4,000 marks to the marquis of Montferrat on the marriage of his eldest daughter, but the manors of Sundon and Hambleden were settled on his daughter Margaret when she married Edmund, earl of Cornwall.[21] *Maritagia* are still found in the fourteenth century but were less common. In the indenture of 1319 for the marriage of Roger Mortimer's daughter Margaret to Thomas de Berkeley, Margaret's marriage-portion amounted to £1,000, and Roger also gave half the manor of Awre in Gloucestershire as *maritagium*. The other half comprised part of the land settled jointly on the couple by Thomas's father Maurice. If Thomas and Margaret were childless the *maritagium* was to revert to Roger.[22]

The money dowry was paid in instalments to the bridegroom's father or guardian. A father with a large number of daughters might well have difficulty in raising dowries for all of them. The sums paid varied widely, reflecting not only the status of the family but also political considerations and probably bargaining skill. Moreover, the amount of the dowry seems to have varied according to the amount of the jointure. As a general rule it can be reckoned that a member of the higher nobility would have to pay a dowry of at least 1,000 marks for the marriage of one of his daughters. Hugh le Despenser the elder paid 1,000 marks in 1313 for his daughter Margaret to marry John de St Amand, whereas Ralph Stafford was paying £800 or £1,000 for the marriages of his three daughters. However, when his heir married Philippa, the daughter of the earl of Warwick, in 1353,

21 *Annales de Dunstaplia* in *Annales Monastici* ed. H. R. Luard (5 vols) Rolls Series London 1864–9 III 253. *Inquisitions and assessments relating to feudal aids* I 76, 92.

22 Watson 'Marriage settlements' *Genealogist* XXV (1919) 96–7. BL Harley MS 1240 fo.41v. Part of this document is missing.

her portion amounted to £2,000. Marriage to the eldest son and heir to an earldom merited a higher dowry. Edward III paid 5,000 marks for his granddaughter Philippa, the heiress of Lionel, duke of Clarence, to marry Edmund Mortimer. Gentry dowries were of course considerably lower, Margery Brews' dowry in the draft marriage settlement being set at 400 marks.

Fathers who died leaving a young family often made provision for their daughters' dowries in their wills. Thomas Stonor in 1431 provided for the money received for the marriage of his son to be spent on the dowries of his five daughters, who were to be married in order of age; each was to receive at least 200 marks. According to his will, Elizabeth Paston's father wanted her to have £200 for her marriage provided that she took the advice of her mother and his executors over her marriage, and he wanted a jointure of lands worth at least £40 a year to be settled on her and her husband.[23] Richard, earl of Arundel left 1,000 marks towards the marriage of his daughter Margaret and was prepared for the sum to be increased to 1,500 marks; he also allowed her 100 marks a year for her maintenance until her marriage.[24]

From the late thirteenth century it became increasingly usual to settle estates jointly on husband and wife, and these jointures, provided by the husband's family, were specified in the marriage contract. The jointure continued to be held by the wife if, as often happened, she outlived her husband, and it gave her wealth and greater security than widows had previously enjoyed. From the point of view of her heirs jointures proved a mixed blessing. With estates remaining in the widow's hands, there was no danger of their passing to the king in the event of a minority, and there was therefore continuity in their administration and exploitation. However, if the widow remarried, as was frequently the case, the lands passed under the control of her husband, and there was some risk that family lands would be lost. A large jointure in the hands of a long-lived widow resulted in the impoverishment of the heir.

Complications also arose if the marriage settlement was drawn up in such a way as to limit the rights of succession by primogeniture. When Gilbert, earl of Gloucester married Joan of

23 *The Stonor letters and papers, 1290–1483* ed. C.L. Kingsford (2 vols) Camden Society third series XXIX (1919) I 47–9. *Paston letters* I 24.

24 J. Nichols *A collection of all the wills of the kings and queens of England* London 1780 133.

Acre in 1290, Edward I arranged that all the Clare estates should be held jointly by husband and wife. As a result the whole inheritance remained in Joan's hands when Gilbert died five years later. The heir was only four years old, and did not suffer from the arrangement as Joan herself died in 1307. More damaging in the long run were the provisions in the 1290 settlement which limited the succession to the children of Gilbert and Joan, and excluded Gilbert's daughters by his first marriage and all other possible heirs. This case can be compared with the marriage settlement between Ralph Neville and Joan Beaufort about a hundred years later. Joan received a very large jointure and the settlement provided for most of the family property to pass to her children. Ralph's grandson and heir to the earldom of Westmorland was considerably impoverished, and the arrangements led to protest by the children of the first marriage and warfare during the 1430s.

Arrangements over dower underwent some change in the later Middle Ages, again providing the woman with greater security and wealth. Before about 1200 the wife's dower in land or goods was assigned to her by her husband at the church door at the time of the marriage, or she might receive one-third of the lands held by her husband at that time. The 1217 and 1225 versions of Magna Carta assigned to her one-third of the land that her husband had had in his lifetime, unless she had been dowered with less at the church door when the marriage was solemnised. The grant of dower at the church door is still found in the early fourteenth century, as when Edmund Mortimer married Elizabeth de Badelesmere in 1316.[25] By the later thirteenth century, however, dower was allocated from the land held by the husband on the day of his death and the widow held her dower for life. This precluded the need for gifts or endowment at the church door.

The provisions for jointure and dower brought considerable economic advantages to noblewomen. As wives their financial security was provided by their husbands, but if they survived to be widows they were better off in the later Middle Ages than they had been earlier. Jointures are not found until shortly before 1300, and for many noblewomen the jointure provision was generous, either as laid down in the marriage contract or arranged later. The widow who especially benefited was the one

25 Watson 'Marriage settlements' *Genealogist* XXXIV (1918) 30–1. PRO DL27/93.

who held nearly all her late husband's estates in this way. As far as dower was concerned, the grant of one-third of the lands held by the husband at the time of his death meant that the widow received more than she would have done in the twelfth century. A widow with both jointure and dower enjoyed financial independence and was in great demand for remarriage; the implications of this will be looked at in the next chapter.

The question, however, arises as to whether all noble marriages were as practical and businesslike as the evidence of the settlements suggests, or whether personal considerations had a part to play alongside the desire for land, alliance and family advantage. Factors such as beauty and character are occasionally mentioned and are likely to have been under-recorded. There was no place in legal documents and marriage contracts for such information, and, as has been seen, the chroniclers who might have made such personal comments rarely did so. The application of the adjective 'dear' to husband or wife in a will cannot be taken at its face value as it may have been included as a matter of course by the clerk. Wills, however, sometimes provide a clue as to the feelings between husband and wife in the nature and distribution of the bequests and the provisions for burial. At the end of the thirteenth century, William Beauchamp, earl of Warwick, wanted his heart to be interred wherever his wife decided to be buried.[26]

Love matches sometimes occurred, but were frowned on by noble society. The Pastons saw marriage primarily in economic terms but could not prevent Margery's marriage to Richard Calle even though they put considerable pressure on her to prevent it. The bishop of Norwich found in 1469 that the vows exchanged were valid and the marriage was therefore accepted. It is likely that part of the problem with this marriage lay in Calle's social inferiority. Margaret Paston's feelings are clearly seen in her failure to mention her daughter in her will. From her point of view love was likely to lead to a disadvantageous alliance.

Margaret Paston had no objection to love, however, provided that a satisfactory settlement was reached, and there is great contrast between her disapproval of the Calle marriage, and her encouragement of John Paston III's courtship of Margery Brews. The valentines which Margery sent to her future husband are

26 *Testamenta Vetusta* ed. N.H. Nicolas (2 vols) London 1826 52.

proof of her feelings. John promised Elizabeth Brews not to broach the matter to Margery until terms had been agreed, but Margery apparently pestered her mother to effect the marriage. John's elder brother commented that he was better pleased with the Brews marriage than with any other projected for John III, because of Margery's person, youth and family, the favour she enjoyed with her parents and their attitude to John. He also considered that her parents' character indicated that Margery would be virtuous and good.[27]

Christine de Pisan considered that love was an insufficient base for marriage, but saw the good husband as inspiring love in his wife. A happy marriage was to be hoped for but the wife had the duty of caring for her husband whatever he was like. Ideally, economic and personal considerations were seen as going together, as with Sir John Neville and Margaret, the widow of John, duke of Somerset, who wanted to marry in 1446 because of their love for each other and in order to look after Margaret's dower lands.[28] In a situation where arranged marriages were virtually universal in noble society it is likely that affection usually developed after marriage rather than before and that men and women accepted this as normal. When marriages were arranged between young children the practice of bringing up a prospective bride in the household of her future father-in-law meant that the couple had the chance to grow up together and to get to know each other before giving their final consent to marriage. The indenture for the projected marriage between Edmund Mortimer and Alice, daughter of the earl of Arundel, provided that the earl of March would maintain the children until they were of age to consent to marriage.[29] The general practice of bringing up noble children in households other than those of their parents must have generated independence and social skills at an early age.

The Paston letters show how affection grew after marriage in spite of the formal tone of much of the correspondence. After ill-treatment at home at the hands of her mother, Elizabeth Paston eventually married Robert Poynings. In a letter to her mother in 1459 she described her husband as her best-beloved, writing of

27 *Paston letters* I 434–6, 500–1, 662–3.

28 *Papal letters 1431–47* 579.

29 *Calendar of Close Rolls 1354–60* 92–4. This marriage did not in fact take place.

his kindness to her and his activity in ensuring her of her jointure; personal and economic considerations were put together in the same sentence. Evidence of affection also appears in some of the letters between John Paston 1 and his wife Margaret. Much of their correspondence was formal and restricted to items of news and business and purchases which Margaret wanted him to make in London, but the letters exchanged after Margaret's visit to John in the Fleet prison in 1465 display considerable affection.[30] Both the Paston and the Stonor letters show that affection existed between many married couples, and it is likely that such affection was widespread. At the same time it is important to bear in mind that love was based on a solid economic foundation.

Most of the marriages arranged lasted for life, but there were cases of marital breakdown and divorce. The Church regarded marriage as indissoluble but accepted that there were certain conditions under which separation or annulment could be granted. Such cases in the later Middle Ages were essentially a matter for canon law. Separations on grounds of adultery were not accepted, although in 1302 a case in the royal courts alleged that Margaret de Camoys had eloped with William Paynel and had subsequently been quitclaimed to him by charter by her husband John.[31] Canon lawyers were ready to consider pleas based on the absence of free consent to the marriage, non-consummation and cruelty. From the point of view of the noble family lack of male heirs might well appear a good reason for annulment, but this was not regarded as valid by the Church. Similarly there might be political reasons why a marriage should be ended, but these were not sufficient on their own in the eyes of the Church. Personal incompatibility might lead to informal separation but not necessarily to a termination of the marriage.

The lack of free consent to the marriage was often cited as the reason for wanting divorce. In 1350–1 the matrimonial case was heard between John, Lord Segrave and Margaret de Brotherton, Margaret claiming that she was contracted to him before she was of marriageable age and had never agreed to cohabit with him. The marriage had taken place in the 1330s, and, as in other divorce cases, there may well have been background factors

30 *Paston letters* 1 206–7, 318–22.

31 F. Pollock and F.W. Maitland *The history of English law before the time of Edward* 1 (2 vols) Cambridge 1898 11 395–6.

unmentioned in the records. Margaret married Walter, Lord Mauny within a year of John's death in 1353 without the king's licence. The speed of her remarriage may be an indication that she and Walter were attracted to each other during John's lifetime. Her only son by John died in 1349 and John may have been anxious to remarry to secure a male heir. Whatever the reasons, the divorce was not granted.[32]

Absence of consent was also cited in the successful divorce petition of Richard, earl of Arundel and Isabella Despenser in 1344, but this case was really based on political considerations and shows that political influence was of major importance in securing a divorce. It was alleged that when Richard was in his seventh year and Isabella in her eighth they were married without their consent; at puberty Richard was forced to consummate the marriage and a son was born, but after that he refused to live with her. (In fact the couple had three children.) Early in 1345 he was secretly remarried in the presence of the king and queen to Eleanor, the daughter of Henry, earl of Lancaster. Here were two alliances made to cement royal favour, Richard's father being anxious to be connected to Hugh le Despenser the younger at the time when he was the favourite of Edward II, and Richard himself, as the close friend and supporter of Edward III, wanting to remarry in order to ally himself more closely with the king's friends. His divorce resulted in his son by Isabella being declared illegitimate and losing any right to inherit from his father. His protest had no effect.[33]

Divorce on grounds of cruelty was granted to Margaret de Clare, the wife of Edmund, earl of Cornwall, in the late thirteenth century. Archbishop Pecham ordered Edmund in 1290 to return to his wife and to treat her with proper affection, but efforts at reconciliation proved unsuccessful and the marriage was annulled. Margaret accused her husband of neglect and cruelty and alleged that she feared for her life. How far her accusations were justified is not known, but the fact that the marriage was childless may have contributed to the difficulties between the couple.[34]

---

32 *Papal letters 1342–62* 381, 391. R.E. Archer 'The estates and finances of Margaret of Brotherton, *c*. 1320–1399' *Historical Research* LX (1987) 266.

33 *Papal letters 1342–62* 176, 254; *Calendar of entries in the papal registers relating to Great Britain and Ireland. Petitions to the pope 1342–1419* 75, 81, 99.

34 M. Altschul *A baronial family in medieval England: the Clares, 1217–1314* Baltimore 1965 35–6.

An earlier marriage contract could also be cited as reason for divorce. This was one of the claims made in the case between John de Warenne, earl of Surrey, and Edward I's granddaughter, Joan of Bar. The root problem here seems to have been the incompatibility of the couple and Joan's childlessness, which meant that the Warenne family died out in the male line in the mid-fourteenth century. Divorce in this case was not granted. At the time of the marriage in 1306, Joan was ten years old and her husband nineteen. Seven years later John applied for divorce on grounds of consanguinity, a claim which was not permissible as Clement V had given a dispensation for the marriage. John therefore changed his tactics, and Joan was cited to answer John's mistress, Matilda de Neyrford, in the divorce case on the grounds of a previous marriage contract between the earl and Matilda. John had sons by Matilda and in 1316 was settling property on them. Matilda subsequently lost favour although it is not clear how far John was reconciled to Joan. Towards the end of his life, however, John was warned by Clement VI to treat Joan with marital affection. When he died in 1347 he was living with Isabel Holland and apparently hoping for an heir by her; she was left substantial bequests in his will.[35]

Divorce meant the loss of dower rights and therefore a separate property settlement is sometimes found. Gilbert de Clare and Alice de la Marche are said to have been divorced in 1271, although the final annulment came fourteen years later when Gilbert's marriage to Joan of Acre was under consideration. The property settlement was made at the same time as the annulment, with Alice being granted the six manors of Thaxted, Wells and Warham, Whiston, Burford and Speenhamland for life.[36]

The number of divorce cases among noble families in the later Middle Ages was small, and most couples marrying for the first time accepted the marriage which had been arranged for them. The attitude of both partners appears passive. The consent insisted on by the Church provided a theoretical safeguard against parental pressure, but there were many ways in which such pressure could be exercised and there were instances where parental ambitions overrode the wishes and feelings of their children. It is only in a few cases that it is possible to see an

35 F.R. Fairbank 'The last earl of Warenne and Surrey and the distribution of his possessions' *Yorkshire Archaeological Journal* XIX (1907) 193–264.

36 *Calendar of Close Rolls 1279–88* 357.

element of love in the marriage arrangements. Affection was seen as developing after the marriage had taken place, and although this can be seen in surviving letters it mostly went unrecorded. What the records show are the economic arrangements for marriage, and these were regarded as essential by all parties.

For the daughter of a noble family marriage, in the eyes of the law, meant passing from the control of her father to that of her husband. Yet far more was involved in practice with her change of status. She was established in her own household, living a life which, as Christine de Pisan shows, was often separate from her husband's, and which therefore meant that there were times when she had to take over at least some of his responsibilities. She had to develop her skills in running the household and bringing up her children. The settlement reached by her parents over her dowry, jointure and dower provided her with land, which was to prove of particular importance once she was widowed as it gave her the opportunity to wield power and influence outside the household in a wider community. Marriage was essentially the foundation of noblewomen's influence in the later Middle Ages, and marked the starting-point of their exercise of power in society. How they carried this out will be examined in the following chapters.

Chapter 2

THE WIDOW AND HER LANDS

As far as the law was concerned, a great contrast existed between the child whose marriage was arranged by her parents and who was then subject to her husband, and the widow who as a *femme sole* was regarded as an independent figure, able to plead in the courts and act as head of her household and estates. She was responsible for making her own decisions as regards her lands, her family and her own relationships. She had no formal training for the duties she assumed as a widow and it is likely that she relied on what she had learned by assimilation during her girlhood and marriage.[1] The appointment of noblewomen to execute wills, and their increasingly favourable treatment over jointure and dower indicate that husbands, fathers and brothers considered that they were quite capable of tackling business matters. Although abilities obviously varied, many widows in the later Middle Ages were vigorous and successful in furthering the fortunes of themselves and their families.

On the death of her husband it was often the widow who had the task of arranging the funeral and of executing the will. Most of the later medieval nobility left wills in which they laid down the type of funeral they wanted, but the appropriate religious ceremonies had to be arranged and the requiem masses provided for. The funeral was often an occasion for great display and the mourners had to be invited and entertained. Marie de St Pol consulted Edward II in 1324 over the burial of her husband, Aymer de Valence, and the decision that he should be buried at Westminster was endorsed by the council. Elizabeth de Burgh,

---

1 This point is made in connection with Margaret Paston by A.S. Haskell 'The Paston women on marriage in fifteenth-century England' *Viator* IV (1973) 463–4.

arranging the funeral of her half-brother Edward de Monthermer in 1339, notified Queen Isabella, Lord Fitzwalter, the abbot of Bury St Edmunds, and knights in Essex and Suffolk, among others.[2] Noblewomen were also responsible for the tomb of the deceased, but this took many years to complete. Masons were making Edward de Monthermer's tomb in the church of the Augustinian friars at Clare in 1352, and work on Thomas, Lord Morley's tomb at Hingham was being carried out by his widow nearly thirty years after his death.[3] It can still be seen against the north wall of the chancel of Hingham church, and shows the importance attached by the nobility to impressive monuments.

The task of executing a husband's will could well take years, and problems arose if resources were inadequate for undertaking the provisions laid down in the will. The executors took an oath before the bishop or churchman with probate jurisdiction to administer the estate faithfully. They had to submit an inventory of the deceased's goods and carried out the majority of the bequests once they received probate. The seals of the deceased had to be surrendered; after the death of Michael de la Pole in France in 1415 his widow reported that his seals were overseas and she was instructed to hand them over later. In this case probate was granted at the widow's home at Wingfield in Suffolk. The executors had to give a full account of their work before being discharged.[4] The amount of work for the executors is exemplified in the inventory and account for Elizabeth, Lady Clifford who died in 1424.[5] The inventory included money, plate and furnishings; livestock and wool were sold and the sale prices listed, an estimate was made of grain which had been sown, and debts owed to the lady were totalled, the whole amounting to nearly £681. The account dealt mainly with the payment of the lady's debts; in addition, £4 was paid to secure probate and the acquittance of the executors, and writing the inventory cost one mark.

2 H. Jenkinson 'Mary de Sancto Paulo, foundress of Pembroke College, Cambridge' *Archaeologia* LXXXVI (1915) 435–6. PRO E101/92/11 m.11.

3 PRO E101/93/12 m.3d. BL Additional MS 34122A m.3.

4 An ordinance concerning probate was issued by Archbishop Henry Chichele in 1416. *The register of Henry Chichele, Archbishop of Canterbury, 1414–43* ed. E.F. Jacob (4 vols) Canterbury and York Society XLII (1937) II 49, 57–60: XLVI (1945) III 16–18.

5 *Testamenta Eboracensia* (6 vols) Surtees Society XLV (1865) III 85–7.

Although the widow was often named as executor, practice varied as to the number of other executors named. What is not known is how active a part each executor played, but it would be a mistake to assume that the widow played a minor role. Ralph Neville, first earl of Westmorland, named four executors including his second wife and their son Richard, earl of Salisbury. When the executors were acquitted, the earl and John Quixley presented the account on behalf of all four, and swore that the account was true and that they had been diligent in their duties. Joan Beaufort was not personally involved in this but she is known to have been active as an executor in other parts of the business.[6]

As well as carrying out her husband's will, the widow had to secure her jointure and dower. All women had their rights to land, even if they were widowed as children. Jointure was laid down in the original marriage settlement, but was added to during the marriage by joint purchases or joint enfeoffments. Dower, amounting to one-third of all the lands the husband had held in his lifetime, was usually allocated by the Crown since virtually all the nobility were tenants-in-chief of the king. According to Magna Carta as issued in 1225 the widow should receive her *maritagium* and inheritance immediately after her husband's death, and she had the right to stay in her husband's house, although not in his castle, for forty days. During that period her dower should be assigned to her, and she should not have to pay anything for her *maritagium*, inheritance and dower. All these lands remained in her hands for life and then passed to her heirs. The expectation that dower would be assigned within forty days proved to be optimistic; Matilda de Lacy was assigned some manors by Henry III within three weeks of Richard, earl of Gloucester's death in July 1262 to suffice until she was assigned a reasonable dower, but the final settlement was not made until early 1263, and was subsequently contested by her son. Widows found that they had to take action themselves to secure their rights. On the death of John de Warenne, his lordships of Bromfield and Yale in Denbigh were granted to the earl of Arundel as it was not known if his widow, Joan of Bar, was alive or not. Joan appeared personally before the Black Prince and his

6 *The register of Thomas Langley, Bishop of Durham, 1406–37* ed. R.L. Storey (6 vols) Surtees Society CLXX (1961) IV 97–8, 132–3.

council to show that she and John had been jointly enfeoffed of the lordships, and she then swore fealty to the prince.[7]

The fact that the widow enjoyed jointure and dower together with her own inheritance meant that there were some very wealthy noblewomen in the later Middle Ages. As a result of joint enfeoffment Joan of Acre took over all the lands of the earldom of Gloucester on the death of Gilbert de Clare in 1295. Margaret de Brotherton succeeded to half the inheritance of her father, Thomas de Brotherton, earl of Norfolk, on his death in 1338, and to the other half in 1382; she had jointure in most of the lands of her first husband, John Lord Segrave, who died in 1353, and she continued to hold all her lands until her own death in 1399. These two women ranked among the highest nobility, but the same customs applied at the lower levels and widows found themselves in possession of a sizeable part of the family estates.

Looking at these arrangements from the point of view of the heir, the situation could be galling, and lead to his impoverishment for a substantial period, even in some cases for life, and possibly to a limitation of his political activities. The widow often remained responsible for the younger children, especially for unmarried daughters. Jointure and dower safeguarded estates from being taken into royal custody during the heir's minority and had the advantage of keeping them in the hands of the family. Yet the long lives of many widows meant that some families, like the Mowbrays, found that they were supporting more than one dowager for a substantial period, and the prospects of gaining the widow's inheritance must have appeared far-distant. Katherine Neville (d. 1483) survived her first husband, John Mowbray, duke of Norfolk, by fifty-one years, outliving also her son, grandson and great-granddaughter. In Warwickshire Margaret Freville survived her husband, Sir Hugh Willoughby, by nearly fifty years, and it was her grandson rather than her son who succeeded her.[8] Among the Pastons, Agnes survived her husband, William I, for thirty-five years, dying in

7 *Register of Edward the Black Prince* (4 vols) London 1930–33 I 111, 114.

8 R.E. Archer 'Rich old ladies: the problem of late medieval dowagers' *Property and politics: essays in later medieval English history* ed. A. Pollard Gloucester 1984 28–31. Carpenter 'The fifteenth-century English gentry and their estates' *Gentry and lesser nobility in late medieval Europe* ed. M. Jones Gloucester 1986 41.

1479, while her daughter-in-law Margaret outlived John I (d. 1466) by eighteen years.

Not only were estates held for years by widows but in some cases waste and loss of land also occurred. Many widows proved to be good administrators but by no means all. The inheritance of Thomas de Courtenay, earl of Devon, was seriously wasted during his minority by the administration headed by his mother, and even when he came of age his mother retained about two-thirds of his estates as her jointure and dower until her death in 1441.[9]

It was very rare and also very difficult for the widow to get rid of the whole family inheritance. It was always accepted that dower was held by the widow for her lifetime, and Edward I's legislation provided a remedy for the heir to recover alienated dower. The succession to jointure lands was laid down in the marriage settlement or other deeds, and according to feudal custom the woman's inheritance passed to the heir by right of primogeniture. Joan de Mohun was exceptional in disposing of the family lands by sale, making use of the device of the enfeoffment to use in order to do so. In 1369 her husband John de Mohun conveyed his principal estates to feoffees on the condition that they should follow his wife's orders in disposing of them. John died seven years later, leaving three daughters who had already made good marriages but no son. Before his death Joan had agreed to sell the lands to Elizabeth Luttrell and she carried this out in 1376; the feoffees conveyed the lands to her for life with remainder to Elizabeth. Joan continued to enjoy the income from the estates and also had the purchase money of £3,333. 6s. 8d.; her daughters and their husbands had, however, no inheritance to look forward to.[10]

On occasion heirs and successors voiced a protest over the widow's dower and jointure. Gilbert de Clare, earl of Gloucester, disputed Henry III's allocation of dower to his mother, Matilda de Lacy, which was contrary to feudal custom including, as it did, the castle of Clare which was the centre of the honour of Clare in the eastern counties. In 1266 he brought a case against her to recover two of his Marcher castles, Usk and Trellech,

9 M. Cherry 'The struggle for power in mid-fifteenth century Devonshire' *Patronage, the Crown and the provinces in later medieval England* ed. R.A. Griffiths Gloucester 1981 125.

10 H. C. Maxwell Lyte *Dunster and its lords, 1066–1881* Exeter 1882 20–2, 44–6.

which were awarded to him.[11] At the time Gilbert was defending his Welsh lands against a possible takeover by Llywelyn ap Gruffydd, and his need for military resources in the Marches probably added to his sense of grievance. The widow's jointure also caused grievance among other relations. Manors in Ulster, Connacht and Munster were settled jointly on Elizabeth de Burgh and her first husband by her father-in-law Richard, earl of Ulster, and her daughter-in-law, petitioning in 1334, clearly felt aggrieved over the extent of Elizabeth's lands, complaining about her small dowry and the inadequate sum assigned by the king for the maintenance of her daughter.[12]

The lord of an estate, whether it was an earldom or the holding of a gentleman, might well resent the situation if he found that at least one-third of his lands was in the hands of a mother, grandmother or other female relation. Yet in the later Middle Ages it was accepted that widows should be generously supported and through the changes over dower and the use of the jointure the support became more generous rather than less. In view of this attitude in society it would be a mistake to look at the situation only from the viewpoint of the heir. There was every reason to believe that the noblewoman herself had an important role to play in society. Setting Joan de Mohun to one side as exceptional in her attitude to her family, dowagers generally acted constructively in the support of their children, the running of their estates and the building up of their affinity. They were important figures in their own locality and in noble society.

It was usual for widows to remarry at least once, and the question of their remarriage was significant not only personally but to their families and sometimes to the king. Their freedom of choice over a second husband improved in the later Middle Ages. By the early thirteenth century the king was accepting proffers that women should not be forced to remarry without their consent and in some cases he allowed them to act as guardians of their children and to arrange their marriage.[13]

11 M. Altschul *A baronial family in medieval England: the Clares, 1217–1314* Baltimore 1965 95–6, 99–100, 117. PRO KB26/177, m. 3, 13-13d. The new dower settlement was recorded in PRO SC11/610 m.1.

12 PRO C81/217/8173. R. Frame *English Lordship in Ireland, 1318–61* Oxford 1982 62–4.

13 J.C. Holt *Magna Carta* Cambridge 1965 45–6, 113–15.

According to the 1225 issue of Magna Carta no widow should be distrained to remarry while she wished to live without a husband, but she had to give security that she would not remarry without the king's consent if she was a tenant-in-chief or without the consent of the lord of whom she held her lands. In the later Middle Ages even if she remarried without consent and her lands were confiscated, she usually recovered them on the payment of a fine; the marriage itself was regarded by the Church as valid provided that the parties had pledged their consent to each other.

Many widows availed themselves of this freedom of choice, often choosing men of less wealth and lower status than themselves; they had sometimes served in the households of their first husbands. Joan of Acre secretly married Ralph de Monthermer, one of Earl Gilbert de Clare's knights, within fifteen months of the earl's death. Her attitude is summed up in the remark which she is reputed to have made to her father, Edward I, that if a noble could marry a poor girl, then a noble lady could marry a poor knight.[14]

At the same time pressure was brought to bear on widows by their families, by would-be husbands, and by the Crown and they did not always enjoy the free choice of a second or subsequent husband. In a society where widows could be children or teenagers it could prove difficult for them to stand up to those around them and make independent choices. The widows who achieved this in the face of opposition were women of strong personality, and even women of this calibre were not invariably successful. They were part of a hierarchical society which stressed family concerns more than individual considerations and thought that decisions should be taken as a result of counsel. Christine de Pisan envisaged that a young widowed princess would be subject to the guidance of her parents and be advised by her friends when it came to remarriage. She considered that a widow who made her own choice without their wholehearted consent was very much at fault. Parents in late medieval England exercised influence over the remarriage of their daughters and this may well have occurred in the second marriage of Thomas of Woodstock's daughter Anne. Her first husband, Thomas earl of Stafford, died in 1392. Her father was

14 *Johannis de Trokelowe et Henrici de Blaneforde Chronica et Annales* ed. H.T. Riley Rolls Series London 1865 27.

in charge of the earl's younger brothers, and she was subsequently remarried to Earl Edmund.

Whatever the forces of mutual attraction, a prospective husband was likely to be motivated by practical considerations.
Social, political and economic advantage all accrued from marriage to a widow. If a knight like Ralph de Monthermer married
a countess, his social status was immeasurably enhanced. So was
his wealth, as he became responsible for his wife's lands, and by
the custom of courtesy of England continued to hold them after
her death. When a widow made several marriages, her dower
and jointure accumulated throughout her life. Political advantage was also gained through his wife's family and other connections, whether these were at court or in the county.

Bearing these advantages in mind, would-be husbands sometimes resorted to abduction in the hope of marriage to a wealthy
widow. Joan, countess of Fife, complained to the king in 1299
that while on her way to England with her possessions to save
them from the Scots she was seized by Herbert de Morham
between Stirling and Edinburgh. Herbert imprisoned her
because she refused to marry him and took from her horses,
jewels and clothes valued at £2,000.[15] Eleanor, widow of Hugh le
Despenser the younger, was abducted in 1328–9 by William de
la Zouche from Hanley castle in Worcestershire and they were
married, although John de Grey of Rotherfield claimed that she
was his wife. Angry words were exchanged between William and
John in the presence of Edward III and his council, and the case
went on appeal to the pope. However, Eleanor remained William's wife.[16] Some widows may have been willing to elope. After
the death of her first husband, John de Burgh, and her return
from Ireland, Elizabeth de Burgh made a runaway marriage
with Theobald de Verdun who may well have been attracted by
the prospect of one-third of the Clare inheritance and Elizabeth's
jointure lands in Ireland. On being summoned before the king's
council, he alleged that he and Elizabeth had been betrothed in
Ireland. He denied that he had abducted her from Bristol castle,
saying that she had come out to meet him.[17]

15 *Calendar of Patent Rolls 1292–1301* 410, 466. Joan subsequently married
Gervase Avenel; ibid. *1317–21* 5–6, 10.

16 *Rotuli Parliamentorum* (6 vols) London 1783 II 62a–b, 65b. *Calendar of entries in
the papal registers relating to Great Britain and Ireland. Papal letters 1305–42* 394.

17 *Rotuli Parliamentorum* I 352–3.

The Crown continued to regard widows, like heiresses, as valuable means of patronage. It is this consideration which explains Edward I's fury over Joan of Acre's remarriage since he planned to marry her to Amadeus V of Savoy and the contract had already been drawn up.[18] Edward II made use of the two widowed Clare heiresses to marry them off to his favourites before partitioning the inheritance in 1317. Of the three sisters among whom the lands were divided, the eldest, Eleanor, was married to Hugh le Despenser the younger, who had long been pressing for the partition to be made. Margaret, the widow of Piers Gaveston, was married to Hugh Audley, one of the king's household knights, in April 1317. Shortly afterwards Elizabeth, whose marriage to Theobald de Verdun had only lasted a few months before his death in the summer of 1316, was married to another household knight, Roger Damory. Considerable pressure was brought to bear on Elizabeth soon after Theobald's death to persuade her to marry Damory, the king using flattery and describing her as his favourite niece in an attempt to get his way. Her daughter by Theobald was born only a few weeks before her third marriage.[19] By 1317 both she and Margaret had more lands to offer their husbands than their share of the Clare inheritance. Margaret held dower land from her first marriage and she and Audley attempted unsuccessfully to secure the restoration of the earldom of Cornwall which had been granted to Gaveston.[20] Elizabeth held estates in dower from her second marriage as well as jointure from her first.

Widows had free choice over remarriage in theory and in many cases in practice, but they were on occasion subject to pressure from family, friends, prospective husbands and the Crown. They had more say than they had over their first marriage, but it cannot be assumed that their choice was absolutely free. Some widows made the deliberate decision not to remarry. Once Damory had died a traitor in 1322, Elizabeth de Burgh spent the thirty-eight years until her death as an independent lady ruling her household and estates. Her daughter-in-law married Ralph de Ufford, justiciar of Ireland, after

18 T. Rymer *Foedera* eds. A. Clarke J. Caley J. Bayley F. Holbrooke and J.W. Clarke (4 vols) Record Commission London 1816–69 I 861.

19 PRO SC1/63/150.

20 *Rotuli Parliamentorum* I 453. *Calendar of Close Rolls 1318–23* 143.

the death of William de Burgh, earl of Ulster, but then entered
the religious life. Marie de St Pol never remarried after the death
of Aymer de Valence. The choice of becoming a nun was always
open to noble widows but it was a mistake to make the decision
too precipitately; Elizabeth de Juliers, countess of Kent, became
a nun but subsequently remarried and was sentenced to a variety
of penances by the archbishop of Canterbury.[21]

Widows, like all members of the nobility, wanted to safeguard
and defend their lands. Normally this could be done through
cases brought before the royal justices, but difficulties arose in
the event of a clash with the Crown or at a time of political crisis.
The question arises as to whether the widow was particularly
vulnerable in this situation. The Crown always reserved the
right to intervene in the inheritance of tenants-in-chief, particularly when there was no direct heir. Under Edward I, two
noblewomen suffered losses at the king's hands. Aveline, countess of Aumale was the wife of Edward I's younger brother
Edmund, earl of Lancaster; she died childless in 1274 and her
heirs were cheated of their inheritance. Aveline's mother, Isabella de Forz, dowager countess of Aumale and countess of
Devon and lady of the Isle of Wight in her own right, was
subjected to pressure from Edward I during her lifetime. In 1276
it was agreed that she should surrender the Isle of Wight and all
her other lands, apart from four manors, which would then be
handed back to her for life. Edward I agreed to pay 20,000 marks
for the inheritance. However, the plan did not go ahead, and it
was only when Isabella was on her deathbed in 1293 that the
Isle of Wight was sold to the Crown.[22] These details throw light
on more than Edward I's persistence in securing lands for his
family and the Crown. The fact that Edward could only secure
the Isle of Wight, and not Isabella's whole inheritance, when she
was dying indicates that during her life Isabella had shown
determination in the defence of her lands. Moreover it was not
only women who lost out to Edward I's ambitions. Robert
Ferrers, earl of Derby had to surrender his inheritance in prison,
Gilbert de Clare and Humphrey de Bohun found that the

---

21 J. Nichols *A collection of all the wills of the kings and queens of England* London
1780 215.

22 K.B. McFarlane 'Had Edward I a "policy" towards the earls?' *The nobility of
later medieval England* Oxford 1973 256–9. F.M. Powicke *Henry III and the Lord
Edward* (2 vols) Oxford 1947 II 707–9.

succession to their earldoms was limited as a result of the settlements on their marriage to the king's daughters, and Roger Bigod's earldom of Norfolk fell into the king's hands. A determined and feared king like Edward I had the edge over the baronage, men and women alike.

The same was found in later reigns; the Crown had inbuilt advantages which an energetic king could exploit when it came to securing land. Anne, countess of Stafford had little option but to accept the new division of the Bohun estates as laid down by Henry V. Joan, dowager countess of Hereford, who had held dower in the Bohun lands since the last earl's death in 1373, died in 1419. Henry V then brought a case for the redivision of the inheritance on the grounds that the profits of his share, inherited from his mother Mary de Bohun, were 100 marks less than those derived from the pourparty of Anne's mother Eleanor. Anne's arguments for accepting the original division were overruled and a new partition drawn up. Although this ostensibly still gave Anne greater profits than Henry, her responsibility for arrears due to the king from Brecon, which was allotted to her, and the growing problems of securing revenues from Welsh lordships, meant that she probably lost on the deal. Anne was also anxious to secure lands held by her father Thomas of Woodstock, and here persistence and determination paid off in the end and she secured the lordships of Oakham and Holderness. It is significant that when her father's attainder was reversed by Henry IV he 'forgot' Anne's claim and granted Holderness to his son Thomas, whose widow refused to surrender the lordship after his death in 1421. It appears that Anne did not secure the lordship until the year before she died.[23]

A further threat to widows' estates was posed by political crises. In law the penalty for treason was severe, involving the forfeiture of estates and in the fourteenth and fifteenth centuries the possible execution of the traitor. In discussing estates held in fee simple, the treatise long attributed to Bracton decreed the perpetual disinheritance of the traitor's heirs so that they were excluded from both their father's and mother's inheritance. The increasing prevalence of jointures, entails and enfeoffment to

---

23 C. Rawcliffe *The Staffords, earls of Stafford and dukes of Buckingham 1394–1521* Cambridge 1978 14–18. PRO SC8/142/7063. *Proceedings and ordinances of the privy council of England* ed. N.H. Nicolas (7 vols) Record Commission London 1834–7 III 209–10. *Rotuli Parliamentorum* IV 416.

uses from the later thirteenth century raised the question as to whether they should be included in the forfeiture or not. Entailed estates were protected from forfeiture by *De donis*, the first chapter of the statute of Westminster II of 1285, by the statute of treasons of 1352, and by the Lords Appellant in 1388; the Appellants, however, declared that estates held to the use of the traitor were liable to forfeiture. Ten years later Richard II was far more ruthless than the Appellants in declaring forfeit entailed estates as well as lands held in fee simple and to use. This was the position taken by the fifteenth-century acts of attainder.[24]

The law was not necessarily fully implemented, as a policy of wholesale confiscations and seizures ran the risk of alienating the baronage and sparking off further trouble, as Richard II found in 1399. Women in particular did not suffer as severely as the legal provisions might suggest. Both the Appellants and the acts of attainder protected the wife's and widow's right to her inheritance and jointure, since she possessed these before her husband committed treason. Her right to dower was not protected since it was allocated after her husband's death and therefore after treason had been committed. In theory the woman could only claim her inheritance and jointure after the death of her husband when she was independent and able to plead in the courts. In practice, especially if she had influential connections, she was able to secure lands earlier. Philippa de Coucy, wife of Robert de Vere and granddaughter of Edward III, was able to make arrangements over jointure soon after the condemnation of her husband for treason by the Appellants, although she was not able to claim dower until Richard II had reversed the treason sentence.[25] Such arrangements were important in ensuring that at least some lands remained in the hands of the family rather than falling into the hands of the Crown and running the risk of being alienated or sold.

Women were vulnerable at a time of political upheaval if their lands were coveted by the king or a favourite and if there were reasons why the Crown wanted a measure of revenge. Even in these cases it is clear that their husbands were equally, if not more, at risk, as they suffered loss of political power and

---

24 C.D. Ross 'Forfeiture for treason in the reign of Richard II' *English Historical Review* LXXI (1956) 560–75. J.R. Lander 'Attainder and forfeiture, 1453–1509' *Historical Journal* IV (1961) 119–151.

25 *Calendar of Patent Rolls 1385–9* 423; ibid. *1391–6* 34.

sometimes death in addition to the imprisonment and forfeiture of estates endured by their wives. These dangers were particularly apparent after Edward II's victory at Boroughbridge in 1322 when penalties for treason and the greed of the Despensers combined to put a number of noble families in danger. The younger Despenser was ambitious to add to his lordship of Glamorgan the Welsh lands of the other two Clare heiresses and of others, and he had already provoked the Marcher rising of 1321, which resulted in his temporary exile. Moreover, the legacy of political bitterness from the crises earlier in the reign explains why loyal members of the nobility also came under attack in the 1320s.

Aymer de Valence, earl of Pembroke advised Edward II to exile the Despensers in 1321 but he never joined the king's opponents who were defeated at Boroughbridge the following year. He died suddenly on 23 June 1324 and his widow, Marie de St Pol, received most of her dower by the end of the year. Aymer had no children by either of his marriages and the coheirs were his nephew John Hastings and his nieces Joan and Elizabeth Comyn. All were harassed over Aymer's lands, goods and debts. Despenser may have been exacting revenge for his exile, but he was also eager to acquire Aymer's land, especially in Wales. Marie complained that Despenser would not allow the escheator to return the information on Aymer's lands at Hertford and Haverford because he wanted them for himself, and Robert Baldock would not allow her to have dower there or in Aymer's lands in Monmouth until she produced the original royal grants. The king granted Despenser land in Monmouth in 1325, and Elizabeth Comyn was imprisoned by the Despensers until she granted them her rights at Goodrich and Painswick. Marie's difficulties continued into the early part of Edward III's reign, when she was forced to make an unequal exchange of lands with the king; again there may have been an element of revenge in view of Aymer's close association as counsellor with Edward II.[26]

Rebel widows lost not only their rights to dower but also their inheritance and jointure until they agreed to hand over what the king and the Despensers wanted. Alice de Lacy, the widow of Thomas, earl of Lancaster, was forced to grant most of her lands to the king and his favourites and had to promise not to make any alienations without royal permission. She received a life

<hr>

26 J.R.S. Phillips *Aymer de Valence, earl of Pembroke, 1307–24* Oxford 1972 233–9.

tenancy on some estates with remainder to the younger Despenser and his heirs, and she also held the lands with which she had been dowered by her husband at the church door.[27]

A comparison can be drawn with the fate of the two younger Clare heiresses and their husbands. Both Hugh Audley and Roger Damory rebelled in 1321–2; Roger died of his wounds before the battle of Boroughbridge; Hugh was taken prisoner at the battle, but his life was spared and he remained in prison until his escape in 1325. His wife Margaret was sent for safe keeping to Sempringham priory, while Roger's widow, Elizabeth de Burgh, was captured at Usk and sent to Barking Abbey. The younger Despenser had secured Audley's lordship of Gwynllwg and set about gaining Elizabeth's lands at Usk. Whereas all Audley's lands remained in the king's hands, Elizabeth had her English and Irish inheritance restored in November 1322.[28]

Elizabeth was not prepared to accept any loss of land. On 15 May 1326 she had a document drawn up giving a full account of her grievances against the Despensers, and this account is corroborated by other evidence.[29] After her capture she was forbidden to marry anyone without the king's special licence and had unwillingly agreed to grant her lordship of Usk to her sister Eleanor and the younger Despenser in exchange for Gower. Elizabeth claimed that the exchange was obtained from her by force at a time when she feared for her own life and that of her son William de Burgh. Further difficulties arose when she was summoned to spend the Christmas of 1322 with the king at York. She was arrested, separated from her council, and again had to quitclaim her Welsh lands. She was compelled to repeat her promise not to remarry or alienate any of her lands without the king's permission. If she failed to comply, her lands would be confiscated. Elizabeth tried to evade these undertakings by leaving York, but this only led to the imprisonment of some of her council. It was in the April of 1324 that William de Braose sued Elizabeth successfully for the recovery of Gower and granted it to the Despensers. Elizabeth did not accept her losses

---

27 R. Somerville *History of the duchy of Lancaster* (2 vols) London 1953 I 33–4.

28 *Calendar of Close Rolls 1318–23* 603–4. The English lands were taken back into the king's hands the following January but this was a temporary resumption; ibid. 624.

29 BL Harley MS 1240 fos 86v–87. G.A. Holmes 'A protest against the Despensers, 1326' *Speculum* XXX (1955) 207–12. *Rotuli Parliamentorum* II 440a.

passively, but petitioned for redress in subsequent parliaments. It is small wonder that she backed Queen Isabella's invasion in the autumn of 1326, and once Edward II was deposed she gained the restoration of Usk and the reversal of her surrenders to the Despensers.[30] Her actions in the 1320s show that she was ready to put up a struggle to keep her estates; she believed in protest even if it did not bring her immediate victory.

Women like Margaret Audley and Elizabeth de Burgh undoubtedly had a difficult time when they found themselves on the wrong side at a time of political crisis. Yet periods of crisis were on the whole shortlived and there was every prospect that the women would recover their position once political circumstances changed. This in fact happened in 1327. Looking at the higher nobility in general there are few signs that either noblewomen or their children were permanently disadvantaged as a result of their families' involvement in rebellion. The amount of intermarriage among the nobility ensured that virtually every family had influential connections, and once the family's estates were restored it could continue to flourish. The marriages made by the children of families which had been opposed to the Crown depended on their status within the nobility, their wealth, and the prospects of inheritance and alliance rather than on reservations over the family's past history. Elizabeth de Burgh's eldest son William, earl of Ulster married the daughter of Henry, earl of Lancaster, and her daughter Isabella, heiress to a share of the Verdun lands, married Henry de Ferrers of Groby, associated with the earl of Lancaster in 1328. The marriage of the younger daughter Elizabeth to John Bardolf of Wormegay ensured that she remained in the peerage but cannot be described as brilliant; Elizabeth, however, was not an heiress.

Throughout the later Middle Ages, widows were an important group among the nobility. Their position grew stronger as the law worked in their favour over dower and jointure. Most of them remarried at least once, but as they grew older some clearly enjoyed the independence which widowhood gave them. As widows they were not completely free of outside pressures, whether from family, suitors or the Crown, but they had more say in making the decisions affecting their own lives, households and estates than they had had as wives. Their responsibilities for land were the same as those of their male counterparts, and they

30 *Calendar of Patent Rolls 1327–30* 32. *Rotuli Parliamentorum* II 6.

had to engage in administration and litigation. Virtually all had a strong sense of their own and their family's rights over patrimony. They were as ready and able to defend and increase these rights as their husbands and sons, but all the nobility faced difficulties when they came up against the interests of the Crown or of parties supported by the king whether it was a time of political crisis or not. Among these noble widows, a few women stand out as especially powerful and formidable, such as Elizabeth de Burgh, Marie de St Pol and Margaret de Brotherton. These were the women who combined wealth, ability, long life and force of personality to exert particular influence on their family and locality, and they epitomise the power which noblewomen could exercise in the later Middle Ages.

Chapter 3

THE HOUSEHOLD

The household constituted the centre of the lady's life and activities. It enabled her to run her affairs, exercise hospitality, go on journeys, and maintain her reputation in the neighbourhood through displays of power and magnificence. It had an important social and economic impact on the region where the lady was living and also further afield. The lady and household functioned as a community, living, eating, working and worshipping together. It was not, however, self-contained or exclusive, but had the flexibility to be able to change according to the lady's needs. Although it had its own cohesion, it fitted into the wider world of the lady's family, kinsmen and affinity.

During the later Middle Ages, the noble household cannot be treated as a single unit: various types of household existed to serve different needs. The great household was usually based at a chief residence, while a smaller household accompanied the lord or lady on journeys. Small skeleton households were maintained at other residences. The exigencies of noble life, with the husband absent at court, on business or on military campaigns, meant that the wife was left to exercise considerable responsibilities. The activities of the lady and her household show that the wife as well as the widow had power and influence.

The widow or the wife whose husband was away was in charge of the great household. It is likely that William and Joan de Valence had great and travelling households, William journeying with the smaller group while Joan remained with the great household and was responsible for its smooth running. When William was with her at Hertford and Brabourne in 1295–6 it was at the costs of the lady. Joan also organised her itinerant household if needed, as when she left Brabourne to pay her husband a short visit at Dover.[1] Richard Beauchamp, earl of Warwick in 1420–1 had both his inner household and the foreign household which accompanied him to France; he spent only a short time with the inner household, which was to all intents and purposes the household of the countess, Elizabeth Berkeley.[2] Anne Neville, duchess of Buckingham had her great and itinerant households when she was married to her second husband Lord Mountjoy and was regarded by her servants as the head of the household.[3]

In addition to being on occasion in charge of the great household, it was usual for wives of the higher nobility to have what amounted to a mini-household of their own, and to meet at least some of their household expenses. Elizabeth, countess of Hereford had her own wardrobe and chamber in 1304, and was paying wages to various servants even when she was with her husband. On her journey south from Scotland to Knaresborough she travelled with an itinerant household which met all her daily needs.[4] Elizabeth, countess of Ulster's household was separate from her husband's and in 1357 comprised ladies, clerks, esquires, yeomen of the chamber, pages and a chaplain. Geoffrey Chaucer was then a member of the household, possibly a page, and went on to serve her husband, Lionel, duke of Clarence, and the king.[5] Under a particular lord and lady these various households overlapped and as need arose men moved from one to another.

Households varied in size according to the status of the lady, the numbers of her family and the level of her activities. Elizabeth Berkeley's household consisted of about fifty people. Anne Neville probably had a household of about sixty in 1473 when it was estimated that £133 was needed for salaries.[6] For knightly families the number of servants was very much less.

1 PRO E101/505/25 m.2, 3.

2 C.D. Ross 'The household accounts of Elizabeth Berkeley, countess of Warwick, 1420–1' *Transactions of the Bristol and Gloucestershire Archaeological Society* LXX (1951) 84.

3 BL Additional MS 29608.

4 PRO E101/365/20 m.1, 2.

5 *Chaucer Life-Records* eds. M.M. Crowe and C.C. Olson Oxford 1966 13–22.

6 C. Rawcliffe *The Staffords, earls of Stafford and dukes of Buckingham 1394–1521* Cambridge 1978 87. BL Additional MS 29608 m.2.

Whatever the size, the household was structured hierarchically. In accounting for the wages of the household servants in 1418–19, Alice de Bryene referred to her maid, chamberlain, squires, chaplains, grooms, clerks of the chapel and boys.[7] Elizabeth Berkeley had six gentlewomen and three women of the chamber, nine gentlemen, several of whom had administrative duties, five yeomen who ranked as upper servants, and fifteen grooms. The yeomen acted as usher, cook, butler and two valets of the chamber, while the grooms included the clerks of the chapel, pantry, buttery, ewery and kitchen, and the head gardener. There were eleven further unnamed grooms who were attached to some of the household offices.

The same sense of hierarchy is apparent in Elizabeth de Burgh's list of liveries of 1343, which covered not only the household but estate officials, relations and members of her affinity. Everyone was graded according to rank; the roll began with the knights and then worked down through the ladies, clerks, esquires, serjeants, lesser clerks and women of the chamber, little clerks, yeomen, grooms and pages. The terms lesser and little clerks referred to their standing in the household. The term used for the yeomen was 'gentz de mester,' which often meant tradesmen or craftsmen; however, yeomen are more appropriate as an intermediate rank between the esquires and the grooms; several of the bailiffs of demesne manors came under this heading. Some of Elizabeth's tradesmen were included among the esquires.[8]

Household accounts indicate that the household was divided into departments to carry out various functions, and the degree of specialisation was greatest within the largest households. Elizabeth de Burgh's daily accounts entered items under the headings of the pantry, buttery, kitchen, poultry, saucery, scullery, stables, and sometimes the hall and chamber. The pantry was responsible for the supply of bread, the buttery for ale and wine, the kitchen for meat and fish, the poultry for birds, eggs and dairy produce, the saucery for sauces and the scullery for dishes. This list was not exhaustive and the chapel, which was an integral part of the household, went unmentioned in the accounts.

7 *Household book of Dame Alice de Bryene 1412–13* ed. V.B. Redstone trans. M.K. Dale Suffolk Institute of Archaeology and Natural History Ipswich 1931 124.

8 PRO E101/92/23.

These departments did not have rigid lines of demarcation between them, and in small households especially there would be flexibility in the arrangements for provisioning. The impression of strict departmental division in the accounts resulted from the need to account for all that was used in the household, whether items of stock or purchase. In Elizabeth de Burgh's household each office made its own account to the clerk of the wardrobe and a few of these accounts survive as for the kitchen, the brewers and the stable. There was a special account for the children in 1327–8 and for the goldsmiths in 1332. Accounts were submitted by the skeleton households, as by Henry de Colingham at Clare in the summer of 1341 when the lady was in Wales. Journeys were accounted for separately, and Elizabeth's personal expenditure was entered on her chamber account.[9] A roll was drawn up of daily expenditure listed under departmental headings and giving details of visitors to the lady. Much of the information in all these accounts was incorporated in the wardrobe and household account for the year, and in the counter-roll which gave on one side the daily and weekly totals of cash and stock expenditure and on the other a shortened version of the wardrobe account. All accounts were audited.

The household was a complex and hierarchical organisation and it was almost completely a male preserve. The lady had her own female attendants but they only comprised a minority of the servants. The laundress was invariably female, and in a household with young children nurses and a mistress of the nursery were employed. Older daughters also came under the charge of a mistress. Isabella, dowager Lady Morley had a household staff of fourteen of whom four were women, namely two gentlewomen, a laundress and one other.[10] Elizabeth de Burgh's livery roll listed seven ladies, four women of the chamber, and a laundress. In her will of 1414 Elizabeth Montague, countess of Salisbury named three ladies, a woman of the chamber, and the laundress, together with thirty-five male servants.[11]

Relatively little is known of these personal attendants, but it is

9 PRO E101/91/15, 16, 19, 30; 92/1, 15, 17; 93/12, 16. Elizabeth's own chamber has to be distinguished from the chamber which was her main accounting office.

10 BL Additional MS 34122A m. 3.

11 *The register of Henry Chichele, archbishop of Canterbury, 1414–43* ed. E.F. Jacob (4 vols) Canterbury and York Society XLII (1937) II 17.

likely that some at least were connected with other members of the household or retinue. Three of Elizabeth Berkeley's six gentlewomen were married to retainers of her husband. Instances of long service are also found. Suzanne de Neketon and Anne de Lexden were in the service of Elizabeth de Burgh in 1343 and were left substantial bequests of plate and clothing in her will which was drawn up twelve years later. Traditions of family service were probably built up. Margaret de Neketon was one of Elizabeth's women of the chamber in 1343. Elizabeth Marshal, who was serving Elizabeth de Burgh in 1351–2 and was married that year, may have been related to Margery Marshal, entered among the ladies in 1343. Elizabeth Marshal received gifts of cloth and fur from her mistress, who attended the wedding.[12]

As far as the men of the household were concerned, the most obscure were the grooms and pages. In Elizabeth de Burgh's household in 1343 many of these were known by the department to which they were attached, such as the grooms Robert and Jevan of the wardrobe and Robert of the chamber, and the pages Adam of the poultry and Adam of the bakery. The page of the palfreys was not even given a Christian name. It was possible to be promoted from page to groom, John Lucesone having made the transition in 1343. Some grooms were mentioned by name in the lady's will; Richard, groom of the chamber and John, groom of the buttery each received two marks. Long service is again found, as a bequest of £3 each was left to John Lucesone, Robert Lucesone, a page in 1343, and Henry Cnappyngs, referred to among the grooms in 1343 as Cnappyngs the carter.

Above the pages and grooms were the yeomen and esquires. Joan de Valence had twenty-three esquires for herself and her daughter-in-law Beatrice, who served among other things as clerk of the chapel, usher, palfreyman, carter and huntsman; it is likely in view of their status that they had a supervisory rather than a menial role.[13] This is borne out by the activities of Elizabeth de Burgh's esquires and yeomen, many of whom spent years in her service and were remembered in her will. Hugh le Pulleter and John de Southam were included among the yeomen in 1343. Hugh was in her service from the mid-1330s and his

12 PRO E101/92/23 m. 1, 2; 93/12 m. 2d, 4d. J. Nichols *A collection of all the wills of the kings and queens of England* London 1780 24.

13 PRO E101/505/26 m. 2d.

main responsibility was the purchase of fish for the household, although on occasion he also bought pigs, sheep, salt, honey, and horse hides for the carts, presumably to cover loads. John de Southam's main duty from 1344–5 was to buy wine. Among the esquires, both Colinet de Morlee and John Gough had entered Elizabeth's service by 1335. Colinet had miscellaneous duties, making a variety of purchases and organising carriage; in 1336–7 he was in London supervising the shearing of cloth, eight years later he was supervising the carting of cloth from London, and in 1351 he was again in London buying cloth, shoes, embroidery thread, keys and other items for the lady.[14] John Gough as avener had to provide hay, oats and litter for the stables, and this meant that he had sometimes to scour the country in order to secure what was needed. In 1337–8 he was making purchases at Stourbridge fair, Cambridge and Wisbech, as well as a number of places round Clare; he made use of Clare and Bardfield markets as well as buying oats and hay at Dunmow, Stebbing, Birdbrook, Glemsford and elsewhere.[15] John Bataille was sometimes involved with provisioning but was more often involved with administrative business and the supervision of demesne manors; he served as an auditor in 1355–6.[16] Similar wide-ranging responsibilities were exercised by some of the clerks. William de Berkway, who was probably clerk of the kitchen, was involved in the purchase and sale of animals and the sale of the issues of the kitchen – hides, sheepskins, rabbit-skins, skimmings of fat. Piers de Ereswell served as Elizabeth's almoner in the 1350s.

The men in overall charge of the household were often clerks and the terms used to describe them varied. Elizabeth de Burgh made use of clerks for her wardrober, who was responsible for the household, and the clerk of the chamber, who was in charge of her finances; from 1350–1 these two positions were combined. Giles de Wenlok described himself as keeper of the household of Margaret de Brotherton in 1385–6 and also acted as her chaplain. Lewis Beale, clerk, was termed both keeper and steward of Elizabeth Berkeley's household, and William Stather, also a clerk, was steward of Isabella Morley's household and

14 PRO E101/92/4 m. 9; 92/27 m. 7; 93/12 m. 1.

15 PRO E101/92/7 m. 2, 4.

16 PRO E101/93/19 m. 8.

also her receiver for 1463–4. Sometimes this responsibility was undertaken by members of the gentry. Anne, dowager duchess of Buckingham made the Buckinghamshire landowner John Heton steward of her household and receiver-general. It was a matter for the lady's decision whether the man in charge of running the household should have estate responsibilities as well.

Household servants were paid wages or fees and were given livery by the lady twice a year. In 1420–1 Elizabeth Berkeley paid the usher, cook, butler and a valet of the chamber four marks each, the valet of the kitchen and the man in charge of her stable £1 each, and the kitchen and buttery boys each received one mark; the total entered came to £18. 3s. 4d., but this was incomplete. Isabella Morley's domestic fees amounted to £33. 3s. 4d., the highest sum of £6. 13s. 4d., being paid to William Stather; her chaplain received £4, her two yeomen £1. 13s. 4d., and £1. 6s. 8d., respectively, and her two gentlewomen £1. 6s. 8d., and ten shillings; the lowest amount of half a mark went to the laundress. Alice de Bryene spent £44 on the wages of her household servants, and just over £35 on their winter and summer liveries. The amounts spent on labour seem to have been quite low compared with certain other costs of the household.

Liveries were graded according to the servant's rank in the household, as seen in Elizabeth de Burgh's livery roll. Her ladies and clerks received both cloth and furs. Suzanne de Neketon received 8¾ ells of cloth and a fur lining of Baltic squirrel and Anne de Lexden twelve ells of cloth, 1½ linings of budge and a lining of lambskin. John de Lenne, who was wardrober between 1337 and 1340, had eight ells of cloth, a lining of budge and a budge hood.[17] Most of the esquires received between six and seven ells of cloth and a lining of lambskin; a few, like Henry de Colingham, were also given a hood of budge. The yeomen, grooms and pages received no furs but had between five and six ells of cloth.

In addition to wages, fees and liveries, there were a number of miscellaneous rewards. Extra payment was given for particular jobs, and messengers were often rewarded by the recipient. Ladies left bequests to servants of all ranks. The greatest rewards were reserved for those at the top of the hierarchy, since service

17 Budge was imported lambskin. Fur linings to clothes were essential for warmth in the winter.

to a noble lady led to promotion and work with other lords and the king. Even when officials stayed with a lady for years, there was no reason for her service to be regarded as a backwater or a dead end. Hugh de Burgh was Elizabeth de Burgh's wardrober between 1326 and 1332 and went on to serve other magnates and to rise in the Irish royal administration.[18] William de Manton was wardrober from 1340 until Elizabeth's death, combining the office with that of clerk of the chamber from 1350–1. He was named in her will as one of her chief executors, went on to serve Lionel, duke of Clarence, and was keeper of Edward III's wardrobe between 1361 and 1366.[19]

Service in a lady's household provided employment, reward and good prospects to a wide range of people. These men had to cater for the domestic needs of the lady, a task which called for organisational skills of a high order and which can be likened to a major business enterprise. The size and complexity of the task is exemplified by the diversity and amounts of goods which the household needed. Not only did foodstuffs for men and horses have to be procured in large quantities, but fuel and lights had to be obtained together with cloth and furs for liveries and iron for the stables. Once purchased the goods had to be transported wherever the lady needed them. Alice de Bryene, as head of a fairly small household, used 64 quarters of wheat for bread in 1418–19, and 124 quarters of malt for ale, and the horses consumed nearly 62 quarters of oats. 46 cattle, 97 sheep and 87 pigs were consumed together with birds and rabbits, and the fish consumption included 2,510 red herrings, 3,060 white herrings, various types of saltfish, three-quarters of a barrel of salmon and a quarter barrel of sturgeon. These figures appear small beside Elizabeth de Burgh's household needs in 1350–1 when 516½ quarters of wheat furnished 106,248 loaves, and 714½ quarters of malt made 40,682 gallons of ale. 968 quarters of oats were needed for the horses. 136 cattle, 147 pigs and 276 sheep were used over the year, together with a commensurate amount of fish.[20] Such quantities were needed to feed the members of the household and to exercise hospitality.

18 R. Frame *English lordship in Ireland, 1318–61* Oxford 1982 69–70.

19 T.F. Tout *Chapters in the administrative history of medieval England* (6 vols) Manchester 1920–33 III 199, 233, 254; IV 149–57; VI 27.

20 *Household Book of Dame Alice de Bryene, 1412–13* Redstone, 125–36. PRO E101/ 93/8.

The obtaining of these provisions meant the lady's household had an economic impact on the region where she was living as well as at the fairs and in the towns where purchases were made. The household's activities contributed to the demand for goods and thus had an effect on the prosperity of towns and traders. Substantial changes took place during the later Middle Ages in the ways in which provisions were obtained. The lady's reliance on merchants increased, partly because of the growth of leasing rather than the direct farming of the demesne manors, partly because of the changing patterns of residence, and because of the desire for luxuries and the emphasis placed by the nobility on conspicuous consumption.[21]

In writing his advice to the countess of Lincoln c. 1240 on the governance of her estates and household, Robert Grosseteste recommended that she should decide at Michaelmas on the places where she was going to live over the next year. By the end of September she knew the state of the harvest and which places would be able best to accommodate her without being impoverished. Grosseteste recommended increased stocking of cattle and sheep on the manors to pay for the countess's purchases of wine, cloth and wax and to meet the expenses of her wardrobe. He assumed that she would mainly live off the produce of her estates.[22] This was only happening to some extent in the later Middle Ages and it became increasingly unusual by the fifteenth century.

The change is particularly noticeable in the provision of grain to the household. Elizabeth de Burgh farmed most of her demesne manors directly and received grain supplies from them. Even so it was usually necessary to make some purchases. Most of the grain came from her manors in the eastern counties,

---

21 The discussion of the provisioning of the lady's household is based mainly on the following accounts: the household accounts of Elizabeth de Burgh, 1325–59, notably PRO E101/91/11–13, 17, 21–9; 92/2–11, 13, 14, 16, 18–22, 24, 25, 27–30; 93/1–15, 18–20; 94/1, 2; the household account for Margaret de Brotherton for 1385–6, BL Additional Roll 17208, printed in *Medieval Framlingham. Select Documents, 1270–1524* ed. J. Ridgard Suffolk Records Society xxvII (1985) 86–128; *Household Book of Dame Alice de Bryene, 1412–13* Redstone; Ross 'The household accounts of Elizabeth Berkeley' 81–105; and the household accounts of Anne, dowager duchess of Buckingham, BL Additional MSS 29608, 34213, and BL Latin Egerton 2822.

22 'Les Reules Seynt Roberd' *Walter of Henley's Husbandry* ed. E. Lamond Royal Historical Society London 1890 144–5.

although some was supplied by the Welsh estates when she was at Usk. Her officials made an estimate of the likely harvest in the spring and the grain was delivered to the household at harvest-time, much of it on 28 September, just before Michaelmas. The ratio of demesne supplies to purchases varied from year to year. Normally most of the wheat, used for bread for the household, came from the manors, but in 1349–50 when the lady was at Usk until April about one-third of the supply had to be bought. The situation changed from one year to the next with barley and oats, essential for ale and feeding the horses respectively. In 1349–50 most of the supply came from the manors, but at other times a considerable amount had to be purchased; over two-thirds of the oats had to be bought in 1350–1. Vigilance and forward planning by the officials were essential. When grain had to be purchased it was normally obtained from the villages and local markets near where the lady was living, but in 1350–1 when the lady was at Clare for much of the year, John Gough went to Wisbech on several occasions to secure beans, peas and oats.

Live animals were obtained for meat, driven sometimes con-siderable distances to the household, fattened up and slaughtered as needed. In 1350–1 Elizabeth de Burgh's household rented twenty-four acres of pasture in Clare for the oxen for the larder. Animals came from manors all over the southern half of England and not just from those near the lady's residence. In 1350–1 pigs came from the demesne manors of Caythorpe, Lincolnshire, Brandon in Warwickshire, Standon in Hertfordshire and else-where; it took six days to drive pigs from Brandon to Clare. Most of the sheep were supplied from Clare itself. Some cattle were purchased locally, but ninety-three oxen and twenty-two cows were bought at Usk. Venison was supplied from the lady's parks, and 839 rabbits came from the demesne manors. Swans were supplied by the demesne manors and also received as gifts. Seventy-seven herons were purchased at Usk. As in the case of the grain supplies, considerable organisation and coordination by the officials were needed if all was to run smoothly.

The scale of Elizabeth de Burgh's operations was far greater than that of Alice de Bryene, but parallels can be drawn between the two ladies' methods. In 1418–19 Alice was living at Acton Hall in Suffolk and was able to supply much of what her household needed from her local estates. Her manors of Acton and Bures were farmed directly, and Acton supplied most of the wheat and oats needed, together with the barley which was malted to make ale; Bures contributed to the stock of oats. Cattle, sheep and lambs were supplied by the bailiff of Acton, and pigs by the bailiffs of Acton and Bures. The household was not, however, self-sufficient as far as meat was concerned and purchases had to be made locally as well as from the nearby town of Sudbury and from Colchester. Cattle were bought live and kept at pasture until needed by the household. The rabbits and most of the poultry were home-produced, swans came from the lady's manors and pigeons from the Acton dovecote. The provisioning of such a localised household was far easier than that of a much bigger establishment with widely scattered estates.

The increasing practice of leasing demesne manors from the later fourteenth century meant that noblewomen came to rely far less on supplies from their estates and this provided additional stimulus to local trade. For Margaret de Brotherton's household in 1385–6 wheat, oats and meat were bought as needed throughout the year, and malt was purchased at about eighty or ninety quarters at a time. Margaret spent much of the year at Framlingham in Suffolk and the town was an important source of her supplies; wheat was purchased there and 108 sheep carcasses were bought from Robert Beverlee between October and December 1385. Local fairs were important for the purchase of livestock such as those of Diss, Loddon and Newmarket. It appears that Margaret's officials were able to secure most of what they needed within Suffolk itself. Margaret's estates were as extensive and widely scattered as Elizabeth de Burgh's but her officials were not making use of estates or markets further afield and the demesnes may already have been leased; by the mid-1390s Margaret's income came from rents rather than direct farming.

Very similar patterns of providing grain and meat are found in the households of Elizabeth Berkeley and Anne, duchess of Buckingham. Elizabeth Berkeley bought ale and wheat as needed. She purchased oxen at Ross-on-Wye while she was at Berkeley in the autumn of 1420, and at Salwarpe when she was living there the following August and September. Anne, duchess of Buckingham likewise relied heavily on local purchases. While she was living at Writtle in Essex in 1462–3 she obtained many of her supplies from nearby Chelmsford, and men like Guy Harling, who provided ale and oats, and William Baker of

Moulsham, who supplied ale, did good business with the lady. Anne, however, obtained much of her meat from her own estates, cattle coming from her manors in Gloucestershire and Northamptonshire and sheep from Fobbing, on the Essex marshes. Venison was obtained from her own parks.

Certain provisions always had to be purchased throughout the later Middle Ages. No household could meet all its needs in fish from its own resources. The principal categories of fish needed were herrings, saltfish and stockfish, which was dried; the last two comprised a number of different types of fish. Smaller quantities were obtained of other kinds of fish. Alice de Bryene's account mentioned salmon, sturgeon and eels. These were all used in Elizabeth de Burgh's household and her accounts mention in addition pike, lampreys, grampus, mackerel, bream, and occasionally shellfish and oysters. A wealthier household was able to afford a greater variety, although this was enjoyed by the lady, her guests and top-ranking officials and not by all the household members.

Elizabeth de Burgh was fortunate in being able to obtain some of her fish supplies from her demesne manors. Southwold owed rent in herrings in 1342, and one last and 9,000 herrings were supplied to the household eight years later;[23] the last was the equivalent of twelve barrels. As with her other provisioning, Elizabeth's officials bought their fish all over the country although certain markets were only used when the lady was in the vicinity; purchases of fish in Bristol were made when the lady was at Usk and at Bury St Edmunds and Colchester when she was in the eastern counties. Salmon usually came from Usk, and lampreys from Gloucester or Wales. A large quantity of herrings was bought at the Yarmouth herring fair in the autumn. Stockfish was often purchased at the east coast ports of King's Lynn and Boston. Occasionally fish was bought in London. Margaret de Brotherton had a similar pattern of purchasing, obtaining her fish from Wales, London and the east coast. Elizabeth Berkeley, who was mainly living in western England with a short stay in London in 1420–1, made her principal purchases of fish in London, Tetbury, Bristol and Droitwich.

Fairs were important for making household purchases and were recommended by Robert Grosseteste to the countess of Lincoln. In the eastern counties, Stourbridge fair at Cambridge

23 PRO SC12/15/19; E101/93/8m.6.

was used by many noblewomen and grew in importance in the later Middle Ages. In 1279 it was held on 13 and 14 September, but by 1516 lasted from 24 August until Michaelmas. Elizabeth de Burgh made some of her fish purchases there, and also bought salt, some spices and wax, and occasionally seacoal. Margaret de Brotherton purchased salt at the fair. It is likely that the fair was of relatively greater importance to smaller households, which relied on it for most of their supplies. Alice de Bryene bought all her saltfish, stockfish and salt at Stourbridge fair in 1418–19. All these purchases of salt were essential in a society which preserved large quantities of meat and fish.

When it came to the purchase of wine, traders in the larger towns were used. Most of the wine was Gascon, with some Rhenish, and in the fifteenth century some sweet wines. In only one case has a noblewoman been found buying her wine in Aquitaine when Elizabeth de Burgh sent her butler, Roger de Medfeld, to the duchy in 1330.[24] Such activity in any case became difficult with the outbreak of the Hundred Years War. Normally Elizabeth's butler made his purchases in Ipswich, Colchester and London with purchases at Bristol when the lady was at Usk. Alice de Bryene's main supplier was John Joye of Ipswich, although she also made some purchases in London. Margaret de Brotherton likewise bought some of her wine in London and also in the port of Orwell, but her main purchase of fifteen tuns of red Gascon wine and two tuns of white was made from Gilbert de Bouge of Ipswich. Elizabeth Berkeley bought wine in London when she was living there and at Walthamstow, but otherwise made her purchases in Bristol or Worcester. All these noblewomen had to bear in mind the cost, not only of the wine but also of transport, and it was often preferable to buy the wine in a town near their residence. Bringing the wine by water was cheaper than land transport but even that would add to the overall expense.

Such considerations did not apply to the same extent to spices, which were usually purchased in London, the centre for the luxury trades in the later Middle Ages. The term comprised not only what are now regarded as spices, but dried fruits, sugar, rice, almonds, turpentine, ointments and medicines. The wealthier the household, the more spices it obtained. The contrast can be seen in the households of Alice de Bryene and Elizabeth de

24 *Calendar of Patent Rolls 1330–4* 1.

Burgh. Alice's household in 1418–19 used among other things five pounds of pepper, two and a half pounds of ginger, thirty-eight pounds of almonds, three pounds of rice, one pound of sugar, and two frails and seventeen pounds of dried fruit.[25] According to Elizabeth de Burgh's stock account in 1350–1, her household consumed 28 pounds of pepper, 32½ pounds of ginger, 886 pounds of almonds, 413 pounds of rice and 223½ pounds of sugar. Purchases of dried fruit varied from year to year, and large amounts were sometimes needed, as when 114 pounds of Malaga raisins were purchased in 1350–1.

In addition to the provision of food supplies, some purchases had to be made for heating and lighting, although faggots could often be obtained from manors and parks and tallow produced at home. Wax was bought at the fairs or from the same merchants who sold spices. Iron was essential for horseshoes and iron imported from Spain or the Baltic had to be bought; Elizabeth de Burgh preferred such supplies to the iron produced on her own estates in the Weald. All these purchases were minor items of expenditure compared with food and liveries.

Cloths and furs were an essential and major item in the provisioning of the lady's household. Quite apart from clothing the lady and her family and supplying liveries, cloth was often used as gifts. For Elizabeth de Burgh's livery in 1344 70½ cloths were needed, each measuring between 22 and 27½ ells.[26] Although London was a major source of supply for both cloths and furs, there was a certain amount of shopping around from one year to the next. In 1340–1 most of the furs were purchased from Robert de Eynesham in London, but a few lambskins were bought at Stamford. Robert Grosseteste had recommended the purchase of robes at the fair of St Ives and Elizabeth purchased cloth there and at Boston fair as well as in London; eight ells of English cloth were bought at Clare for the gardener, and wool was bought at Caythorpe to be made into two cloths for the lady and Marie de St Pol and one for the little clerks. In 1344–5, however, nearly all the cloth was bought in London, and most of the furs at Boston fair.

Close relationships were forged between the household and its suppliers. John de Wynterton stands out among the merchants

25 The frail was a basket and the size is not known.

26 PRO E101/92/26. The ell measured forty-five inches, one and a quarter yards.

provisioning the household of Margaret de Brotherton, and he was probably the same man who held property in Norwich in 1397.[27] He was certainly engaged in the Norfolk coastal trade. He operated at Stourbridge fair where he sold salt to the household; he supplied all the malt it needed and also stockfish, eels, salmon and sturgeon. Elizabeth de Burgh gave her livery to some of her suppliers, listing them among the esquires in 1343, and these men usually received her custom for several years. They included Nigel Tebaud of Sudbury who sold her rice and lambskins in 1339–40, Robert de Eynesham, the skinner of London, and Thomas Coteler of Ipswich, who provided wine, Spanish iron, and sometimes salt and spices between 1337 and 1345. Elizabeth also had good relations with Colchester traders; she bought wine from John atte Forde in 1350–1 and 1355–6. Her most eminent and longstanding supplier was, however, the Italian grocer, Bartholomew Thomasin of London, from whom she bought spices, confections, wax and fruit. Although born overseas, Bartholomew was described in 1351 as a citizen of London and as living permanently in the city with his wife and children. Elizabeth was trading at least from 1336 until 1352 with Bartholomew, who for part of the period was also supplying the royal household. Elizabeth obviously chose one of the best London suppliers.[28]

Provisioning a noble lady's household was a complex and time-consuming business. To ensure that the household had what it needed when it needed it was no mean feat. The lady was well advised to employ able, honest and efficient servants and these men were in a position to give traders of all kinds considerable business. For certain goods like wine, spices, furs and quality cloths it was essential to use London and the large towns or to frequent the major fairs, but local markets also benefited from the presence of a great lady in the vicinity. It is possible that more business was generated as the lady came to rely less on her own estates for bread, ale and meat. Where it was deemed essential to obtain supplies from a distance, slow communications were not a deterrent to the household officials.

27 *Records of the city of Norwich* eds. W. Hudson and J.C. Tingey (2 vols) Norwich 1910 II 247.

28 *Calendar of Patent Rolls 1350–4* 22. PRO E403/336–7, 339, 347, 353, 355, 359, 362, 377, 380, 391. I would like to thank Ms Helen Bradley for drawing my attention to these references to Bartholomew.

Running costs varied according to the status of the lady, her lifestyle, and the size of the household. The totals given in the household accounts have to be regarded as minimum figures, as certain essential items were almost invariably omitted. Although Elizabeth de Burgh's accounts give the purchases of cloths and furs for liveries, it is very rare to find a figure for fees and wages. Margaret de Brotherton's account was primarily concerned with food supplies. Daily expenses inevitably added considerably to the overall total. In 1420–1, Elizabeth Berkeley spent £511. 6s. 8d. on provisions for the year, while the day-to-day expenses amounted to £257. 17s. 7d. The total of £769. 4s. 3d. did not include the full wage bill and there was no reference to clothes for Elizabeth or her daughters. It is likely that the full cost of the household was well over £800.

The figures available necessarily vary widely. Isabella, Lady Morley paid £80 for living in the household of her son-in-law, John Hastings esquire, in 1463–4. In addition she spent nearly £36 on various purchases including cloth, furs and spices, on medical expenses and on gifts. Fees amounted to just over £47. Alice de Bryene's expenses for the year amounted to £161. 15s. 11½d., and covered provisions, wages and livery; in addition it has to be borne in mind that she obtained supplies from her demesne manors. Expenses for great noblewomen were in excess of £1,000 a year. Margaret de Brotherton spent just short of £1,117 in her account of 1385–6, mainly on provisions, and Anne, duchess of Buckingham spent nearly £1,616 in her great and foreign households over eighteen months in 1472–4.

Elizabeth de Burgh's yearly expenditure on supplies for the household amounted to about £1,200 or £1,300, with about 25 per cent of the expenditure going on provisions from the demesne manors and about 75 per cent on purchases. The supplies from the demesne manors were always costed in the household account, and allowance was made to the individual reeve or bailiff in his own account. The totals for each type of goods always included the cost of transport. Although total yearly expenditure remained fairly steady, there were fluctuations in particular items from year to year. Partly this was due to price levels and the relative availability or scarcity of goods, and partly to the amount of stock which the household was carrying forward from the previous year. Live animals were kept at pasture; spices and, with luck, salt fish would keep. It was rare for the officials to buy too much of a particular commodity; in 1350–1 they bought too much wheat and this was sold, but they used up the barley and had less than six quarters of oats left. About half the expenditure went on the basic foodstuffs of bread, ale, wine, meat and fish. The livery accounted for about a quarter of the money spent, and the stables, with their needs of oats, peas, beans, hay and iron, could take nearly one-fifth.

The household was paid for mainly by the revenues of the lady's estates, and it is likely that households' reliance on credit was widespread. Money was disbursed by the lady or by her financial officials. Gifts constituted a minor source of receipts, and Anne, duchess of Buckingham received household gifts worth nearly £33 in 1465–6. Small amounts of money were made by selling what the household did not need. Sales of hides, woolfells, sheepskins, fat and spare barrels at Acton in 1418–19 brought in £3. 10s. 11½d., but the steward financed most of his purchases with the money he received at different times throughout the year from the lady, totalling £43. 13s. 4d. Many of the payments, amounting to nearly £110, were entered as being made by the lady herself. A similar situation is depicted in the account of Margaret de Brotherton, where money for purchases is said to have been received from the lady. It is, however, more likely in a great household that the money for household supplies was handled by officials, in some cases the officials of the lady's husband. The keeper of Elizabeth Berkeley's household received the money he needed from the receiver of the Lisle estates, Elizabeth's own inheritance, and from the earl of Warwick's receiver-general.

In Elizabeth de Burgh's household the money for provisions was handled by the wardrobe, in charge of the household itself, and the clerk of the chamber, the equivalent of the treasurer or receiver-general in other households. The wardrobe and household accounts listed on the receipts side the goods received from the demesne manors, sales of household stuff, and a lump sum received by the wardrober from the clerk of the chamber. The indentures between the clerk of the chamber and the wardrober and the chamber accounts themselves show that this sum was dispensed in small amounts throughout the year.[29] Varying sums were handed over weekly, and the wardrober was also given money for specific major purchases such as wine, oats, cloth, furs

29 E.g. PRO E101/91/23; 93/5, 8. The offices of clerk of the chamber and wardrober were amalgamated in 1350–1.

Table 1 The cost of Elizabeth de Burgh's household supplies[a]

	1340–1			1355–6		
	Supplies from manors	Purchases	Total	Supplies from manors	Purchases	Total
Wheat	92	2	94	138	18	156
Barley	27	57	84	60	52	112
Dredge[b]	15	9	24	19		19
Malt	7	21	28[c]	3		3
Wine		115	115		176	176
Cattle	14	44	58	31	24	55
Pigs	31	15	46	20	17	37
Sheep	15	7	22	13		13
Other meat	1		1[d]		8	8[e]
Herrings		30	30		26	26
Stockfish		18	18		24	24
Cod and conger		12	12		48	48
Salmon		16	16		12	12
Other fish		32	32[f]		32	32[g]
Salt		20	20		17	17
Spices and confections		65	65		85	85
Oats	58	72	130	27	60	87
Peas and beans	1		1	15	2	17
Hay	60	24	84	14	39	53
Iron		4	4		11	11
Cloths		196	196		232	232
Furs		150	150		84	84
Total	321	931	1,252	340	967	1,307

[a] The figures are taken from PRO E101/92/13 and 93/19, and are given to the nearest pound.

[b] Dredge is a mixture of oats and barley and was used for malt.

[c] The malt in 1340–1 was made from barley, dredge, wheat and oats, barley constituting the largest item.

[d] This item comprised herons and swans.

[e] This item comprised rabbits, herons and swans.

[f] This item comprised pike, lampreys, sturgeon, eels, grampus and mackerel.

[g] This item comprised pike, lampreys and sturgeon.

Table 2 Proportion of total expenditure on supplies for Elizabeth de Burgh's household (%)

	1340–1	1355–6
Wheat	8	12
Barley ⎫		
Dredge ⎬	11	10
Malt ⎭		
Wine	9	13
Meat	10	9
Fish	9	11
Salt	2	1
Spices ⎫	5	7
Confections ⎭		
Oats ⎫		
Peas, beans ⎬	18	13
Hay		
Iron ⎭		
Cloth ⎫	28	24
Furs ⎭		
Total	100%	100%

and spices. It is unlikely that Elizabeth played much part in the organisation of supplies, but she always had an authorising role, together with her council and auditors. All the accounts were audited yearly, and the lady had the final decision as to whether officials could be released from their debts.[30] Appeal to the lady was the final resort of any official. It is likely that many ladies realised the importance of close supervision if they were not to be cheated.

The lady's household, whether large or small, provided the organisation and expertise to enable her to maintain her dignity and status and to enjoy a noble lifestyle. Through the household the lady affected the society and economy of the world around her. She provided employment for a considerable number of people, often on a long-term basis, and within the household she built up a hierarchical community of servants and officials. These men ran the household and carried out the complex task of supplying it with food and other necessities, stimulating trade

30 E.g. PRO E101/93/8 m. 3, 10.

through their purchases. The household constituted the hub of the lady's life and activities, enabling her to bring up her family, run her estates, live a full social life, and carry out her religious obligations. As well as being a community in its own right, it was also part of a much wider world.

Chapter 4

LIFESTYLE AND TRAVEL

Late medieval noblemen and women enjoyed luxury, splendour and display. This is apparent in their castles and houses, where increasing emphasis was put on privacy and comfort and where considerable sums of money were spent on new building, rich and colourful furnishings, and plate. It is also seen in the clothes and jewels of the time which were regarded as an essential appurtenance of rank, since dress indicated a person's position in the social hierarchy. The love of magnificence shows itself in the art of manuscript illumination and in the embroidery, which called for imaginative design and a high level of technical skill. Jousts and tournaments were the occasion for splendour and display, as were the feasts with their lavish food, and varied and colourful dishes. All this conspicuous consumption was condemned by preachers, but was an essential and significant part of noble life. It proclaimed the position of the lord and lady in society and enabled them to take what they regarded as their rightful place in the social hierarchy. They provided not only for themselves but for their households, retainers, kinsmen and friends, as well as for the poor and those who depended on them for their livelihood, and their residence furnished a centre for hospitality in their neighbourhood.

When at home, husband and wife participated together in this noble lifestyle. The Luttrell psalter shows Sir Geoffrey Luttrell seated at table with his wife, two sons, his daughter-in-law, and two visiting friars.[1] Wives accompanied their husbands to ceremonial occasions, as when Isabella Despenser, second wife of Richard Beauchamp, earl of Warwick, attended Henry VI's coronation in Paris. Yet husbands' absences on campaign and

---

1 J. Backhouse *The Luttrell Psalter* British Library London 1989 43.

business meant that it often fell to the wife to maintain the status and dignity of the family at home, and in order to do this she had to maintain herself and her household and to offer hospitality and entertainment in accordance with her husband's and her own rank and expectations. Similarly, the widow normally enjoyed a style of living commensurate with her status and with the influence she wished to exert on society.

This way of life involved being much in the public view; there was little privacy for the individual in the modern sense of the term. The layout of castles and large houses about 1300 meant that both lord and lady were rarely alone. Their lives centred on the hall, the chapel and the chamber and it was only in the latter that they had comparative privacy. Although large castles had separate chambers for the principal officials, important visitors and members of the family, in most residences the accommodation was far more limited. Goodrich Castle, where Joan de Valence spent considerable time in 1296–7, was largely rebuilt in the early 1280s round a courtyard with towers at the corners and a strongly fortified gatehouse. The Norman keep remained but was not the main living area in the late thirteenth century. Instead the great hall was built in the west range of the castle, with buttery, pantry and kitchen at one end, and at the other a private chapel and chamber. The main chapel was next to the gatehouse. Accommodation such as this, although up to date, hardly gave much privacy to the widow of a leading member of the baronage, and at this time it appears that privacy was not expected. By the end of the Middle Ages more provision was made for it among the nobility and their families, but even then it was considered important for the lord and lady to be seen by the members of their household, guests and strangers.

Christine de Pisan's description of the day of the wise princess in *The treasure of the city of ladies* indicates that there was little time when the lady was on her own.[2] The wise princess rose quite early every day and said her prayers. When she was ready she heard her masses, the number being determined by her sense of piety and the amount of time she could spare; if she had responsibilities for governing in the absence of her husband she would be excused in God's eyes from spending as much time in prayer as those who had more leisure. She gave alms to the poor

---

2 Christine de Pisan *The Treasure of the City of Ladies or the Book of the Three Virtues* trans. S. Lawson, Harmondsworth 1985 59–62.

and heard petitions as she left her chapel. If she was responsible for government she went to the council after mass on the days when meetings were held, acted as president, and listened to the full discussion of the matters raised. Some councillors she saw every day on necessary business, and Christine stressed the need for her to judge who were the wisest and most virtuous advisers. After the morning council she had her dinner, which was usually in the hall where seating was according to precedence. After grace she received and talked to the company before retiring to her chamber. Here she rested and worked with her women until vespers which she heard in the chapel or said privately. Afterwards, in the summer, she walked in the garden until suppertime and listened to anyone who wished to speak to her. Prayers and bedtime ended the day.

Admittedly, Christine was writing in general and somewhat idealistic terms; she was, after all, describing the day of the wise princess. Yet her description is largely borne out by household accounts, manuscript illuminations and incidental details in the romances. All these types of evidence show the lady in her chapel, at the high table in the hall, working in her chamber and enjoying her recreations. It is the responsibilities for government and business that mostly go unrecorded in illuminations and literature, but evidence of the lady's work with her council is found in the estate documents of widows. Wherever she was and whatever she was doing the lady was living very much a public life, her activities always coming under the scrutiny of her family, household, visitors and strangers. Although Christine was describing the life of the married princess, the life of the single noblewoman would have been very similar, although she would not have had the duty of attending the council and executing business. Before her marriage, the noblewoman lived in her parents' or another noble household and would have been expected to participate in all its activities.

Christine de Pisan's division of religious devotion between private prayer and attendance at services in chapel was typical of noblewomen in the later Middle Ages. Many possessed their own books of hours which contained the eight services comprising the Little Office of the Virgin Mary together with other devotions. Some noblewomen like Cicely, duchess of York virtually lived a religious life during their widowhood. For all the nobility attendance at mass was an essential part of their lives, an obligation which they shared with their families and households. Elizabeth de Burgh's chamber account of 1351–2 regularly gave details of the offerings made by the lady and her household at mass, and the anniversaries of members of the family and of some of the councillors and officials were observed. The number of masses varied, three being recorded on Christmas Day.[3]

Christine de Pisan did not go into any detail over the work of the princess and her ladies in her chamber, but it is likely that all engaged in sewing and embroidery. Not only are such scenes recorded in manuscript illuminations, but household accounts, like Elizabeth de Burgh's chamber account, refer to the purchase of embroidery thread, and wills occasionally make bequests of items embroidered by the testator. Noblewomen also enjoyed games and romances which they may have read themselves or had read aloud while they were working. The books of romances mentioned in the wills of noblewomen, as in that of Elizabeth Darcy, are probably only a tiny proportion of those they owned or had enjoyed during their lifetime. Such books were owned by gentry as well as top noble families; Anne Paston had a copy of Lydgate's *Siege of Thebes*. Books were borrowed as well as owned; Elizabeth de Burgh and her sister Margaret had borrowed four romances each from the royal collection in 1327. Occasionally the romance had a strong family connection; Eleanor de Bohun left her son Humphrey a history of the knight of the swan, the swan being the Bohun badge.[4]

Christine de Pisan mentioned amusements such as hunting and hawking, but left the details to the preference and wishes of the ladies and their husbands, simply warning that these amusements should be taken in moderation. Women are depicted with hawks on their hands and using the bow in hunting, and both sports appear to have been widely enjoyed. At the end of August 1421 Elizabeth Berkeley went on a three-day hunting excursion to Bordesley on the edge of the forest of Arden with her daughters and a few servants. Elizabeth de Burgh had her own falconers and birds in the late 1330s and 1340s and bought falcons at

---

3 PRO E101/93/12.

4 *The register of Bishop Philip Repingdon, 1405–19* ed. M. Archer (2 vols) Lincoln Record Society LVIII (1963) II 265. *Paston letters and papers of the fifteenth century* ed. N. Davis (2 vols) Oxford 1971–6 I 575. J. Vale *Edward III and chivalry. Chivalric society and its context, 1270–1350* Woodbridge 1982 Appendix 9. J. Nichols *A collection of all the wills of the kings and queens of England* London 1780 181.

King's Lynn and Norwich in 1341–2. The sport cost the household little, £8. 12s. 10½d. being the highest sum recorded in 1340–1. There is no reference to falconry in the household accounts after 1345, by which time Elizabeth had reached the age of fifty.[5]

Recreations such as jousts and tournaments received much attention from the writers of romances, and women had their part to play as spectators, giving inspiration to the knights, and at the banquets and dancing which were an integral part of the proceedings. Tournaments were a major social occasion from the early thirteenth century, and the numerous jousts of Edward III's reign were spectacular and colourful and widely enjoyed. When Edward III founded the Round Table at Windsor in February 1344 he invited the Prince of Wales, earls, barons and knights. The queen and queen-mother were there together with countesses, baronesses and ladies. As well as continuous jousting for three days, there was feasting and dancing. At the end, the king took an oath that he would establish a Round Table in the same way as King Arthur had, to the number of three hundred knights. To the sound of trumpets and drums the company then moved to a final feast with rich food and abundant drink, which all thoroughly delighted in.[6]

It has to be emphasised, however, that noblewomen spent most of their lives at home and their principal celebrations took place at the great religious festivals. These were the times for music, dancing, games and play-acting. References to traditional games are occasionally found, such as the payment to the boy bishop on the eve of St Nicholas (5 December) 1351 in Elizabeth de Burgh's chamber account. Minstrels were often employed at festivals. Alice de Bryene had a harper eating with her household over Christmas and New Year, 1412–13, and eight years later the minstrel of the duke of Clarence entertained Elizabeth Berkeley. Christmas was also a time for plays, and local players

---

5 C.D. Ross 'The household accounts of Elizabeth Berkeley, countess of Warwick, 1420–1' *Transactions of the Bristol and Gloucestershire Archaeological Society* LXX (1951) 89. PRO E101/92/13 m. 10; 459/24 m. 2d.

6 R. Barber and J. Barker *Tournaments, jousts, chivalry and pageants in the Middle Ages* Woodbridge 1989 32, 206–7. *Chronica Adae Murimuth et Roberti de Avesbury* ed. E.M. Thompson Rolls Series London 1889 231–2. The description of the founding of the Round Table in 1344 in Adam Murimuth's chronicle is given in translation in *English Historical Documents* ed. D.C. Douglas (12 vols) IV *1327–1485* ed. A.R. Myers London 1969 74–5.

from Slimbridge and Wotton visited Berkeley castle at the same time.[7]

Such festivities when the lady, with or without her husband, presided in the great hall were not simply for the benefit of family and household, although the element of personal enjoyment was doubtless there. The noblewoman's exercise of hospitality throughout the year, not just at festivals, was one of her most important social functions. It was the occasion when she displayed the power and status of herself and her family to the locality through the food and drink that she offered, the entertainment she provided, and the splendour and magnificence of her setting. This was an essential part of her lifestyle, whether she was of gentry, knightly or baronial rank. What she provided constituted a further tie between herself and her servants, officials, retainers and neighbours. The hospitality was as significant in its way as the wages, fees and liveries and can be regarded as part of the two-way relationship of service on one side and reward on the other.[8]

The types of food served were to a large extent determined by the fasts and feasts of the Church. On at least two days a week and during the whole of Lent the eating of meat was forbidden; dairy produce and eggs were also prohibited during Lent. Sundays and the great festivals were the occasion for a more lavish spread and greater expenditure. The principal items of diet were wheat bread and either meat or fish, with ale or wine to drink depending on one's position in the household. Vegetables and fruit were not widely used. While the household accounts give the basic ingredients of the diet, cookery books from the late fourteenth and fifteenth century show the importance attached to taste, texture, colour and presentation, especially at feasts. Food was well flavoured with spices and dried fruit being mixed with the meat, or used in sauces. Sauces were considered an important accompaniment to roast meat and fish. Cookery books often concentrated on the more elaborate recipes. One divided its contents into pottages, leches and

7 PRO E101/93/12 m. 1. *Household book of Dame Alice de Bryene, 1412–13* ed. V.B. Redstone trans. M. K. Dale Suffolk Institute of Archaeology and Natural History Ipswich 1931 25–8. Ross 'The household accounts of Elizabeth Berkeley' 93.

8 The importance of the lord's largesse is discussed by C. Dyer *Standards of living in the later Middle Ages* Cambridge 1989 86–91.

bakemeats, each section including sweet and savoury dishes and both meat and fish; pottages can be described as a type of thick soup, leches were sliced like brawn and gingerbread, and bakemeats comprised food cooked in a pastry-case.[9] The main meal of the day was dinner, eaten about midday, with supper being taken in the late afternoon or early evening, and few people partaking of breakfast; on Sunday 5 March 1413 Alice de Bryene's household had eighteen people for dinner and supper, but only six at breakfast.

It was up to the individual lord or lady to decide which feasts were to be major celebrations. Expenditure on food on Sunday was higher than on weekdays; in 1330, Elizabeth de Burgh's household spent just over sixty-four shillings on food on Sunday 30 September, while the sums for the following week ranged from thirty-two to fifty-seven shillings a day.[10] All households celebrated the twelve days of Christmas, and the feast of Easter; the main celebration at Christmas sometimes came on 1 January rather than 25 December. It was on 1 January 1413 that Alice de Bryene held a dinner for her friends and neighbours, her household, the bailiff, harvest-reeve and vicar of Acton, and 300 tenants and strangers. Elizabeth de Burgh's expenditure was higher at these festivals than on Sundays; in 1349–50 expenditure on food on Christmas Day came to just over £6 and at Epiphany to about £4. 12s. 0d., while on Easter Sunday the sum amounted to a little over £7.[11] Other festivals and saints' days were celebrated according to the wishes of the lady. For Elizabeth de Burgh the most important was the feast of Corpus Christi when about £18 was regularly spent on food throughout her widowhood. Although this feast was authorised in 1264, it was not ordered to be adopted until the council of Vienne of 1311, and it then rapidly became popular in Europe.

The hospitality offered by the lady on these and other occasions extended to men and women of all conditions. Elizabeth Berkeley entertained her women friends, churchmen, officials and servants of her husband, and strangers and travellers who were unknown to her. A similar picture emerges from

9 *Two fifteenth-century cookery-books* ed. T. Austin Early English Text Society original series xci (1888) 1–4.

10 PRO E101/91/25 m. 1.

11 PRO E101/93/4 m. 7, 8, 15.

Eleanor de Montfort's household roll in 1265.[12] The whole range of potential guests can be seen in the accounts of Elizabeth de Burgh and Alice de Bryene. The daily account rolls of Elizabeth de Burgh's household show that the most lavish feasts were prepared for her most distinguished guests. The large quantities of food prepared were needed to feed their retinues as well as Elizabeth's own household. The number of people fed is not known but an indication is provided in the increase in the number of horses in the account for the stables. On Edward III's visit for the weekend of 27–29 May 1340, hay and fodder had to be provided for about 180 horses, with a special allowance of horse-bread for the king's horse; this compares with about 100 horses in the stables immediately before and after the visit. The food is noteworthy not just for its quantity but for the variety which was set before the lady and her most important guests. Saturday was a fish day, and as well as the usual herring, stockfish, and various sorts of salted white fish, salmon, crabs, crayfish and whelks were also served. On Sunday 28 May the dishes included boar, veal, several types of poultry, and five swans, six herons and three bittern. The size of the company and the variety of the food are reflected in the expenditure of £7. 8s. 8d. on the Saturday, and £16. 14s. 3d. on the Sunday.[13] This visit constituted an exceptionally large entertainment; Edward was on his way to the Continent and the battle of Sluys was won on Midsummer Day. On later visits by members of the royal family the retinues were considerably smaller. However, Elizabeth always entertained lavishly, setting a great variety of dishes before her noble guests.

Elizabeth ranked among the highest nobility and for the most part the accounts record visitors of her own status and high-ranking churchmen. Doubtless she also provided for less important people and strangers, but these went unrecorded. The household book of Alice de Bryene of Acton, however, brings out the full range of late medieval hospitality. This is apparent not only at the New Year feast in 1413 but throughout the year. In addition to neighbouring gentry and churchmen and their servants, workers on the estate received food as part of their

12 *Manners and household expenses of England in the thirteenth and fifteenth centuries* ed. T.H. Turner London 1841 1–84. Ross 'The household accounts of Elizabeth Berkeley' 92–5.

13 PRO E101/92/12 m. 8d, 9d.

remuneration. Boon-workers at harvest-time were given food by custom, but unnamed carters, roofers, carpenters and ploughmen were entered from time to time as eating a meal in the hall, as were the six women gathering rushes on 19 June. Friars were entertained on their journeys from local houses like Sudbury and Clare, and also from Colchester, Ipswich and Norwich. Some local people who were fed were identified by the place they came from, like the man of Boxted on 21 December. Strangers, however, even when they had some status remained anonymous; on 5 November a meal was given to a priest, and on 17 November to a merchant. Hospitality appears to have been given with little attention being paid to the personal details of the visitor.

Noblewomen occasionally entertained officials and religious communities near their residences. In the summer of 1265 Eleanor de Montfort, who was concerned to secure the loyalty of the Cinque Ports to her husband, entertained the burgesses of Winchelsea and Sandwich.[14] Elizabeth de Burgh regularly entertained the religious communities in the places where she was living, such as the prior and convent of Anglesey in 1344, the prioress and convent of Usk five years later, and the Augustinian friars at Clare in 1355 and 1357. On her visits to London towards the end of her life she regularly entertained the Minoresses outside Aldgate, in whose precinct she was living. On occasion a member of the nobility or the royal family was a guest at the same time, like the duke of Lancaster in 1355 and the Black Prince three years later on the feast of the Assumption of the Virgin Mary. She is known to have entertained the mayor and sheriffs of London in June 1358.[15]

Almsgiving to the poor was a duty stressed by the Church and noblewomen responded in various ways. It was customary for the leftovers of noble meals to be distributed among the poor, and Robert Grosseteste recommended the countess of Lincoln to see that her alms were properly distributed among the poor, the sick and beggars, and not taken out of the hall by worthless grooms.[16] Some of the nobility fed a specific number of poor people in their household; Katherine de Norwich fed thirteen

14 *Manners and household expenses* Turner 47–8, 50, 62.

15 PRO E101/92/24 m. 13; 93/4 m. 6; 93/18 m. 2, 5; 93/20 m. 1, 11d, 20d.

16 'Les Reules Seynt Roberd' in *Walter of Henley's Husbandry* ed. E. Lamond Royal Historical Society London 1890 134–5.

poor on bread and herrings in 1336. Special distributions of food were sometimes made at particular times of the year. Eleanor de Montfort fed 800 poor people on 14 April, 1265, and Elizabeth de Burgh regularly throughout her widowhood distributed bread and herrings on the feast of St Gregory, 12 March, the anniversary of the death of Roger Damory, her third husband, in 1322. At the end of her life she made money disbursements to the poor wherever she happened to be living as well as giving casual alms. Amounts given to the poor by the nobility were small in comparison with other items of their expenditure; Eleanor de Montfort's account in early May recorded that half a quarter of grain and thirteen gallons of ale had been given to the poor over eight days while three quarters of grain had been expended on bread for the dogs.[17]

Hospitality and the maintenance of one's position involved more than the giving of food and entertainment. The setting was also of great importance, and noblewomen enjoyed expensive clothes and jewellery, splendid furnishings and possessions, and comfortable residences both for themselves and for what they represented to the outside world. Their love of striking clothes and jewels is reflected in manuscript illuminations, and they were influenced by fashion, and by the materials available. The adoption of set-in sleeves about 1340, for instance, enabled clothes to be made which were tighter fitting, and the shape of the sleeves could be altered according to the dictates of fashion. Head-dresses and hairstyles were also subject to fashion as can be seen on the tombs and monumental brasses of the fourteenth and fifteenth centuries. Jewelled head-dresses were popular throughout the period. Hair came to be dressed closer to the head in the 1340s and women arranged it in stiff plaits either side of the face. These developed into the tightly plaited *cornettes* of the later fourteenth century. Married women wore veils, and these varied from the crimped style of the later fourteenth century with several layers of frills surrounding the face to the much larger head-dresses of the fifteenth century.[18] The difference is highlighted in a comparison of Lady de la Pole's brass of about 1380 at Chrishall in Essex with Lady Camoys' brass at Trotton, Sussex, of about 1419.

17 BL Additional Roll 63207. *Manners and household expenses* Turner 20, 29. PRO E101/93/4 m. 14; 93/12 m. 1; 93/18 m. 2.

18 S.M. Newton *Fashion in the age of the Black Prince* Woodbridge 1980 3–4.

The robes which were mentioned in household accounts and wills were outfits, not individual garments, and consisted of a shirt of linen, and a tunic, over-tunic, cloak and hood of wool or more expensive material. These woollen garments were frequently fur-lined, and the fur can often be seen at the neck and cuffs in manuscript illuminations. The three gowns mentioned in Lady Peryne Clanbowe's will were all furred with Baltic squirrel, one with the grey back winter skins, one with skins from the bellies, which were white with a little grey in the surround, and the third with whole squirrel skins.[19] The outfits owned by noblewomen ranged from those for ceremonial occasions to those for everyday. Elizabeth de Burgh put her six best robes in order of importance when bequeathing them to her ladies and at the other end of the scale left her russet robe, of poorer woollen material, to the Minoresses.[20]

Jewels were much prized and often worn. Some were purchased by the noblewomen themselves, others were gifts or bequests. Rings and brooches were most often mentioned in wills, but jewelled head-dresses and girdles are also found. Isabella Despenser, countess of Warwick referred to the jewels she wore on her forehead, which contained pale rubies, and Elizabeth FitzHugh left chaplets of pearls to her daughters. Crosses, sometimes containing relics, were also the subject of bequests; Eleanor de Bohun left her son a gold cross hanging by a chain with an image of the crucifix on it and four pearls round, saying that this was her best-loved possession.[21]

The richness of clothes and jewels extended to the furnishings of the hall, chapel and chamber. Members of the nobility were concerned to put on as good a show as they thought they could afford, and factors of comfort, piety and investment were also taken into consideration. The tastes of noblewomen in furnishings are best seen in the accounts and wills of widows, especially of those who had been widowed for a long time, as during their widowhood they would have had the chance to exercise their

19 *The fifty earliest English wills* ed. F.J. Furnivall Early English Text Society original series LXXVIII (1882) 50–1. E.M. Veale *The English fur trade in the later Middle Ages* Oxford 1966 228.

20 Nichols *A collection of all the wills* 24–5, 30.

21 Ibid. 181–2. *The fifty earliest English wills* Furnivall 116. *The register of Thomas Langley, bishop of Durham, 1406–37* ed. R.L. Storey (6 vols) Surtees Society CLXIX (1954) III 62–4.

own preferences without being influenced by fathers or husbands. A comparison between the possessions of dowagers and noblemen, however, points to much similarity of taste, and a love of magnificence, colour and expensive materials. The difference between women of knightly and of higher rank lay in the amount rather than the type of their possessions.

All noblewomen had their collections of plate. This made an impressive show when set out on the tables of the hall or put on display. Few pieces of late medieval plate have survived, but the Bermondsey dish and the King John cup of silver and enamel show the sumptuousness and workmanship of the time.[22] Plate was also an investment, as it could be sold during the lady's lifetime if there was a need for money or after her death to carry out her will. Philippa, countess of March left plate to her executors with this end in view, and Matilda de Vere bought silver from the executors of Elizabeth de Burgh, which she subsequently left to her children.[23] Inventories and wills have to be regarded as giving the minimum rather than the maximum amount of plate. The inventory of 1305 for Elizabeth, countess of Hereford is unlikely to have been comprehensive as the main item was twenty goblets of silver-gilt and twenty-four of silver; reference was made to enamelled dishes, but not to the great array of silver dishes and bowls which noble families possessed.

An indenture of 1332, by which Elizabeth de Burgh's clerk of the wardrobe handed over the possessions in his custody to his successor, gives a more varied picture, although very few drinking vessels are mentioned.[24] The plate was to be found in various departments of the household, and altogether the indenture listed eight plates, thirty-two spoons, thirty-four dishes, thirty saucers, six basins, four ewers, one goblet, one cup, eleven pots, one measure and four chargers. All these were of silver, and in addition there were two silver-gilt spoons and two silver-gilt mazers. Much of the plate was marked with the arms of the lady and most of the spoons had the letter E, but some of the silver still had the arms of Roger Damory or the arms of Gloucester

22 Both these pieces are illustrated in *Age of Chivalry: Art in Plantagenet England 1200–1400* eds. J. Alexander and P. Binski London 1987 166, 257–8, 435–6.

23 Nichols *A collection of all the wills* 102. G.M. Benton 'Essex wills at Canterbury' *Transactions of the Essex Archaeological Society* new series XXI (1933–7) 264.

24 PRO E101/367/1; 91/28.

and Ulster, presumably having belonged to Elizabeth's brother and sister-in-law. It is likely that Elizabeth added to her collection of plate throughout her widowhood as a far greater quantity is mentioned in her will and this did not represent the sum total; to take just three items, there were eighteen chargers, fifty-six saucers, and fifteen plates.

The hall, chapel and chambers were hung with tapestries which provided warmth and colour. The hangings were not necessarily made of expensive materials; Elizabeth de Burgh left her daughter Elizabeth Bardolf a set made of worsted with blue parrots and cockerels on a tawny ground. It was on the beds that the most costly fabrics and furs appear, like the tapestries they provided colour and warmth; the best beds were treasured possessions which were left to favourite relations. The term bed, as used in wills, stood for the expensive hangings and covers rather than the frame. The bed which Elizabeth de Burgh left to Elizabeth Bardolf was of green velvet striped with red, the coverlets lined with pured minever and with gris.[25] Joan Beauchamp, lady of Abergavenny, left her most magnificent beds to her grandchildren: a bed of cloth of gold embroidered with swans, with green tapestry hangings with branches and flowers of different colours, a bed of cloth of gold embroidered with leopards with her best red worsted hangings, a bed of black and white velvet, and a bed of blue brocaded silk with blue worsted hangings. Widows of knights also used expensive materials on beds; three of the beds mentioned in Elizabeth Trivet's will were of silk and one of velvet, one of them being of green silk embroidered with eagles, with hangings of green tapestry.[26]

The same impression of richness and colour was found in the chapel, with its hangings, paintings and images of saints, silver candlesticks, and chalices and other altar vessels of silver and silver-gilt. Occasionally a chalice was made of gold. The books used in the chapel were often illuminated and richly bound. Vestments were provided for all seasons of the Church's year and were made of costly materials and embroidered. Among the vestments which Elizabeth de Burgh left to Clare College in

---

25 Nichols *A collection of all the wills* 34–5. Both the furs were from the Baltic squirrel, gris being the grey back of the winter skin, and pured minever being the white belly skin with no grey surround.

26 *The register of Henry Chichele, archbishop of Canterbury, 1414–43* ed. E.F. Jacob (4 vols) Canterbury and York Society XLII (1937) II 495–7, 536–7.

Cambridge, there was one of black camaca for requiems, one of white samite for Lent, one of white tartaryn also for Lent, and one of red camaca embroidered with gold which was worn at festivals.[27] Joan Beauchamp left the Dominican friars at Hereford her best set of vestments of cloth of gold embroidered with peacocks.

Their wealth, tastes and lifestyle meant that many noblewomen were patrons of the decorative arts like metalwork, embroidery and illumination. Luxury trades developed in response to demand, and craftsmen are found working in the noblewoman's household. Elizabeth de Burgh had goldsmiths working at Clare and Bardfield in the 1330s, and also at Walsingham, the family priory which she patronised; they were making jewellery, plate, images and religious vessels. Noblewomen also patronised illuminators. In 1265 parchment was purchased to make a breviary for Eleanor de Montfort's daughter, which was subsequently written at Oxford. Elizabeth de Burgh had an illuminator working in her household in 1339, and in March 1352 a friar minor of Cambridge was paid for illuminating a book for the lady.[28] Although information is sparse, it is likely that noblewomen commissioned at least some of the books of hours, religious works, histories and romances which they mentioned in their wills as well as receiving them as bequests and gifts. The Bohun family were the greatest patrons of manuscript illumination in the fourteenth century, the works with which they are associated being produced between about 1360 and 1390. The last Bohun earl of Hereford died in 1373, and the later works are associated with Mary de Bohun who married Henry Bolingbroke. The Fitzwilliam psalter was probably made at the time of her marriage, and another volume shows her at prayer in adoration of the Virgin Mary.[29]

Most noblewomen lived in the castles and houses built by their ancestors or husbands, but some engaged in building activity on their own account. Elizabeth de Burgh was involved in several building projects, reflecting her changing preferences

27 These materials were all types of silk, camaca being a gold-patterned silk, and samite plain silk cloth.

28 PRO E101/91/27 m. 4; 91/30 (the goldsmiths' account for 1332); 92/2 m. 1, 2, 14; 92/9 m. 10; 93/12 m. 3. *Manners and household expenses* Turner 9, 24.

29 *Age of Chivalry* Alexander and Binski 155–6, 501–4. L. F. Sandler 'A note on the illuminators of the Bohun manuscripts' *Speculum* LX (1985) 364–72.

as to where she lived. She had a new chamber built for herself at Clare castle in 1346 and 1347, and in 1344 building was in progress at Bardfield, which was a residence much favoured by her and where the accommodation was inadequate for her household; in 1334 baking and brewing had to be done at Clare because of the lack of room at Bardfield.[30] Elizabeth also built a London house in 1352 in the precinct of the abbey of the Minoresses outside Aldgate. The house was built by Richard de Felstede, a carpenter and London citizen, who is known to have worked elsewhere in London and also for Henry of Lancaster at Kenilworth. Elizabeth's house must have been substantial as Richard was paid £171. 14s. 5d. for the work.[31]

The nobility of the fourteenth and fifteenth centuries were not as constantly on the move as earlier in the Middle Ages. The greater noblewomen maintained more than one residence but spent substantial periods living in one place. Elizabeth Berkeley spent the autumn and winter of 1420–1 at Berkeley castle. A residence might be favoured at one time and not at another; Elizabeth de Burgh spent 1343–5 mainly at Clare, Bardfield and Anglesey, but her last recorded visit to Anglesey was in 1346–7 and when she was in the eastern counties in 1354–6 she divided her time between London, Bardfield and Clare. She also had her castle at Usk and her longest visit there was for about eighteen months between 1348 and 1350. She is not known to have made the journey to Wales after that, possibly because of age.

Most of the wealthier noblewomen of the later Middle Ages are known to have spent time in London. This reflects the growing importance of the city and the increasing tendency of the king's court to be based at palaces nearby. Many ladies had their own houses in London which could be rented out when they did not need them, a policy which was followed by Margaret de Brotherton and by Alice de Bryene.[32] Alternatively, a family

---

30 PRO E101/92/2 m. 13; 458/4 m. 1; 459/25 m. 2, 3; 459/26 m. 1. G.A. Thornton *A history of Clare Suffolk* Cambridge 1930 79–84.

31 PRO E101/93/12 m. 2d, 3, 3d, 4d. M. Carlin *St Botolph Aldgate Gazetteer. Holy Trinity Minories: abbey of St Clare, 1293/4–1539* Centre for Metropolitan History 1987 37–9; I would like to thank Dr Derek Keene, Director of the Centre for Metropolitan History, for allowing me to see this unpublished report. L.F. Salzman *Building in England down to 1540* Oxford 1967 433–4, 436–7.

32 College of Arms, Arundel MS 49 fo 11b. PRO SC6/1245/16 m. 1; 1245/17 m. 1.

with estates within easy reach of the city might choose to stay there; Elizabeth Berkeley spent most of the spring and early summer of 1421 at Walthamstow as well as in London. A stay in London enabled the lady to frequent the court, see her friends, participate in religious life, carry out business, and have ready access to the luxury trades of the capital.

Even though the nobility of the fourteenth and fifteenth centuries used fewer residences than they had done earlier, travel still constituted an important part of their lives. Women travelled both with their husbands and on their own, whether they were changing residences, making visits, overseeing their estates, or going on pilgrimage. They proclaimed their status by travelling with a suitable retinue, and their journeys entailed considerable preparations and careful organisation, as recorded in their household accounts. Most of the journeys took place in Great Britain, although a few noblewomen went abroad. The information is fuller for great ladies than for the wives of knights, but it is likely that the same considerations apply to both, although less important women were accompanied by a smaller retinue.

The amount that a noble lady travelled in a year depended both on circumstances and inclination. Journeys were made during pregnancy, Elizabeth, countess of Hereford, the daughter of Edward I, travelling from Scotland to Knaresborough for the birth of her son.[33] Age did not necessarily curtail a lady's journeys. Admittedly, in the last six years of her life Elizabeth de Burgh's travels were limited to journeys between Clare, Bardfield and London, but it has to be remembered that she died in 1360 at the age of sixty-five. Women in their fifties certainly engaged in long journeys, as Elizabeth did herself. Her travels can be compared to those of Joan de Valence, who at the time when her surviving household rolls were drawn up in 1295–7 must have been about sixty, having married Henry III's half-brother in 1247.[34] The autumn of 1295 saw her making short journeys round Hertford, mostly on her own. Early in the New Year she was with her husband in Kent, where she remained when he died and was buried in London in May 1296. She spent much of June and July at Hertford before embarking on an extensive tour of the Midlands in August, finally arriving at Goodrich castle in

33 PRO E101/365/20.

34 PRO E101/505/25–7.

November, where she stayed until the following May. She
journeyed to London for the anniversary of her husband's death,
spent much of June and July at Swindon, was at Moreton
Valence in August, and was back at Goodrich in mid-September.
For the twelve months from the autumn of 1295 Joan was more
continuously on the move than a noblewoman would have been
a hundred years later; Elizabeth Berkeley's year was divided
between Berkeley, Walthamstow, London and Salwarpe near
Worcester.

There were several ways in which the noblewoman could
travel. One way of travelling was to ride, usually astride;[35] when
Elizabeth Berkeley had to return to Gloucestershire in June 1421
she travelled on horseback in order to get there more quickly.
The greatest ladies had their own travelling carriages of the type
portrayed in the Luttrell psalter.[36] These were highly decorated
four-wheeled covered waggons, enabling the ladies to look out in
front and behind and through openings in the sides. The interior
of the carriage was furnished with tapestries and seats covered
with cushions, and it was drawn by five horses harnessed in line,
with riders on the fifth horse, next to the carriage, and on the
second. As well as the new carriage which she bought in London
in 1332, Elizabeth de Burgh also purchased a litter which was
carried by two horses, one in front and one behind. She also had
a travelling carriage for her ladies. These carriages were costly
and highly valued, and Elizabeth bequeathed hers to her daughter, Elizabeth Bardolf. The horses were likewise expensive as
they had to be strong; one bought in 1332 cost £26. 13s. 4d. at a
time when £2. 13s. 4d. was paid for a carthorse and £8 for a
palfrey.[37]

Occasionally noble ladies travelled by water. Ferries had to be
taken across major rivers, and on her return from Kent in 1296
Joan de Valence travelled up the Thames to London from
Gravesend, using a ferry which retained its importance into
modern times. In certain parts of the country such as the Fens
travel by water was the obvious choice, and Elizabeth de Burgh
regularly did part of her journey by boat when she visited Marie
de St Pol at Waterbeach and Denny. For those staying in

35 J.J. Jusserand *English wayfaring life in the Middle Ages* London 1891 100–5.

36 Backhouse *The Luttrell Psalter* 50–1.

37 PRO E101/91/27 m. 4; 91/29.

London and wishing to visit Greenwich, Westminster and Lambeth, travel by barge was the answer, as Anne, duchess of Buckingham found in 1465.[38]

Journeys were undertaken in daylight. It was the realisation that her husband was facing a growing military threat which forced Eleanor de Montfort to travel from Odiham to Portchester by night, guided by Dobbe the parker, on 1 June, 1265.[39] Speed of travel depended on the means employed and the urgency of the business. When Elizabeth Berkeley travelled back to Gloucestershire, she rode the 150 miles from Walthamstow to Wotton in two and a half days, covering sixty miles in a day. On her return she covered the ground in approximately twice the time. Thirty to forty miles a day was a good distance to cover, and many noblewomen travelled more slowly. After a short stay at Porchester, Eleanor de Montfort travelled to Dover in three days in daily stages of between about twenty-five and thirty-five miles. Joan de Valence travelled up to thirty miles a day, but the stages were usually shorter. Coming from Goodrich to London in the spring of 1297 she took a week, not stopping at any place for more than one night, and travelling via Moreton Valence, Cirencester, Dorchester, Maidenhead and Kingston. On her journey south from Scotland to Knaresborough in 1304, the countess of Hereford travelled up to twenty miles a day. Elizabeth de Burgh normally travelled between twelve and eighteen miles a day. On her journeys to Canterbury she regularly stopped at Dartford, Rochester and Ospringe, and on those from Bardfield to London at Standon and Waltham. Her journey from Usk to Clare in 1350 took her seventeen days, including a weekend spent at Tewkesbury and another at Chicksands. It was possible to do this journey much more quickly; it took a group of her officials seven days to go from Clare to Usk in 1328–9, in stages of up to thirty-five miles a day.[40]

The noblewoman's journeys were undertaken for pleasure and business. Moves from one residence to another, visits to members of the family and to friends, and sometimes the enjoyment of recreations such as hunting, involved a certain amount of travel.

38 PRO E101/505/25 m. 10; 92/7 m. 6. BL Additional MS 34213 fos. 70v, 72v, 73r, 74r, 77v.

39 *Manners and household expenses* Turner 33, 42.

40 PRO E101/505/26 m. 23d; 365/20 m. 1, 2; 91/20 m. 1; 92/12 m. 9d–11d; 93/4 m. 13d, 14, 14d, 15; 93/18 m. 2.

Many noblewomen regarded pilgrimage as an important part of their spiritual lives, and although most restricted themselves to England, some visited shrines on the continent like that of St James of Compostella. Travel was not, however, undertaken solely for personal reasons and the lady's journeys were often concerned with the management and defence of her estates. It was important for her to display the power and status of her family, and journeys had to be undertaken to deal with legal business as well as to oversee demesne manors. Although the estates were run by officials, women like Elizabeth de Burgh considered it important to show themselves on their lands and whether Elizabeth was at Usk or in the eastern counties she periodically visited the manors nearby. In a few cases, like that of Marie de St Pol, it was necessary to supervise estates in France as well as in Britain. Many journeys combined personal enjoyment with more serious concerns; Elizabeth de Burgh's visits to Norfolk gave her the chance to see her daughter Elizabeth, married to John Bardolf of Wormegay, go on pilgrimage to Walsingham and Bromholm, and see to any questions arising on her lands in the county.[41]

Whatever the purpose of the journey, considerable organisation was needed, especially when the noblewoman was moving from one residence to another and the main furnishings of hall, chapel, chamber and service quarters had to be transported. Horses and carts were assigned specifically to household departments and officials. The account for the countess of Hereford's journey to Knaresborough in 1304 mentioned carts for the chamber, wardrobe and buttery, two carts for the kitchen, and a hackney carrying the equipment of the poultry.[42]

Even when only part of the household went on the journey the number of people and horses constituted an impressive company which reflected the rank and importance of the lady. The countess of Hereford travelled with thirty-six horses, including five for her carriage, six packhorses and fourteen carthorses. This is comparable with Joan de Valence coming from Goodrich to London with about fifty horses and thirteen grooms in her

41 PRO E101/92/2 m. 12, 13.

42 PRO E101/365/20 m. 1, 2. The accounts for travelling rarely give the total number of people in the company, but the account for the stable gives the number of the different types of horses; these figures vary slightly from day to day during the journey.

retinue. When Elizabeth Berkeley set out to join her husband at Walthamstow in March 1421, she had a retinue of thirty-two people, including her daughters, together with fifty-seven horses and eleven hackneys. Such a company befitted her status as a countess, but pales in comparison with the numbers that accompanied Elizabeth de Burgh on some of her journeys, as when she went to Canterbury in 1340 with about sixty-five horses and twenty-one hackneys, the stable also accounting for two esquires, forty-nine grooms and eleven pages. She had an even bigger company on her journey from Usk in 1350, but then she was returning to Clare with all her household after a lengthy absence; the numbers varied slightly from day to day, but the stable account recorded about 130 horses, twenty-eight hackneys, twenty-two oxen, two esquires, about sixty grooms, and nineteen pages.[43]

Because of the amount which had to be taken on journeys, it was usual to hire horses and carts, often from religious houses. On her journey to Dover Eleanor de Montfort borrowed the carriage of the countess of Arundel and its five horses, hired two carts to take her equipment from Portchester to Winchelsea and then a boat to take it to Dover. Elizabeth Berkeley borrowed horses from the abbot of Gloucester, the prior of Llanthony, and the master of the hospital of St John the Baptist at Warwick. In addition to hiring, Elizabeth de Burgh obtained horses for her return journey from Usk by exacting customary labour.

The journey had to be carefully planned in order to ensure that there would be suitable accommodation for the lady each night. It was sometimes possible to stay at a demesne manor or with relations. Houses of officials or retainers were used on occasion. On her return from Usk in 1350 Elizabeth de Burgh's last stop before Clare was at Radwinter, then held by one of her councillors, Andrew de Bures. Another possibility was to spend the night at the house of a friend among the nobility, as when the countess of Hereford was entertained at Dunbar by Earl Patrick. The most frequently used stopping-places in the later Middle Ages were abbeys and priories. Joan de Valence stopped at Gloucester Abbey on her way to Goodrich in 1296, and Elizabeth Berkeley was entertained at the abbey of Malmesbury on her way to London.

43 Ross 'The household acounts of Elizabeth Berkeley' 87. PRO E101/92/12 m. 10d–11d; 93/4 m. 13d, 14, 14d, 15.

The lodging was rarely provided free of charge, and household officials had to make arrangements for both money and food for the journey. Compared with other noblewomen, the countess of Hereford was fortunate in 1304. At Dunbar she had nothing to pay for food and drink for her retinue and horses because this was the gift of Earl Patrick, supper at Tynemouth was provided by the prior, and she was able to make use of royal stores of bread, wine and meat as she came south; for the rest her officials had to make provision, but they had less to find than was usually the case. Sometimes, part of the company was given free hospitality; the abbot of Malmesbury entertained Elizabeth Berkeley and twenty-four of the people with her. Alternatively a gift was made of some of the company's needs. The abbot of Gloucester contributed some of the oats needed for Joan de Valence's horses, and when Elizabeth de Burgh spent a night at Pleshey in 1344 the earl of Hereford gave hay for forty-three horses and eight hackneys.[44]

Certain provisions were generally taken on the journey, notably bread, meat and fish, and all the wine which would be needed. Ale on the other hand was bought daily and consumed in large quantities; on the journey from Usk Elizabeth de Burgh's officials were purchasing about eighty gallons a day. If it was impossible to replenish supplies by staying at demesne manors, basic foodstuffs were bought as needed along with firewood and rushes. Luxuries were occasionally purchased on the journey, like the basket of figs bought by the countess of Hereford so that she could eat fruit on the feast of St Laurence (10 August). Officials sometimes had to travel over a considerable area to secure supplies. When Elizabeth de Burgh stayed at Westacre in Norfolk in 1347, meat was brought from King's Lynn and Watton, several miles away.[45]

On a journey it was usual for some of the household officials to go ahead to make sure that all was ready for the lady at the next stopping-place. Preparations were also essential as she approached her destination. John the baker and Isaac were sent ahead of Joan de Valence to make bread and see to the meat at Goodrich castle. When Elizabeth de Burgh moved from Anglesey to Clare in 1334, brewing and baking had been taking place

44 PRO E101/92/2 m. 9.

45 PRO E101/92/30 m. 10d.

in advance of her arrival.[46] Apart from the occasional case of a servant or horse having to be left behind because of illness, household accounts give the impression that all the arrangements for journeys went ahead smoothly. In view of the size and complexity of the operation, it is likely that this was not always the case.

Most of the expenditure for the journey went on provisions, and the stable was generally the most expensive department since pasture, hay and oats normally had to be bought. Incidental expenses were few and those which were entered in the accounts mainly concerned river-crossings. The passage of the countess of Hereford and all her equipment over the River Tweed at Berwick cost two shillings, and the same amount was paid to eight men getting Elizabeth de Burgh's carriage and carts across Rochester bridge in 1340. This journey from Essex to Canterbury took Elizabeth five days, with the Saturday and Sunday nights being spent at Ospringe. Daily costs ranged from £4. 4s. 3¼d. to £5. 8s. 9d., the sum total for the journey amounting to £28. 14s. 7¾d.[47] These totals were considerably higher than normal expenditure at home. The seventeen-day journey from Usk to Clare cost just over £99, and of this the stable's purchases amounted to a little over £39. The expense of the horses on a journey is brought out in the daily breakdown of purchases; at Tewkesbury on 15 April, the buttery's purchases totalled £0. 8s. 4d., the kitchen's £1. 3s. 4½d., the poultry's £0. 3s. 11¼d., and the stable's £3. 6s. 7½d.[48]

Late medieval noblewomen used their wealth to live in a comfortable and, in many cases, a luxurious lifestyle, although there were obvious differences in what the wife of an earl and the wife of a knight could achieve. Most women, however, loved magnificence and splendour, and were ready to spend their money on jewellery and plate, furs, high-quality cloths for their robes, costly vestments, brightly-coloured embroidered furnishings and painted and carved travelling carriages. In making their purchases they provided patronage of the arts, and fostered the employment of craftsmen. There was more to the situation, however, than just personal enjoyment, although that element

46 PRO E101/505/26 m. 5; 92/2 m. 3.

47 PRO E101/92/12 m. 10d–11d.

48 PRO E101/93/4 m. 13d, 14, 14d, 15.

was certainly there. Conspicuous consumption was not only the result of the nobility's love of luxury for its own sake, but was an essential part of the role which it was expected to play in society. Noblewomen, whether they were wives or widows, used display and hospitality to uphold their own reputation and that of their families in the community. Their prestige was linked to their generosity to their servants and retainers, and also to neighbours and strangers. Both at home and on her journeys the noblewoman enjoyed comfort and luxury but her lifestyle had a far wider social significance as well.

Chapter 5

CHILDREN, KINSMEN AND FRIENDS

The birth of an heir to a noble family was greeted with joy in the later Middle Ages, and the importance of this event was recognised at the time and has been stressed by historians. Yet comparatively little is known of the noblewoman's relations with her children or with her relatives and friends. It was through her personal relationships that she exercised influence on noble society and her role as mother, grandmother, sister, aunt and cousin, as well as friend and distant kinswoman, is therefore significant. The nature and strength of the ties varied from one individual to another and at different stages of life, but noblewomen were able to foster close family connections and to form strong and long-lasting friendships.

The formal tone of many of the documents, even letters, does not completely conceal the family and friendship networks which existed. Certainly, emotions were rarely divulged, but even a short, factual letter can throw considerable light on relations between parents and children or between siblings. Certain caveats in wills are a pointer towards family tensions, while bequests provide a guide to close friendships. Household accounts in many ways are the best guide to social contacts and relationships because they show the lady's exercise of hospitality; by giving the names of visitors it is possible to see who came most frequently and who stayed longest, and the lady's own visits are also documented. If these sources are used in combination the noblewoman can be seen in the circle of her family and friends. What is more difficult to discover is how relationships changed during the lady's lifetime. Wills reflect her feelings only at the end of her life, and it is rare to have a series of household accounts covering more than one or two years. It is here that Elizabeth de Burgh's accounts are of particular value

93

in that they extend over more than thirty years and indicate how her relations with children, kinsmen and friends developed.

Wives were expected to have children, preferably sons, and it was the responsibility of the midwife and the women of the household to officiate at the birth. The dangers of childbirth to the mother were realised, and in 1304 two monks travelled with relics of the Virgin Mary from Westminster to Knaresborough at the time when Elizabeth, countess of Hereford gave birth to her first son, Humphrey.[1] Once the child was born, there was occasion for general rejoicing. Both the baptism of the child and the churching of the mother were times for a social gathering and celebration. *The history of the foundation and founders of the abbey of Wigmore* went into detail over the baptisms of the children of Edmund Mortimer, earl of March and Philippa, daughter of Lionel, duke of Clarence. Baptism and confirmation took place within a few days of birth and were carried out by a prominent churchman. The godparents were either churchmen or members of the nobility. The heir, Roger, was born at Usk in 1374 and baptised by William Courtenay, bishop of Hereford, with the bishop of Llandaff, the abbot of Gloucester and the prioress of Usk as godparents. Entertainment was probably provided afterwards, just as happened after churching. When Margaret, the wife of Piers Gaveston, was churched at York in 1312 after the birth of their daughter Joan, Edward II paid the minstrels forty marks for playing to the assembly, and minstrels provided the entertainment after the churching of Elizabeth, countess of Hereford eight years earlier.[2]

In view of the widespread infant mortality these celebrations might well turn out to be hollow and premature. The countess of Hereford's son Humphrey died soon after birth, and within four days of his mother's churching his body was brought south to be buried in Westminster Abbey.[3] It has been suggested that the uncertainty of the child's survival led to the parents deliberately distancing themselves from the child,[4] but any distancing

---

1 N. Orme *From childhood to chivalry* London 1984 8–9. PRO E101/365/20 m. 8.

2 Sir William Dugdale *Monasticon Anglicanum* eds. J. Caley, H. Ellis and B. Bandinel (6 vols) London 1817–30 VI part 1 354. J.S. Hamilton *Piers Gaveston earl of Cornwall, 1307–12* Detroit 1988 93–4. PRO E101/365/20 m. 8.

3 PRO E101/365/17.

4 P. Ariès *Centuries of childhood* London 1962 368.

was more likely to be the result of social conventions and circumstances rather than a deliberate cutting off of emotional ties. The paucity of references to a loving relationship does not mean that it did not exist; rather it stems from the nature of the records and from contemporary ideas on the upbringing of noble children.

Noble mothers had nothing to do with the physical care of their children. This was the duty of nurses and servants, and in greater households children were put in the charge of masters and mistresses. The life of the noblewoman and her responsibilities for her estates meant that she could not have devoted herself fully to her children even if she had wanted to and even if this had been the contemporary convention. Absences were unavoidable, as when Elizabeth de Burgh had to go to her Welsh estates to oversee them personally in 1327-8 and left her two daughters at Clare.[5] Yet mothers were concerned for the upbringing of their children, for their education and their social training. Widows often exercised particular responsibility, as when Agnes Paston's husband in his will left her in charge of the upbringing of their youngest son Clement and their daughter Elizabeth.[6] The support of children had to be carefully considered on remarriage; Thomas, duke of Clarence is found giving money to his wife for the support of his stepchildren, the earl of Somerset and his brother Thomas.[7]

Unfortunately, the evidence for the education of noble children is scattered and patchy. References are occasionally found to the mother herself educating her children. In the mid-thirteenth century, Walter de Bibbesworth wrote his treatise for Denise de Montchensy to help her to teach her children the French language they would need for estate management.[8] In a great household, however, the teaching was undertaken by the masters and mistresses, and in any case the usual practice was to send the child elsewhere, to a monastic establishment, school, or another noble household. The children returned home from time

---

5 PRO E101/91/15 comprises the household account for the children.

6 *Paston letters and papers of the fifteenth century* ed. N. Davis (2 vols) Oxford 1971-6 I 23-4.

7 K.B. McFarlane *The nobility of later medieval England* Oxford 1973 242-3.

8 M.T. Clanchy *From memory to written record* London 1979 151-2; the Denise referred to was possibly the wife of Warin de Montchensy, who died in 1255.

to time, and mothers are known to have watched their progress as well as paying their expenses.

Of the options available, nunneries appear to have been the most popular places to send young noble children in the later Middle Ages. The house at Amesbury was patronised by Edward I and Edward II, and Piers Gaveston's daughter Joan, and Eleanor, the daughter of Earl Humphrey and Countess Elizabeth of Hereford, were both brought up there. Philippa, daughter of the widowed countess of Suffolk, spent 1416–17 with the prioress of Bungay; the countess' granddaughter Elizabeth, aged five, was also there for part of the year, but was then sent to the abbey of Bruisyard where she was taught by one of the friars. It was customary in this household for the children to be sent away at an early age but to be sent to places reasonably near the countess' residence at Wingfield in Suffolk. Elizabeth's younger sister, Isabella, was with her nurse in the next village of Fressingfield. The priory of Bungay was paid three shillings a week for Philippa's board and that of the lady with her; Elizabeth's expenses at Bruisyard came to one shilling a week, and her servant was paid 6s. 8d. Philippa spent two weeks at Wingfield with her mother during the year.[9]

The practice of sending noble children to school and university, and not only those intended for the Church, became more widespread in the fifteenth century. Both the younger sons of the countess of Suffolk were receiving formal education. Thomas, who was going to enter the Church, was at Oxford; Alexander, who became a knight, was at school in Ipswich, spent the summer at Wingfield and then started at Cambridge. Mothers took an interest in the progress of their children, and in 1458 Agnes Paston recommended his teacher to punish her son Clement if he did not do well.[10]

The households of noblewomen were in demand for the placing of children in the later Middle Ages. The lady also had wards in the household who were heirs to lands in her or her husband's feudal jurisdiction, or whose wardship had been purchased from the Crown. Parents placed both their sons and daughters with noblewomen. Edward II's son, John of Eltham, was put into the care of Eleanor, wife of Hugh le Despenser the

9 Hamilton *Piers Gaveston* 99–102. McFarlane *The nobility of later medieval England* 244–5. BL Egerton Roll 8776 m. 3–5.

10 *Paston letters* Davis I 41.

younger. Henry Bolingbroke's son John was in the household of Margaret de Brotherton in 1397. Margaret Paston urged her eldest son to arrange for his sister Margery to be with the countess of Oxford or another noblewoman; she offered to contribute towards the cost and commented that she and Margery were not getting on well.[11] Parents had to pay the expenses of their children and supply them with suitable outfits. In a letter to his brother, John Paston II sounded aggrieved over the improbability of his mother paying the expenses of his sister Anne; he said that he would pay the money himself, but it was not as if Anne was his daughter. Among the Stonor letters is a reported complaint from the duchess of Suffolk that if William Stonor's sisters were not better arrayed she might not keep them.[12]

The placing of noble children in other households enabled them to gain valuable social contacts and possibly future patronage and an advantageous marriage, as well as an education in the widest sense of the term. Noblewomen were virtually acting as foster-mothers to other children as well as being mothers to their own families. Children brought up in this way learned social skills and self-reliance. It is likely that parents felt that, as in more modern times, they were doing the best they could for their children by sending them away from home. Their realistic and businesslike approach to children's upbringing is comparable to their attitude to marriage alliances, and it should not be assumed that love and affection were excluded.

Love could certainly exist in family relationships when the children had grown up, as can be seen in surviving letters, accounts and wills, but there is also evidence of family tension, grievance and dislike. The type of relationship was bound to differ from one individual to another, partly because of personal factors and also as a result of settlements concerning land and money. There were times when the widow's dower and jointure caused resentment, as when Gilbert de Clare, earl of Gloucester went to law with his mother in 1266 in order to take back some of her dower land in the Marches. The quarrel between Isabella de Forz and her mother ostensibly centred on their landed

---

11 PRO E101/382/12. McFarlane *The nobility of later medieval England* 243. *Paston letters* Davis I 339.

12 *Paston letters* Davis I 451. *The Stonor letters and papers, 1290–1483* ed. C.L. Kingsford (2 vols) Camden Society third series XXX (1919) II 14.

revenues and they found it impossible to continue their joint administration of Holderness; it is probable, however, that the root cause was political, as Isabella was a supporter of Simon de Montfort in the mid-1260s while her mother was royalist in sympathy.[13]

The Paston letters show how parental exasperation arose on a number of other occasions. Relations between mother and daughter were tense when problems arose over marriage. Agnes Paston seems to have become angry over the failure of various negotiations for the marriage of her daughter Elizabeth and is reported to have beaten her daughter frequently. Margaret Paston had no patience with her daughter Margery when she fell in love with the bailiff, Richard Calle, and complained that she and her daughter were tired of each other. It was at this juncture that she asked her eldest son to arrange for Margery to be placed with a noblewoman. Margaret also found that her eldest son John II did not come up to her expectations; she complained of not hearing from him and was critical of his lack of effort in family concerns. John reciprocated her feelings, saying in one letter that his mother did him more harm than good.[14]

Mothers were, however, usually supportive of their sons who found that they could have a home with them, even after marriage. Margaret Paston provided a home for her sons, John III and Edmund, but in 1472 John III wrote to his elder brother that she was trying to get them both out of the house as she was thinking of the money needed for their younger brothers and for Anne's marriage.[15] Margaret's relations with John III, however, remained good, and she helped him financially over his marriage to Margery Brews. Nearly two hundred years earlier Aymer de Valence, then in his early twenties, made frequent visits to his mother from the spring of 1296, when he returned from abroad, until the spring of 1297. During this time his first wife, Beatrice de Clermont, was living with Countess Joan. Several of Aymer's leading retainers were also frequent visitors at this time, such as

13 N. Denholm-Young 'The Yorkshire estates of Isabella de Fortibus' *Yorkshire Archaeological Journal* XXXI (1934) 410–15. *Select cases in the exchequer of pleas* eds. H. Jenkinson and B.E.R. Formoy Selden Society XLVIII (1931) 58–60.

14 *Paston letters* Davis I 287, 349, 371–3, 379–81, 456–8.

15 Ibid. 576–7.

Sir Roger Ingpen senior, Sir John de la Ryvere, Sir John de Hastings and Sir Thomas de Berkeley.[16]

In some cases the mother provided more than living quarters and actively promoted her son's fortunes. This is apparent in Elizabeth de Burgh's efforts for her son William. William was less than a year old when his father, John de Burgh, died in 1313, and it is likely that he spent at least part of his childhood with his grandfather, Richard de Burgh, earl of Ulster. Shortly after the earl's death in June 1326 William was living in Elizabeth's household. Although he was under age, he received his grandfather's lands in February 1327. Soon afterwards he married Henry, earl of Lancaster's daughter Matilda and set up his own household, but this was supplied with various items from Elizabeth at Clare, and some of Elizabeth's officials passed into William's service. When William returned to Ireland in 1328, Elizabeth spent £859. 15s. 9d. on horses, armour, cloth, furs, table-linen and other household goods. More important, she took action to help him in Ireland. As early as August 1326, she was writing to various Irish magnates, and the following year her councillor, Thomas de Cheddeworth, sent her detailed information about her and William's interests in Ireland, and recommended that William should be sent over with a military following. The advice was taken, but William was murdered in June 1333.[17] In view of the amount of support and money which Elizabeth lavished on him, it is likely that there was a close relationship between mother and son.

Although daughters posed problems to the Pastons, there is evidence in other families of affection between mother and daughter. Elizabeth de Burgh remained close to her two daughters, as is seen in the evidence of visits, bequests and practical help. Isabella married Henry de Ferrers of Groby, while Elizabeth became the wife of Sir John Bardolf of Wormegay in Norfolk. Both visited Elizabeth from time to time and received gifts from her, and Elizabeth appears to have been ready to uphold their interests. Immediately after Henry de Ferrers' death in the autumn of 1343 some of Elizabeth's household were sent to Groby to bring Isabella to Bardfield. Quite apart from personal considerations, Isabella's jointure and dower had to be

16 PRO E101/505/25, 26. J.R.S. Phillips *Aymer de Valence, earl of Pembroke, 1307–24* Oxford 1972 5, 296–306.

17 PRO E101/91/12 m. 1, 3; 91/17 m. 2; 91/18. PRO E30/1536.

secured, and that summer Bartholomew Burghersh and his wife had petitioned for the division of the knights' fees and advowsons on Theobald de Verdun's lands among his four daughters, Bartholomew having married the second and Isabella being the fourth. That Elizabeth and her council had a role to play in these matters is indicated by Bartholomew Burghersh's visits to her in December 1343 and April 1344.[18]

Isabella survived her husband by only six years, dying in the summer of 1349. Elizabeth Bardolf remained in close touch with her mother throughout her life. Her mother visited her in Norfolk, and she and her husband made frequent visits. When she was travelling on her own, she often made the journey from Norfolk to Anglesey, there to be picked up by her mother's travelling carriage and brought to Bardfield or Clare.[19] Elizabeth de Burgh's attachment to her daughter is seen in her bequests to her of her green velvet bed, tawny worsted hangings with blue popinjays and cockerels, and the travelling carriage itself.

The close relationship between the noblewoman and her children was extended to the grandchildren. Again the long series of Elizabeth de Burgh's household accounts enables this to be traced. Her heir was her son William's only child, Elizabeth, countess of Ulster, who came into the king's wardship and was married to his second son, Lionel of Antwerp. Elizabeth paid numerous visits to her grandmother, at least from the age of twelve, and often stayed longer than the usual time of one or two days. All the Ferrers grandchildren spent time living in Elizabeth de Burgh's household, Elizabeth, countess of Athol being there for much of the year 1351-2. It is possible that Elizabeth de Burgh and her officials had some hand in their marriages, but the evidence is suggestive rather than definite. William de Ferrers married Margaret Ufford in 1344, and it was in 1343-4 that Margaret's father, the earl of Suffolk, paid six visits to Elizabeth. William continued to visit his grandmother after his marriage. The earl of Warwick stayed with Elizabeth from time to time, and by the spring of 1351 William's sister Philippa had married the earl's eldest son. Elizabeth remem-

18 PRO E101/92/24 m. 1d, 4, 7. *Calendar of Close Rolls 1343-6* 192, 203, 212-14, 227, 275-9, 342-6, 372-3.

19 For example, PRO E101/92/2 m. 12d-13d; 92/12 m. 8.

bered her grandchildren in her will, Isabella and Agnes Bardolf receiving plate and furnishings to help them to marry.[20]

An examination of the evidence of the Paston letters and Elizabeth de Burgh's household accounts shows both the tension and the affection which existed in family relationships. Family ties were strong and mothers and children were often close to each other in spite of being separated when the children were growing up. This closeness is reflected in the mother's practical support, whether in providing a home, giving financial help, or defending landed interests. The occasional outburst of exasperation was only to be expected. Mothers were concerned that their children should do well in the world, that sons and daughters should make good marriages, and the sons achieve success and good fortune in their lives.

This concern points to a concentration on the immediate nuclear family, and the impression is reinforced by noblewomen's wills which make much more reference to children than to other relations. Elizabeth de Burgh left bequests to her surviving daughter and grandchildren, but not to the Despensers and Staffords who were the direct descendants of her two sisters. Eleanor de Bohun in 1399 divided her possessions among her children, with a very small bequest to her mother. In 1427 Elizabeth Lady FitzHugh bequeathed her jewellery, books and household stuff to children and grandchildren with no mention of other relations. The extended family had its importance when it came to the division of inheritances, and when there was concern to ensure that the estate would pass to a male heir and not to a daughter. However, the extent to which noblewomen kept in touch with siblings and cousins depended to a large extent on personal liking and whether their relations were living in the vicinity. The bond of kinship remained and was remembered, and it was always possible to call on the help of a kinsman if unforeseen circumstances arose. Elizabeth Poynings asked for the help of her nephew, John Paston II, when she ran into difficulties over carrying out her husband's will.[21]

Attitudes to brothers and sisters were subject to as much variety as those in the immediate family. Some noblewomen

---

20 PRO E101/92/12 m. 10; 92/24 m. 1d, 3d, 4d, 5, 6d, 10, 10d; 93/4 m. 10d, 12d, 13d; 93/9 m. 17d; 93/10 m. 1; 93/12 m. 1d, 2, 2d, 4. J. Nichols *A collection of all the wills of the kings and queens of England* London 1780 34–7.

21 *Paston letters* Davis 1 207–9.

were certainly close to their siblings. When the future Edward II quarrelled with his father in 1305, his sister, Joan of Acre, countess of Gloucester, put her belongings at his disposal, sent him her seal to use, and asked him to come and see her. Elizabeth de Burgh looked after her half-brother, Edward de Monthermer, who was mortally wounded at Vironfosse in October 1339, until his death in early December.[22] He was probably unmarried and his sister may have seemed the obvious person to turn to. Elizabeth Berkeley had her brother Thomas, probably the illegitimate son of Thomas, Lord Berkeley, living in her household.[23] Joan de Bohun, countess of Hereford was on very good terms with her brother Thomas Arundel, bishop of Ely and subsequently archbishop of Canterbury. There was a regular exchange of visits both in the country and in London, and these were marked by festivities of various kinds. Joan's visit to Wisbech in the summer of 1383 included an excursion to King's Lynn, supper and breakfast being provided by the Augustinian friars, and a boat-trip being taken down the River Ouse.[24]

Once siblings were married and living at a considerable distance from each other, it is likely that their relations often ceased to be close. Brothers and sisters were mentioned less frequently than children in noblewomen's wills. Political events might also cool a relationship. Elizabeth de Burgh was in touch with her two sisters and their husbands on matters of business, but there is no surviving indication that either of her sisters visited her. Possibly the activities of her brother-in-law, Hugh le Despenser the younger, in the 1320s left a legacy of bitterness.

The wife was expected to identify with her husband's family and connections. Women like Eleanor de Montfort, Joan de Valence and Elizabeth Berkeley spent much time entertaining their husbands' retainers. Eleanor de Montfort participated in her husband's cause in 1265, and entertained his supporters, including female guests like the countess of Oxford and Isabella

22 *Letters of Edward prince of Wales, 1304–5* ed. H. Johnstone Cambridge 1931 60, 74. PRO E101/92/12 m. 7–10.

23 C.D. Ross 'The household accounts of Elizabeth Berkeley, countess of Warwick, 1420–1' *Transactions of the Bristol and Gloucestershire Archaeological Society* LXX (1951) 94.

24 M. Aston *Thomas Arundel* Oxford 1967 172–3, 181–91, 194–200.

de Forz.[25] How far the connection with the husband's family was maintained after his death depended on a variety of circumstances, such as the widow's responsibility for the execution of his will, her duties towards their children, the family estates which she held, and her possible remarriage. Factors such as personal likes and dislikes, other family deaths, removal to a distance, and living in a new social circle could all have an effect, and the widow's connection with her husband's kinsmen might become only a business relationship. Elizabeth de Burgh's contacts with members of the de Burgh family in Ireland ceased after the death of her son, she was only in touch with the children of Theobald de Verdun's first wife when questions arose over the partition of his inheritance, and there were few links with the Damory family apart from her retaining Roger Damory's nephew Nicholas. Alice de Bryene was widowed in 1386 and her husband was buried at Slapton in Devon. By moving across the country to Acton and living on her own Suffolk inheritance, she was out of touch with her husband's locality, and the only sign of a link in 1412–13 was a visit from two priests of Slapton.[26]

These developments again point to the relative unimportance of the extended as against the nuclear family. In fact, the evidence shows that even during the husband's lifetime the wife did not only remain in touch with her relations but she also had her own friends. This is seen in the way a noblewoman entertained in the absence of her husband, and in the frequent practice of noble wives making visits on their own. The woman's circle of friends, many of them in her own neighbourhood or within reach of her residence, was clearly highly valued. It is not possible to draw a rigid distinction between kinsmen and friends, since the nobility was extensively interrelated and noblewomen were selective as to the relations they treated as friends. It can be difficult to define the difference between a woman's friends and her business and social acquaintances, as business and pleasure certainly overlapped in the noblewoman's life. However, the friends are likely to have been those with whom contact was regularly maintained, who visited frequently or over a

25 *Manners and household expenses of England in the thirteenth and fifteenth centuries* ed. T.H. Turner London 1841 15–16, 37.

26 *Household Book of Dame Alice de Bryene, 1412–13* ed. V.B. Redstone trans. M.K. Dale Suffolk Institute of Archaeology and Natural History Ipswich 1931 68.

considerable period, and who received substantial gifts or bequests.

Some noblewomen, but by no means all, had friends among churchmen. The friendship of Eleanor and Simon de Montfort with Robert Grosseteste is probably the best known, but while she was at Odiham in 1265 Eleanor entertained the abbot of Waverley, a house which she patronised, and twice gave hospitality to the nuns of Wintney. Joan de Valence had the prioress of Aconbury as a guest several times in 1297. Elizabeth Berkeley enjoyed the company of churchmen, some of them staying in her household for several weeks, and the local parish priest was usually invited for Sunday dinner wherever Elizabeth happened to be.[27] On the other hand, Elizabeth de Burgh entertained churchmen occasionally but not often enough to indicate that they were numbered among her particular friends.

It is from Elizabeth de Burgh's accounts that it is possible to see the development of friendships over a long period.[28] She appears to have enjoyed entertaining, and with residences in the eastern counties, at Usk and, in the last years of her life, in London she was able to keep in touch with a large circle of friends, many of whom were also kinsmen. She had her special women friends among her contemporaries, but many of her friends were younger than herself, sometimes much younger. However, once a close relationship was established it lasted for life.

Elizabeth was first cousin to Edward III and from the time of his father's deposition enjoyed friendly relations with the royal family, especially with the king's three eldest surviving sons, the Black Prince, Lionel of Antwerp, who married her granddaughter, and John of Gaunt. There is no sign of visits being exchanged with Edward III's mother Isabella, although contact was maintained by letter. With Edward III and Queen Philippa visits were exchanged, and their sons made frequent visits from the time they were children, a habit which they maintained throughout Elizabeth's life. At her death Lionel came into her inheritance,

27 *Manners and household expenses* Turner 5, 6, 11, 26. PRO E101/505/26 m. 13–15, 19, 22; 505/27 m. 5. 'The household accounts of Elizabeth Berkeley' 93–4.

28 Details of Elizabeth de Burgh's friends have been taken from her will (Nichols *A collection of all the wills* 22–43) and from the following household accounts: PRO E101/91/16; 91/19; 91/21; 91/25; 92/2; 92/3; 92/7; 92/9; 92/11–14; 92/24; 92/28; 92/30; 93/2; 93/4; 93/8; 93/9; 93/12; 93/18; 93/20.

she left the king's college at Windsor a gold cup for the Host and a silver-gilt cup with three cherubs for the chalice; the Black Prince received among other precious objects a gold tabernacle with the image of the Virgin Mary and two cherubs carved in gold, a great silver-gilt cross with the Virgin and St John, and a gold ring set with a ruby. The value of the bequests testifies to lifelong friendship.

Elizabeth had numerous kinsmen who were also friends among the higher nobility. Henry of Grosmont was a frequent visitor at Clare, Bardfield and in London between 1345 and 1358; he sent Elizabeth a present of venison in 1352. He was bequeathed a reliquary cross with a piece of the true cross in it and her little, richly-bound psalter. Elizabeth's niece, Margaret Audley, and her husband Ralph Stafford made numerous visits whether Elizabeth was at Clare, Bardfield, Usk or in London. The same is true of her nephew, Hugh le Despenser, and his wife.

Although these friendships were undoubtedly highly valued, the closest social ties were bound to be built up with those who lived near at hand. Elizabeth de Burgh established a strong social circle with members of the nobility who had residences in Essex, and her relationships with them were based on the interchange of visits and gifts. When in the eastern counties, Elizabeth saw a considerable amount of her Bohun cousins, John, earl of Hereford and Essex, his brother and heir Humphrey, and their brother William, earl of Northampton. With John there were visits to each other's castles at Clare, Saffron Walden and Pleshey, which were within easy travelling distance, and four of Elizabeth's officials attended John's funeral. Elizabeth received presents from Humphrey, but there were no visits, possibly because of the earl's ill-health. William and his wife made numerous visits to Clare and Bardfield and later in London. Their sister, Margaret, countess of Devon, living mainly in the south west, made a single visit to Elizabeth, in June 1344. Other members of the nobility who were included in this local circle were John de Vere earl of Oxford and his wife, and Lady Fitzwalter.[29] John's centre at Castle Hedingham was within easy reach of both Clare and Bardfield. The usual practice for married couples was for husband and wife to make separate visits, and it was only occasionally that they made the visit together. These

29 Lady Fitzwalter was probably Joan, granddaughter of Richard de Burgh, earl of Ulster, who was widowed in 1328.

three families constituted the leading noble families of Essex, and with Elizabeth formed a social group which interlocked with members of the nobility elsewhere.

Because of her wealth, extensive estates and her travels, Elizabeth de Burgh was in a better position than most noblewomen to keep up with a wide circle of friends. Her relations with the Bohuns and the de Veres show, however, that she valued the social circle of men and women of her own rank based on the area where she spent most of her time. Most noblewomen depended on their neighbourhood for their friends, and looked for them among people of their own degree. The link between locality and friends for Elizabeth de Burgh is not fortuitous, as it is found in the accounts of other noblewomen. Alice de Bryene provides a good example of a woman who had a lower ranking in the nobility but who, like Elizabeth, enjoyed the company of friends.[30] Her circle was based on the knights and gentry living near her in Suffolk and north Essex. The Waldegraves of Bures St Mary were related to her by marriage, and she often entertained her half-brother Richard, sometimes on his own, sometimes with members of his family. Other regular visitors included Sir Robert Corbet of Assington, Sir Peter Crek of Cockfield, and Sir John Porter of Boxford. More occasional guests were Sir John Howard, and men whose lands lay in north Essex like John Doreward and John Goldyngham. Like Sir Richard Waldegrave, they came both on their own and accompanied by wives and family, and they always had a suitable retinue of servants. Alice, like Elizabeth, based her social life on a group of people of similar rank to her own, and, as her travelling was limited, she relied on the resources of the locality. This pattern was to last for many centuries.

Wives as well as widows had their own special friends. These were likely to be women; Christine de Pisan highlighted the dangers of slander and scandal if women became particularly friendly with men. Judging by the frequency of her visits, Elizabeth Berkeley's closest friend was Matilda, the wife of Sir Roger Salveyn, who was Treasurer of Calais early in Henry v's reign. Elizabeth de Burgh's special friendships were probably forged in the difficult years of Edward ii's reign and then lasted throughout her life. Joan, countess of Warenne, was at that time threatened with divorce; she subsequently visited

30 *Household Book of Dame Alice de Bryene* Redstone *passim.*

Elizabeth from time to time, and Elizabeth bequeathed her a gold image of St John the Baptist in the desert. Elizabeth's greatest friendship was with Marie de St Pol, countess of Pembroke and widow of Aymer de Valence, to whom she left a little gold cross with a sapphire in the middle, and two gold rings, one set with a sapphire and one with a diamond. The two women kept in touch by letter, and they regularly exchanged gifts of cloth. There was a constant interchange of visits, Elizabeth going to Anstey, Waterbeach and Denny to see Marie, and Marie coming to Clare, Anglesey and Usk. Their friendship resulted in close co-operation in their religious, educational and philanthropic work.

The late medieval noblewoman's principal concern lay with her children and her immediate family. Her interest in her children and their affairs lasted for life, and was epitomised by the valuable bequests she left them in her will, the possessions sometimes having sentimental associations. Although often separated from her children while they were growing up, there is no reason to deny the existence of maternal love, and her affection took the form of ensuring that they gained the training and connections which would benefit them in later life. This practical interpretation of love continued when the children were grown up, but the relations between mother and adult son or daughter are known to have generated tension in some families. Relations with kinsmen were by no means as significant as those with husband and children, but many noblewomen kept in touch with sisters and brothers, cousins, nieces and nephews, sometimes because they were part of their social circle or because they had to do business with them, sometimes because they felt that they could be of assistance in furthering their interests. The ties of kinship overlapped with those of friendship, and all noblewomen had their circles of friends which were not restricted to the husband's friends and relations. Personal and geographical circumstances and the lady's rank imposed some limitations on choice of friends, and, with some exceptions for the higher nobility, friends had to be found in one's own locality. The friendship networks formed enabled the wife and widow to lead a full social life among her peers, and to use her contacts to exercise her influence in the region and to increase the power and standing of her family.

Chapter 6

ESTATES AND REVENUE

All noblewomen relied on their estates for the greater part of their income; revenues from the profits of lordship and jurisdiction constituted a minor share, and grants of wardships and marriages were occasional, although welcome, windfalls. Given the lifestyle enjoyed by the nobility, their love of luxury, exercise of hospitality, fees to retainers and patronage of the Church, it was vital to exploit the land as efficiently as possible in order to maximise income, as well as to preserve the inheritance for future generations of the family. It was easier to do this in the later thirteenth century, at a time of growing population and expanding markets, than about a hundred years later when the population was declining and plague was endemic, and when war and political problems made it increasingly difficult to exploit estates in Ireland and, to a lesser extent, in Wales. Only a few noblewomen had to grapple with the difficulty of running estates both in England and France during the Hundred Years War.

The size of estates in the hands of noblewomen varied enormously, ranging from a small group of manors in one locality to lands situated in many parts of the British Isles. Women like Isabella Morley and Alice de Bryene had a small group of manors in a single region, Isabella's jointure and dower lying in Norfolk, and Alice's inheritance being situated in Suffolk and just across the Essex border. In contrast, Elizabeth de Burgh, Anne Stafford and Margaret de Brotherton had lands as extensive as many of the wealthiest noblemen. Elizabeth's Clare inheritance gave her manors in the eastern counties, Dorset, Gwent and Ireland; as a result of jointure and dower from her three marriages she had additional estates in Ireland, together with English lands in the Midlands.

The extent of the demesne lands often changed during the

widow's lifetime through transfer of manors to members of the family or retainers, or through purchase or acquisitions by inheritance. Isabella de Forz received her dower on the death of her husband William, count of Aumale in 1260 and this comprised one-third of Holderness, half the barony of Cockermouth, and the three manors of Borley in Essex, Clopton in Suffolk and Radston in Northamptonshire. Her son was a minor and came into the king's wardship, and Isabella and her mother purchased the wardship of Holderness, while Isabella was granted the honour of Skipton until the heir came of age. After the death of her brother in 1262 Isabella became countess of Devon and lady of the Isle of Wight in her own right.[1] Whereas her dower lands had been concentrated in the north, her brother's inheritance gave her extensive interests in the south. She lived increasingly in the south, spending much time at Carisbrooke and Radston. This change in her circumstances and landed wealth is mirrored in the lives of other widows, such as Margaret de Brotherton, Anne Stafford, and Joan Beauchamp, lady of Abergavenny.

In view of the extent of their estates and the length of time for which they held them, these widows were a significant part of landholding society and it is important to see how effective and successful they were in running their estates. Yet it is a mistake to assume that it was only widows who were involved in estate administration and that married women had no part to play in connection with the management of lands. The wife often had a definite role in this, and not only during the absence of her husband. While John Paston I was away from home, his wife Margaret had to see that the money he needed was forthcoming. John sent her instructions as to how he wanted his household and livelihood governed, and Margaret had the assistance of officials like the bailiff Richard Calle, but she bore the final responsibility.[2] The same is found higher up the social scale. Elizabeth Berkeley, the first wife of Richard Beauchamp, earl of Warwick, was heiress to the Lisle barony, and up to the time of her death in 1422 most of her lands kept their own identity under their own receiver, who paid the greater part of the receipts to the keeper of Elizabeth's household, not to the earl's receiver-

---

1 N. Denholm-Young 'The Yorkshire estates of Isabella de Fortibus' *Yorkshire Archaeological Journal* XXXI (1934) 389–91.

2 *Paston letters and papers of the fifteenth century* ed. N. Davis (2 vols) Oxford 1971–6 I 125–31.

general. This practice was not repeated with the inheritance of the earl's second wife, Isabella Despenser.[3] Whether this was because Elizabeth was more forceful and effective is not known. Anne, duchess of Buckingham continued to be involved in the running of her estates after her marriage to Lord Mountjoy. In 1467 her receiver in Staffordshire asked her to command her auditor to make him various allowances for business undertaken in her service and to sign the bill with her own hand; Anne agreed.[4]

Once the lady was widowed she had to take responsibility for her estates. Not every noblewoman wished to do this, and it is likely that some women remarried in order to have a husband to take control. Margaret, the widow of John, duke of Somerset, and Sir John Neville stated that they wanted to marry for love and for the preservation of Margaret's dower lands.[5] There were times when the widow sheltered behind her council. When Isabella Morley sought the payment of a relief for Sparham from an unwilling John Paston 1 in 1448, Margaret Paston wrote to him that Isabella said that she was only a woman and had to respect her council's advice. More to the point, she said that she had written evidence that the payment had been made in the past.[6] There is no means of knowing whether Isabella genuinely felt that she must obey her council, or whether she adopted this approach for diplomatic reasons because she considered that John Paston would not accept her word alone.

Whatever Isabella Morley's point of view, there were plenty of formidable widows in the later Middle Ages who played an active part in running their estates, not necessarily being involved in daily routine but in major policy decisions and times of difficulty and crisis. At Skipton in 1267 a dispute arose over the arms which had been handed over to the former constable, and its resolution was put off until the next arrival of Isabella de Forz or her steward. Isabella is known to have been present at

3 C.D. Ross *The estates and finances of Richard Beauchamp, earl of Warwick* Dugdale Society Occasional Papers no. 12 (1956) 6–7.

4 B.L. Egerton Roll 2210.

5 *Calendar of entries in the papal registers relating to Great Britain and Ireland. Papal letters 1431–47* 579.

6 *Paston letters* Davis 1 221, 225. C. Richmond 'Thomas Lord Morley (d. 1416) and the Morleys of Hingham' *Norfolk Archaeology* xxxix (1984–6) 3.

the audit of accounts on several occasions in Holderness, and at Carisbrooke and Radston.[7] Elizabeth de Burgh made personal interventions on a number of occasions, authorising payments, pardoning debts, and sending letters to the auditors concerning the levying of fines. These women consulted their councils but the final decision was theirs. In 1339–40, pardons were issued by Elizabeth de Burgh in the presence of her steward, Andrew de Bures, and others of her council, and in 1343 the question of the fines which could not be collected was discussed in council before Elizabeth wrote to the auditors.[8] The lady had to gain the respect of her councillors and officials and to appoint those who would serve her well. Officials could not be left to their own devices but had to be supervised, particularly if they were working on estates not visited by the lady. Only by doing this would the lady reap maximum profit.

During the later Middle Ages administration became increasingly professional and bureaucratic, even on small estates. Estate officials were usually men with a considerable fund of administrative experience and legal knowledge. Terminology varied, but the grouping of manors into bailiwicks accountable to the central financial officials and supervised by auditors and councillors was virtually universal. To a certain extent it was possible to use traditional arrangements, but the creation of jointure and dower and the splitting up, or in some cases reunion of inheritances meant that there had to be flexibility in the administrative arrangements and a readiness to adapt as circumstances changed.

At the local level demesne manors about 1300 were in the charge of bailiffs and reeves. These were the men responsible for farming the land and acounting to the auditors at the end of the year. They supplied the household with food when needed and sold surplus produce on the market. The bailiff received his fee and livery; in her livery list of 1343 Elizabeth de Burgh listed the bailiffs of the demesne manors among her yeomen and also included the reeves of two of her Suffolk manors, Hundon and Clare.[9] With the growth of demesne leasing from the later fourteenth century, the lady and her council dealt increasingly

7 N. Denholm-Young *Seignorial administration in England* Oxford 1937 73–4, 142.

8 PRO E101/92/11 m. 14; SC6/1110/9.

9 PRO E101/92/23 m. 2–3.

with lessees and no longer had as close a connection with the actual farming of the land.

The grouping of demesne manors into bailiwicks was based either on the geographical concentration of the lands or on administrative convenience; and in some cases of inheritance it was possible to take over existing bailiwicks which already had an established administrative structure. Isabella de Forz treated Holderness as a separate bailiwick because of the extent of her Aumale lands there, and she was able to take over the existing organisation when she inherited the earldom of Devon and the Isle of Wight. Concentration of estates and the possibility of making use of some of the previous administration explain why three of Elizabeth de Burgh's bailiwicks were centred on Clare, Usk and Cranborne in Dorset, and why Anne Stafford had bailiwicks for her lands in Gloucestershire, Rutland and Essex. Alternatively, when manors were scattered over a wide area, it was administratively convenient to treat them together. Elizabeth de Burgh's fourth bailiwick of Brandon, Warwickshire, comprised jointure and dower lands in Brandon itself and in Leicestershire, Lincolnshire and Buckinghamshire. Similarly, Anne Stafford's valor of 1435 grouped her estates in Warwickshire, Bedfordshire, Buckinghamshire and Northamptonshire into one bailiwick.[10]

Each bailiwick had its own officials who received fees and robes from the lady; the bailiff of Holderness received £4 for his livery and a £10 fee in the time of Isabella de Forz, while the bailiffs of Cockermouth and Skipton each had £10.[11] On other estates the term steward was used in preference to bailiff. Each of Elizabeth de Burgh's bailiwicks had its own steward and at least one receiver. The receiver of Clare also had the title of constable of the castle, an office which had become redundant by the fourteenth century. His account for 1340–1 shows that he accounted for money from the demesne manors and from the bailiffs in charge of knights' fees, paid out various fees and wages, including those for building work in Clare castle and at Bardfield, accounted for taxes due to the king, and met various household expenses. He himself received a fee of £6. 13s. 4d. and

10 PRO SC11 rolls 799, 801, 816.

11 Denholm-Young *Seignorial administration* 35.

the lady rewarded him with an extra £3. 6s. 8d. during the year.[12] The steward enjoyed higher status than the receiver, and a correspondingly higher fee; John de Hertford as steward of Clare was paid a fee of £20 in 1340–1. It became increasingly common in the later Middle Ages for the steward to be a member of the gentry or nobility, who often performed his duties by deputy. Lord Hastings was the steward of Anne, duchess of Buckingham for Oakham in Rutland in 1474, also served as constable of the castle, and received a fee of £13. 6s. 8d.; his understeward was paid £1 by the duchess.[13] In the bailiwick the steward's most important duties concerned the holding of courts, but he was also usually a member of the lady's council and so had a voice in the shaping of estate policy. Isabella Morley, however, distinguished between her chief steward and the steward of courts on her manors, who also acted as auditor.[14]

The officials at the centre were essential for the supervision and co-ordination of the estates. The receiver-general or his equivalent was in supreme control of financial resources. Terminology varied; Joan Beauchamp had her exchequer at Abergavenny.[15] Under Elizabeth de Burgh the central financial office was the chamber and its principal official the clerk of the chamber. His accounts for 1329–30 and for 1349–50 included receipts of money from all over Elizabeth's lands in England and Wales, and he met the expenses of the household, the lady's chamber, and her fees, alms and gifts. All financial officials were, however, subject to the scrutiny of the auditors, and there are signs by 1350–1 that the existing arrangements were not working satisfactorily. The clerk of the chamber, William de Oxwik, had debts amounting to nearly £276 which had to be paid off, and from this time until Elizabeth's death the wardrober, William de Manton, also served as clerk of the chamber, and combined wardrobe and chamber accounts were produced.[16]

In addition to the central financial officials, the lady also needed legal experts. All noblewomen had their attorneys to defend their interests in the courts and in some cases to take on

12 PRO E101/459/24 m. 2–2d.

13 BL Additional MS 29608 m. 3.

14 BL Additional MS 34122A m. 3.

15 J.A. Bradney *A history of Monmouthshire* (4 vols) London 1904–32 II 4–5.

16 PRO E101/91/22; 93/5; 93/8; 93/19.

estate responsibilities as well. Elizabeth de Burgh's attorneys in Ireland had the general duty of taking her place on her lands and dealing with royal officials; Elizabeth did not visit Ireland after her return to England following the death of her first husband. Thomas de Cheddeworth, appointed in 1323, had the right to appoint estate officials, carry out the audit of accounts, make grants of forest rights, and make leases for periods of up to ten years. He was also responsible for feudal incidents, ensuring the payment of relief when a vassal succeeded to a holding, and making arrangements for wardship if the heir to land was under the age of twenty-one.[17] The attorneys she appointed served her for many years and built up considerable expertise in Irish affairs.

In overall charge was the lady herself and her council. The council in the late thirteenth century was probably informal, and there is only one explicit reference to Isabella de Forz' council in 1274.[18] In the fourteenth and fifteenth centuries councils were professional and paid, and comprised the most important of the noblewoman's officials and other advisers. The membership of a lady's council was rarely recorded but it is likely that Isabella Morley's was made up of the men to whom she paid fees, totalling £14, in 1463–4. Officials included her chief steward, attorney and the auditor and steward of courts. William Stather, clerk, doubled as steward of the household and receiver in return for a fee of £6. 13s. 4d. Like other noblewomen, Isabella made use of the local gentry; her chief steward was John Heydon, who received £3. 6s. 8d., William Jenny was retained as a legal expert on her council at a fee of £1. 6s. 8d., and Edmund Buckenham esquire received a fee of £4.[19]

The councillors acted as feoffees and executors, as well as carrying out their duties on the estates, but the exploitation and defence of the lady's landed interests were the most important part of their work. Elizabeth de Burgh relied heavily on her council. One of her complaints against the Despensers was that she was forced to make another quitclaim of her Welsh lands after being separated from her council at York at the end of

17 R. Frame *English lordship in Ireland, 1318–61* Oxford 1982 66.

18 Denholm-Young *Seignorial administration* 29.

19 BL Additional MS 34122A. Richmond 'Thomas Lord Morley' 3.

1322.[20] At the time of the invasion of Queen Isabella, the councillors were used in work which had to be kept secret and they took steps to further the lady's support of the queen. During her widowhood, grants were made and pardons issued on the advice of the council. Councillors travelled round the estates to take the view of account halfway through the year, conduct the final audit and oversee the state of the manors. They dealt with legal business and attended parliament on the lady's behalf. They also represented her on ceremonial occasions, as when four councillors and household officials attended the funeral of Earl John de Bohun in 1336. Taking all their activities together, the councillors had varied, responsible and demanding work involving a considerable amount of travel. Men like Thomas and Robert de Cheddeworth, Andrew de Bures and John de Wauton can be said to have earned the fees which Elizabeth paid them.[21]

Looking at the period from the thirteenth to the fifteenth century, it appears that noblewomen's lands were as well run as in the time of their husbands and fathers. Comparisons can also be drawn with a number of Church estates such as the archbishopric of Canterbury and the bishoprics of Ely and Worcester.[22] The successful running of the estate depended in the first instance on efficient and well supervised officials, and many noblewomen were well served. Late medieval landowners, whether men or women, needed to be aware of the factors of profit and loss, and the realisation of the importance of this was widespread. Above all, it was essential for the landowner to be pragmatic, to be aware of and ready to exploit all possible sources of revenue, and to adapt the approach according to changing economic circumstances. This did not simply involve a once-for-all decision to exploit lands directly or to lease them, but a careful assessment of the situation on the ground and the

---

20 BL Harley MS 1240 fo. 86v.

21 PRO SC6/836/7 m.3; 868/19 m.5; 868/21 m.3; 868/22 m.2. PRO E101/91/ 11 m.1; 91/12 m.1d, 2d, 3, 3d; 92/3 m.6; 92/11 m.13; 92/13 m.11, 12.

22 Studies of noble and Church estates which have been published in recent years include: M. Altschul *A baronial family in medieval England: the Clares, 1217–1314* Baltimore 1965; F. R. H. Du Boulay *The lordship of Canterbury. An essay on medieval society* London 1966; C. Dyer *Lords and peasants in a changing society. The estates of the bishopric of Worcester, 680–1540* Cambridge 1980; E. Miller *The abbey and bishopric of Ely* Cambridge 1951; C. Rawcliffe *The Staffords, earls of Stafford and dukes of Buckingham 1394–1521* Cambridge 1978.

potential of individual estates. Both Elizabeth de Burgh and her brother before her adapted their farming methods with an eye to the possibilities of marketing. About 1400, the archbishop of Canterbury, Margaret de Brotherton and Anne Stafford were all adopting a pragmatic approach to leasing and deciding to keep certain assets in their own hands. The most effective men and women landowners were those with determination, drive, a sense of realism and an eye for profit. A few were unfortunate enough to have lands in areas affected by war and revolt in France, Wales and Ireland, but were still able to profit from their English estates.

Noblewomen were ready to add to their lands by purchase and exchange, and it was to their advantage to acquire manors near existing concentrations of estates in order to ease administration. In an exchange with the king in 1337, Elizabeth surrendered the manors of Kennington and Vauxhall, which she had held jointly with Roger Damory, in return for Ilketshall in Suffolk. She already had important estates in the county whereas she had no other lands in Surrey. Acquisitions on a larger scale were made by Joan Beauchamp, lady of Abergavenny in the early fifteenth century; these included the lordship of Grosmont granted to her for life by Henry IV, and numerous manors in southern England and the Midlands obtained from John, earl of Arundel and Sir Hugh Burnell.[23]

It was easier for the nobility to make a profit from their lands in the thirteenth century when markets were expanding and costs were low than in the later fourteenth and fifteenth centuries when the fall in population led to the contraction of demand, much higher wages, and the decline of villein services. Yet even in the thirteenth century it was essential for the noblewoman to be ready to make changes where necessary if she was to maximise her income. Receipts from rents, villein dues and profits of jurisdiction were all important, but the largest share of revenue generally came from the profits of arable and livestock husbandry and it was in this area that adaptability was called for. Isabella

---

23 *Calendar of Charter Rolls 1327–41* 426–8. *Calendar of Close Rolls 1409–13* 144; ibid. *1419–22* 86–90, 156, 167–8. *Calendar of Patent Rolls 1416–22* 305–6; ibid. *1422–9* 486. *Calendar of Fine Rolls 1430–7* 255, 293, 315. C. D. Ross and T. B. Pugh 'Materials for the study of baronial incomes in fifteenth-century England' *Economic History Review* second series VI (1953–4) 188–9.

de Forz' lands in Holderness are a case in point.[24] Here, receipts from the sale of wool grew between 1261 and 1277 from about a quarter to just under a half of her whole income. This came about as a result of rising wool prices, not an increase in the size of the flock; possibly Isabella was unable to do this because of shortage of pasture. However, once 5,158 sheep had been seized in 1278 to pay off part of her debt to the Crown, she diversified into grain production, and also increased receipts from the sale of pasture until murrain struck in 1285. Although in the early years after she took over the lands in Holderness expenditure was high on repairs and purchases of stock, costs later dropped. Like other thirteenth-century landowners, she was concerned to keep the manors in good running order without excessive expenditure. Isabella and her advisers gave careful thought to the type of farming likely to prove most profitable and when necessary policies were changed.

Elizabeth de Burgh developed and adapted her predecessors' policy of direct demesne farming. She lived in an era of economic stability rather than expansion. Her tenure of her inheritance in the early years of her widowhood was precarious due to Roger Damory's forfeiture and her loss of Usk to the younger Despenser. Her English lands were restored to her on 2 November 1322, although they were temporarily re-confiscated two months later. It appears that Edward II intended that the manors should be stripped of assets before their restoration; all grain and stock were sold, together with the crops growing in the fields. It may be doubted whether the king's orders were carried out. The crops were sold to the prior of Stoke, the Benedictine house which had a long and close connection with Clare, and the custodian of the lands was Robert de Bures, who had been steward of the honour of Clare in 1308–9 and whose son Andrew later served as Elizabeth's steward and councillor.[25]

Elizabeth's policies over demesne farming are apparent in her estate accounts and in two valors of her English and Welsh lands for 1329–30 and 1338–9.[26] The valors are particularly informative as they analyse manorial value according to the individual

24 M. Mate 'Profit and productivity on the estates of Isabella de Forz (1260–92)' *Economic History Review* second series XXXIII (1980) 326–34.

25 PRO SC6/1147/9 m.5–15.

26 The figures have been tabulated by G. A. Holmes *The estates of the higher nobility in fourteenth-century England* Cambridge 1957 143–57, 161–3.

sources of profit or loss; the valor of 1338–9 assessed the manors under the headings of rents, profit or loss on arable husbandry, sale of wool, profit of livestock, profits of the courts, and other issues. Grain yields were carefully scrutinised and a calculation made of profit or loss compared with the preceding year. It was especially necessary to make a close investigation in 1338–9, as the total valuation then represented a fall compared with nine years earlier, £2,368 as against £2,723. It was clear even before 1338–9 that arable husbandry was no longer a major source of profit, and diversification and the exploitation of non-farming sources of revenue were essential. Elizabeth and her officials were ready to make changes as far as farming practices were concerned.

There was no question in Elizabeth's lifetime of leasing the majority of the demesne lands as was to become widespread practice by about 1400, although single manors were occasionally let on short leases.[27] It was realised, however, that there was no point having as great a demesne acreage of grain as had been the case in 1300. At that time the emphasis, especially on the Clare lands in eastern England, had been unequivocally on corn-growing, and animal husbandry had been virtually non-existent on a number of manors. Elizabeth had to ensure that sufficient grain was produced to supply her household, whether she was living in England or Wales, but by the end of the 1320s the acreage under cultivation had already dropped markedly. At Standon in Hertfordshire, one of the largest manors, the demesne acreage of 444 acres in 1311–12 fell to 357 acres in 1328–9, and to about 200 acres by the mid-1330s; apart from 1348–9, it remained at that level until Elizabeth's death. At Clare, however, about 500 acres remained under cultivation in the 1320s and 1330s because of the importance of the manor for the provision of the household; in 1330–1 nearly 219 quarters of wheat and 83 quarters of oats were supplied.[28]

The major diversification was into sheep-farming, and the risks of murrain and high royal taxation were considered worth taking. In 1329–30 there were already flocks of sheep on the Dorset lands and at Caythorpe in Lincolnshire. At Cranborne the profit from arable farming and the sale of wool amounted to

27 PRO SC2/212/40 m.8.

28 PRO E101/91/24 m.1.

9% and 9.7 per cent respectively of the total valuation of £133. 10s. 7d.; the flock consisted of 641 sheep and 355 lambs. The figures for wool were more impressive at Caythorpe, where profit from arable farming made up 7.3 per cent and the sale of wool 19.5% out of a total profit of £230. 13s. 0d. Here the flock comprised 904 sheep and 640 lambs. Sheep farming continued to be important in both these areas, but during the 1330s the manors of the Clare bailiwick were also running sizable flocks. The beginning of this policy can be seen in the valor of 1329–30 when 124 sheep were bought to stock the manor of Claret. Flocks were subsequently established in other places at minimum cost, with sheep being transferred from one manor to another; by 1338–9 there were altogether 6,175 sheep on the English estates. It is likely that this policy of wool production continued until Elizabeth's death; in 1358 two years' production, amounting to 6,241 fleeces from the Clare bailiwick, was sold to the London merchant Richard Toky for just over £207.[29]

The changing economic circumstances of the later fourteenth and fifteenth centuries made it unprofitable to continue demesne farming, and noblewomen, like other landowners, had again to adapt their approach. Noblewomen had to decide when it was best for them to lease their lands, and it was up to them and their councils to obtain the best terms they could from lessees. Joan de Bohun was still farming some of her lands directly in the late 1370s. An account for Hatfield Broad Oak, Essex, for 1377–8 shows that the sale of corn and stock brought in about £30, but she received about £41 from rents and farms and about £23 from the sale of works and customs.[30] When her manors came into Henry v's hands on her death in 1419 they were held at farm.

The lady had to decide how many of her demesne manors to lease. Usually she kept little in her own hands, and there is hardly a sign in the valors of Margaret de Brotherton and Anne Stafford of income derived directly from agriculture organised by the lady. In some cases, however, the need for household supplies led to the retention of some direct demesne farming. According to her receiver's accounts of 1428–9 and 1431–2, most of Alice de Bryene's manors in Suffolk and Essex were held at farm, mills were leased separately, and her London house was

29 PRO SC6/993/16.

30 Essex Record Office D/DQ 18.

rented out. Acton was still run by a bailiff and her household accounts indicate that Alice kept the manor in her own hands in order to secure her basic supplies. In 1394–5 arable and livestock farming was carried on; pigs and more particularly sheep were important (346 fleeces were sold), and the estate-servants besides the bailiff included a harvest-reeve, two carters, six ploughmen, one cowman, two shepherds, one pigman and a maid.[31]

The account for the lands of Margaret de Brotherton in 1394–5, and the valors of the estates of Joan Beauchamp, lady of Abergavenny of 1425–6, and Anne, countess of Stafford of 1435–6 all show that it was possible to obtain a high revenue from lands in England in an age of demesne leasing.[32] All three women, like Isabella de Forz and Elizabeth de Burgh earlier, showed themselves determined and efficient in the exploitation of their estates. They kept a close eye on both their officials and their revenues. That receipts were carefully scrutinised is seen in the distinction drawn in Joan Beauchamp's valor between the clear arrears, which it was hoped to collect, and the debts which were described as desperate. Even in her Welsh lordships only a small proportion of the money owing was written off.

Although different criteria had to be adopted when dealing with leasing rather than direct demesne farming, there was in fact much continuity in the later Middle Ages regarding other forms of estate revenue. Rents and profits of jurisdiction were considered of major importance throughout the period, and possessions such as parks provided revenue as well as opportunities for sport. Noblewomen showed themselves aware of the significance of all these sources of income, made use of their customary rights and increased receipts where possible. For Elizabeth de Burgh the value attached to rent and jurisdiction varied according to the situation of the lands. Most of her borough revenues came from these sources, as did a varying proportion of the receipts from her English manors. On her manors in Dorset, rents contributed between 34% and 66% of manorial values, and at Cranborne in 1338–9 rents and farms yielded nearly £65 to the total value of a little under £116. Rents

31 PRO SC6/989/6; 1245/16, 17. *Household book of Dame Alice de Bryene 1412–13* ed. V.B. Redstone trans. M.K. Dale Suffolk Institute of Archaeology and Natural History Ipswich 1931 85–93, 103, 116–39.

32 College of Arms Arundel MS 49. PRO SC11/25, 816. Bradney *A history of Monmouthshire* II 4–5.

were significant even on manors which played a big part in supplying the household; at Hundon, Suffolk, in 1338–9, rents and farms made up 22% of the profit, compared with 4% profit on arable husbandry and 10% on wool. Jurisdictional profits varied, but where the lady was responsible for hundred courts and petty criminal business they could be considerable. The 1338–9 valor valued Elizabeth's hundred courts in Dorset at nearly £63, the highest amount, of nearly £44, being for Cranborne. There are signs that both rents and the profits of courts were being increased, probably a reaction to the cutback in arable farming.

The situation on Elizabeth's Irish lands was somewhat different in view of her being an absentee landlord. Her lands were scattered; her share of the Clare inheritance lay in Kilkenny, her jointure from her first marriage in Ulster, Connacht and Munster, and her dower from her second marriage in Meath and Louth. The emphasis was put on rents and leases.[33] Although some direct farming took place on the Welsh lands, rents and farms accounted for over half the receipts on the majority of Elizabeth's holdings in 1338–9. Although Usk and Caerleon were highly Anglicised lordships, they contained their distinct Welshries of Welsh population living in the uplands. The profits of these bedelries added significantly to the total value of the lands, the principal revenues coming from judicial perquisites and rents. It is likely that Elizabeth developed both; rents were increased when property changed hands and waste was reclaimed. Certainly the value of the Welsh lordships grew between 1317, when it was set at £757, and 1329–30, when it amounted to £928. To take an individual example, in 1317 the demesne manor of Liswerry and the bedelries of Edelegan and Llefnydd were valued at about £90; in 1338–9, the total value of all three amount to about £136.

The proportion of receipts from rents and farms increased with the growth of demesne leasing. The main headings in Margaret de Brotherton's account of 1394–5 covered rents and farms, profits of the courts, and occasionally profits of parks. On the manors of her Segrave jointure, rents and farms comprised the bulk of her revenues, and the same is true of many of the manors of her own inheritance. At Dovercourt and Harwich,

33 Frame *English lordship in Ireland* 62–4. T.E. McNeill *Anglo-Norman Ulster* Edinburgh 1980 136–47 tabulates the account rolls for 1353–60.

rents and farms, together with the rents for the inshore fisheries, amounted to 89% of the total, while the profits of courts contributed 7%. However, a certain amount of variety is found; at Framlingham the percentages for rents and farms, and the courts were 35% and 14% respectively.

It is easier to see the relative importance of the various sources of revenue on the lands of Anne, countess of Stafford as her valor of 1435–6 separates rents and farms. It covers all her English lands apart from Holderness, which she had probably not yet finally secured.[34] Taking the estates as a whole, rent brought in 37% of her revenue, farms 52%, casual yearly issues 6%, and perquisites of courts 5%. There was, however, considerable variation among the bailiwicks, with farms providing most of the revenue in Essex and rents supplying most in Rutland and Gloucestershire. Most of the property was rural but Anne had towns at Thornbury, Rothwell, Oakham and elsewhere.

Parks and woodland were always regarded as a source of income, albeit one which varied from year to year depending on woodland management and expenditure on repairs and wages. Cranborne Chase was given a low valuation in Elizabeth de Burgh's valors but the sale of wood brought in a substantial occasional profit; the sum of £41. 11s. 2d. was entered in the valuation of 1329–30. Forest resources were greater in the lordship of Usk, and the sale of wood in the forest of Trellech brought in about £233 in 1329–30, and about £106 in 1338–9. Elizabeth was also lady of Southfrith forest near Tonbridge, where she developed ironworks at Tudeley. These were alternately managed directly or leased out; problems occurred as the lessees fell into arrears of rent, but they were considered an asset worth developing, as in 1350 when the works were rebuilt.[35] Profits from parks included the sale of pasture and hay. It was usual for the lady to keep woods and parks in her own hands when the demesne lands were leased out. This was done by both Margaret de Brotherton and Anne Stafford. Receipts could be substantial; in 1394–5 Margaret received nearly £41 from her-bage at Framlingham, out of a total revenue of about £118.

By using their administrations to exploit all available resources

34 C. Rawcliffe *The Staffords, earls of Stafford and dukes of Buckingham 1394–1521* Cambridge 1978 18.

35 M.S. Giuseppi 'Some fourteenth-century accounts of ironworks at Tudeley, Kent' *Archaeologia* LXIV (1912–13) 145–64.

Table 3 Revenues of Anne, countess of Stafford, 1435–6, from her English lands[a]

	Rents		Farms		Casual yearly issues[b]		Perquisites of courts		Gross value[c]
	£	%	£	%	£	%	£	%	£
Gloucestershire	295	68	59	13	42	10	39	9	435
Warwickshire Bedfordshire Buckinghamshire Northamptonshire	75	24	190	61	22	7	25	8	312
Rutland Nottinghamshire	198	71	57	20	13	5	10	4	278
Kimbolton and its members	80	54	47	32	16	11	5	3	148
Norfolk Suffolk	43	23	111	60	11	6	21	11	186
Essex	56	9	553	88	12	2	5	1	626
Kent Surrey Sussex	25	20	91	74	4	3	4	3	124
Hampshire Wiltshire	19	34	28	51	3	6	5	9	55

[a] All the figures are taken from PRO SC11/816 and are given to the nearest pound.
[b] This figure includes the profits of parks.
[c] This is the total valuation recorded in the manuscript before the deduction of expenses.

and by developing their estate policies to meet changing situations, noblewomen were able to manage their lands effectively and profitably. War and revolt, however, posed problems for some noblewomen. War in Ireland in the later fourteenth century made it increasingly difficult for absentee nobles to exploit their estates. Elizabeth de Burgh was little affected by this, but she lost control of her lands in Connacht in 1357–8 when no one dared to go there on her behalf because of war.[36] The profits which Elizabeth de Burgh was able to reap from her Welsh lands were not repeated in the early fifteenth century. Several factors contributed to this: economic decline, the difficulty of raising the communal fines which comprised an important source of revenue

36 PRO SC6/1239/33.

in the Marches, absentee lordship and administrative inefficiency, and the effects of Glyn Dŵr's revolt. As a result of the rebellion, Anne Stafford's revenues from the lordship of Newport fell to nothing, although in 1408 Edward, duke of York took on the farm of the lands in return for paying her £100 a year. Anne also lost out from the redivision of the Bohun inheritance in 1421 under which she acquired the Marcher lordships of Brecon, Huntington, Talgarth and Hay. These were already in decline before the rebellion and it proved impossible to exploit them fully and collect the revenues.[37] Joan Beauchamp also faced serious problems over collection of revenue from her Welsh lordships of Abergavenny and Ewyas Harold.[38]

The Hundred Years War posed problems to families with lands in France, and here Marie de St Pol was the noblewoman most affected. She held dower lands in England and France from her marriage to Aymer de Valence and also had French lands of her own. She made several visits to France both before and during the war. There was no question of confiscating her English possessions; Edward III's order of 1337 that the lands of all aliens were to be taken over by the Crown did not apply to her. She lost her French lands temporarily about 1346, but it was not until 1372 that she lost them permanently. Unfortunately, it is not known how her lands fared.[39]

The incomes of noblewomen in the later Middle Ages varied as much as the size of their estates. Because of the nature of the evidence it is only possible to gain an approximate idea of income, and in the absence of a good run of central financial material for one estate the yearly fluctuations and overall rise or decline in revenues cannot be traced. Crown surveys, whether inquisitions *post mortem* on the death of a tenant-in-chief or dower assignments, are of limited help as they often give too low a valuation of the lands and do not include jointures or manors in the hands of feoffees. The accounts of receiver-generals give some guide to income but have to be carefully assessed as they do not necessarily include all the receipts from all the bailiwicks and were designed to show the liability of the official, not the income

---

37 Rawcliffe *The Staffords* 15–18, 107–8. *The Marcher lordships of South Wales, 1415–1536* ed. T.B. Pugh Cardiff 1963 151–2.

38 Bradney *A history of Monmouthshire* II 4–5.

39 H. Jenkinson 'Mary de Sancto Paulo, foundress of Pembroke College, Cambridge' *Archaeologia* LXXXVI (1915) 406–10.

of the lady.[40] In Elizabeth de Burgh's chamber account of 1349–50 the clerk of the chamber totalled his receipts at nearly £1,884; in 1355–6 they amounted to a little under £3,047.[41] These sums include arrears and the sale of issues of the household, but most of the money came from the estates. The difference is explained by the inclusion of all the estates in 1355–6 but not six years earlier, possibly because of disruption as a result of the Black Death.

In the absence of valors, accounts, despite their drawbacks, give the best indication of income. Isabella Morley's account of 1463–4 gave the receipts from her estates and profits of jurisdiction as about £170. Some manors were doing better than others; she received about £42 from Aldeby, which had been worth about £25 in 1426–7, but only about £19 from Foulsham, which had been worth £11 more seven years earlier. Arrears do not appear to have been a major problem; her clerk of moneys, William Stather, owed nearly £40 from the previous year, but this had been cut down to about £18 by Michaelmas, 1464.[42] Arrears were a bigger problem on the lands of Alice de Bryene, where they amounted to £154 in 1428 and about £120 three years later. Excluding Acton, Alice should have received nearly £182 from her estates, but only about £117 was paid to her, and the expenses allowed on the account only came to about £15. Allowances had to be given on many of the farms, and it is likely that Alice found that she was faced with a declining income.[43]

Margaret de Brotherton, in contrast, ranked among the wealthiest members of the nobility. The account for 1394–5 gave the sum received from the profits and issues of her Segrave jointure as nearly £667 and from her inheritance as about £2,173; the sum total came to a little over £2,839. These figures included arrears as well as her main sources of income, but there do not appear to have been major problems in collecting revenue. The receipts did not all come into Margaret's hands as income; some were needed for necessary expenditure on the estates, and there is no indication as to what this amounted to. Margaret's income

40 R.R. Davies 'Baronial accounts, incomes and arrears in the later Middle Ages' *Economic History Review* second series XXI (1968) 213.

41 PRO E101/93/5 m.1; 93/19 m.1–4.

42 BL Additional MS 34122A. Richmond 'Thomas Lord Morley' 4.

43 PRO SC6/1245/16, 17.

was lower earlier in her widowhood, and it was only after 1382 that she enjoyed the revenues of the whole Brotherton inheritance.[44]

Where valors survive it is possible to gain a clearer idea of the value of the estate and the likely income from it; a succession of valors indicates how revenues changed. Valors do not all follow the same form; some give the gross value of lands, others deduct estate and other expenses and provide what was termed the clear value. Some, like Elizabeth de Burgh's in 1329–30 and Joan Beauchamp's in 1421 and 1425–6, dealt with arrears, but some of the nobility, like Anne Stafford, kept separate arrears' rolls. All three of these noblewomen enjoyed substantial incomes. Joan Beauchamp's valor deducted expenses on buildings, mills and parks, and valued her English estates, excluding Rochford in Essex, at just over £2,121; once £137 of fees and annuities were allowed for, the clear value remained at just over £1,984. Her lordships of Abergavenny and Ewyas Harold were valued at about £635 and £29 respectively. Anne Stafford's valor made similar allowances for repairs and annuities; wages were also included under expenses and occasionally the purchase of stock. The clear value of all her English estates except for Holderness came to just over £1,765, as compared with the gross value of nearly £2,187.[45]

With Elizabeth de Burgh it is possible to use the partition of the Clare inheritance of 1317 and the valors of 1329–30 and 1338–9 to see how income fluctuated.[46]

Elizabeth enjoyed an income of between about £2,500 and £3,000 a year. In 1317 she had the revenues of the Brandon bailiwick as well as her Clare inheritance, and a notional figure of at least £600 needs to be added to the total for that year to give a fair idea of her income from her English lands. Her Irish revenues from her first and second marriages also have to be added. Taking Kilkenny into account as well, these remained reasonably stable during her widowhood; she received on average £462 a year in 1333–7, and £440 in 1353–4.[47] Finally, there

---

44 College of Arms Arundel MS 49. R.E. Archer 'The estates and finances of Margaret of Brotherton, c. 1320–1399' Historical Research LX (1987) 266, 277.

45 PRO SC11/25, 816.

46 PRO C47/9/25, 26; SC11/799, 801, 808.

47 Frame English lordship in Ireland 64 tabulates Elizabeth's annual income from her Irish lands.

Table 4   Revenues of Elizabeth de Burgh[a]

	1317[b]	1329–30	1338–9
Bailiwick of Clare	1,039	791	661
Bailiwick of Cranborne	244	498[c]	393
Bailiwick of Usk	757	928[d]	867[e]
Bailiwick of Brandon		612	547
Share in Kilkenny	169		
Total	£2,209	£2,829	£2,468

[a] Figures have been taken from PRO C47/9/25, 26, and SC11/799, 801, 808. Figures are given to the nearest pound, and represent gross values before expenses were deducted. The figures for individual manors in 1329–30 and 1338–9 are printed in G A Holmes, *Estates of the higher nobility in fourteenth-century England* Cambridge 1957 143–4, and the 1338–9 profits are analysed on 145–7.
[b] These figures include the dower lands of the widow of Gilbert, earl of Gloucester, which passed to Elizabeth after the widow's death in 1320.
[c] In addition the sale of wood brought in £42.
[d] In addition the sale of wood brought in £233.
[e] In addition the sale of wood brought in £106.

were occasional temporary increases of income as a result of sales of wood. The fluctuations in revenues show the advantage of exploiting rents and profits of jurisdiction, as in the lordship of Usk. The greatest drop in income took place in the bailiwick of Clare, and was mainly due to the decline in profitability of arable farming; there was a great difference between the famine prices of 1317 and those at the end of the 1330s. A fall in feudal revenues also contributed to the changing situation at Clare. Such changes of income had to be faced by all noblewomen in the fourteenth and fifteenth centuries, and explain the necessity of constant supervision and administrative efficiency in order to minimise falls in revenue.

In the absence of both accounts and valors the income taxes of the first half of the fifteenth century provide some guide to noblewomen's incomes and the tax of 1436 has been used in this connection.[48] It was levied on income from land, rents, annuities and offices in England, but revenues from Welsh lands were

48 H.L. Gray 'Incomes from land in England in 1436' *English Historical Review* XLIX (1934) 607–39. T.B. Pugh and C.D. Ross 'The English baronage and the income tax of 1436' *Bulletin of the Institute of Historical Research* XXVI (1953) 1–28. Richmond 'Thomas Lord Morley' 3.

excluded and this has to be taken into consideration when evaluating the usefulness of the tax evidence to the historian. Where the tax assessment can be compared with evidence from the lady's estates, it is clear that its accuracy varies widely. Isabella Morley's tax estimate of £200 was probably accurate for her income in 1436 and her revenues then fell somewhat by 1463–4. Anne Stafford's income was assessed at £1,958, which compares reasonably with the gross value in the valor of nearly £2,187, provided that she had not yet recovered the lands in Holderness; allowance has to be made for her receipts from the Marches but she had difficulty in levying her revenues there. On the other hand, the tax assessments for women like Joan Beaufort and her daughter Katherine, dowager duchess of Norfolk, were well below their actual landed incomes. In the cases where it is not possible to check on the tax assessment, it is safest to take it as only an approximate guide to income.

In running their estates noblewomen faced the same economic situation as their husbands and sons, they used the same administrative methods, and in a number of instances inherited or shared their personnel with other members of their families. It is not to be expected that there would be major differences in methods and policies. Yet in an age when estates often came into women's hands by way of inheritance, jointure and dower, it was important from the point of view of the noblewoman, as well as of her successors, that the land should be exploited efficiently and that profits should be maximised. Although most noblewomen came into these responsibilities as widows, wives had to take on these duties in the absence of their husbands or in relation to their own inheritance. The evidence of accounts and valors shows that many noblewomen tackled the management of their estates with determination and adaptability, seeing the need for flexible estate policies to deal with changing economic circumstances. At their deaths the lands passed to their successors as a going concern.

Chapter 7

LORDSHIP AND PATRONAGE

The exercise of lordship in the fourteenth and fifteenth centuries is usually seen in terms of the noble's retainers, whether they were living in his household or further afield, and noblewomen built up their own retinues during their widowhood. At the same time the nobility also had rights over the vassals whose predecessors had been granted land in the late eleventh and twelfth centuries in return for the performance of knight service. This was rarely demanded in the later Middle Ages, but the vassals continued to owe relief, aids and suit to the honour court. The payment of relief was made when a vassal succeeded to a holding, and aids were due at the knighting of the lord's eldest son, the first marriage of his eldest daughter, and for the ransoming of the lord's person. Moreover the vassals' lands were subject to wardship in the event of the succession of a minor, unless avoiding action had been taken by joint enfeoffment or the entrusting of the estate to feoffees. It became increasingly difficult for the nobility to keep track of their vassals and enforce their rights of lordship, but they had no desire to relinquish these.

The noble lady's ability to maintain her feudal rights depended very much on the situation she inherited and the vigour and ruthlessness of her own administration. Isabella de Forz derived only a small part of her revenue from feudal sources; her court of Plympton for the honour of Devon was only worth about £8 or £9 a year, and although the court of Skipton was held every three weeks it only brought in about £15 a year.[1] In contrast, Elizabeth de Burgh inherited a much more active and lucrative honour court at Clare. The 1317 partition valued this at nearly £71, and if the perquisites of the forinsec or

1 N. Denholm-Young *Seignorial administration in England* Oxford 1937 96–8.

outlying courts of the honour are included the total comes to a little under £100.[2] Profits fluctuated and the yearly total was occasionally boosted by the payment of a large relief. The valor of 1329–30 gave the figure of £160 as received from bailiffs of fees, and the valor of 1338–9 £109; it is likely that these sums included rents and profits of leet jurisdiction as well as feudal revenues.[3]

The honour court was held at Clare on Wednesdays, generally every three weeks. Freeholders and military tenants in Norfolk, Suffolk, Essex and Cambridgeshire owed suit of court, although it was very rare for the most important vassals to attend. The steward of the honour was usually president and had some discretionary power as in pardoning fines. The lady was aware of what went on and initiated matters like the inquiry into service and suit of court in 1326 by sending mandates to the steward. She may occasionally have been present; an entry fine by one of the leading vassals was said to have been made in the lady's presence.[4] In addition to feudal business, the court dealt with minor personal actions concerning such matters as entry fines, trespass, debt, and the taking or detention of goods and chattels. Much of the success of the court was due to the work of the bailiffs of fees, one for each of the counties of Norfolk, Suffolk and Essex, who made distraints and attachments, summoned juries, carried out inquiries and the decisions of the court, collected information and gave testimony in court. They received a money-fee, and worked under the close supervision of the steward and auditors and ultimately of the lady.

It is clear from the honour court rolls that Elizabeth was not willing to relinquish rights over vassals. She could not put the clock back and force all her vassals to perform suit of court, nor stop them from taking steps to prevent their lands from falling into her hands during a minority; in any case, many of the most valuable custodies belonged to the king because of his right of prerogative wardship. What Elizabeth and her officials could do was to keep track of tenants and insist on the performance of as

2 Most of the forinsec courts were in Norfolk and supplemented the work of the Clare court by taking essoins and holding inquiries. They were probably held in conjunction with meetings of the manor court.

3 PRO SC11/799 m. 8; 801 m. 4d where the bailiwick of Suffolk included the revenues from Southwold.

4 PRO SC2/212/43 m. 2, 4d, 5.

many feudal obligations as possible. On recovering her lands in November 1322 Elizabeth sent out an order to all her vassals in Norfolk, Suffolk and Essex to do homage and fealty, the ceremony in which they knelt before her, placed their hands between hers, and swore to be loyal, in this way admitting her lordship. Over the next few courts a number of her most important military tenants performed fealty; a reluctance to perform homage is found even in the early years of the fourteenth century when honour court rolls begin. Suit of court was not allowed to disappear by default; Richard de Talworth, a prominent vassal, was ordered to produce his charters by which he claimed exemption from suit. There is no reference to knight service, but castleguard was demanded, presumably for financial reasons. It is likely that military tenants regarded this demand as outmoded; in 1326 the knight William Fitz Ralph agreed to make a payment for castleguard at Clare castle if his peers did the same.[5]

Reliefs could not, however, be evaded although vassals took time to pay. They were levied at the rate laid down by Magna Carta of £5 for a knight's fee, and brought in occasional but sometimes large sums; the heirs of Richard Fitz Simond owed £48. 15s. 0d. in 1350 on 9¾ knights' fees in Essex and Norfolk;[6] these holdings had been granted to their ancestors by the Clare family after the Norman Conquest. Elizabeth inherited a procedure on the death of a vassal which was similar to the Crown's and under which an inquisition *post mortem* was taken. An order was issued in the honour court for the dead tenant's lands to be taken into the hands of the lady, the inquisition was carried out, and then the lands handed over to the heir if he was of age. Dower was assigned in the honour court, and at the end of a minority the jury was used in the proof of age.

The way in which this procedure worked in practice is seen on the death of John de la Kersonere in 1325.[7] His eldest son John came to the court and asked to be admitted to his father's lands. The jury established that his father had held various lands in Hawkedon, Suffolk, of the lady by the service of half a knight's fee and suit to the honour court, and that John was the son and

5 PRO SC2/212/39 m. 1–5, 11d; 212/43 m.2.

6 PRO SC2/213/10 m. 8.

7 PRO SC2/212/42 m. 3.

heir and of full age. John then performed homage and fealty, and it was arranged that he was to pay his fifty shilling relief in two instalments at the following Pentecost and Michaelmas. This case can be compared with one of 1323 when the order was issued in the honour court to take the lands of William Walgor into the lady's hands because of the minority of the heir, and to make William's widow come to the court to give security that she would not remarry without permission.[8] In instances of wardship such as this, the custody was used either as a source of revenue or of patronage.

Compared with other honours, the court at Clare appears to have been exceptionally active in the early fourteenth century, and the amount of business diminished by the end of Elizabeth's life. This type of lordship continued to be exercised to some extent into early modern times, but the profits that noblewomen received from feudal dues in the fifteenth century were very low. Anne Stafford employed in Gloucestershire an official known as a feodary who was in charge of the feudal business of the honour of Gloucester, but the receipts were only just over £4 and once the wages of the bailiff were deducted the clear value was barely more than £1. The profits of the feodary of the honour of Hereford in the same county came to about £5 in clear value. Wardships still occurred occasionally; estates in Anne's hands during the minority of the heir of Richard Culpeper were valued at £4 a year.[9]

The lordship which was exercised over vassals whose families had long been established on the honour was usually impersonal. By the thirteenth century it was primarily a financial rather than a service relationship, and it diminished in importance and effectiveness during the later Middle Ages. Subinfeudation, the granting of land to a man and his heirs in return for knight service, was becoming less common in the later twelfth century, probably largely because lords came to realise the dangers of alienating in perpetuity too large a proportion of their demesne land. Such grants had often been made as rewards for service, but it became essential to use some other form of reward. During the thirteenth century and later, service continued to be needed by the nobility and on an increasing scale, in retinues, and in the

8 PRO SC2/212/39 m. 7d.

9 PRO SC11/816.

professional administration of household and estate. However, from the thirteenth century it came to be rewarded by money fees and livery; if the reward took the form of land, often the estate was only granted for life and not to the heirs. The personal ties between noble and retainer in the later Middle Ages have often been described as bastard feudalism, and were more important to both sides than the fossilised feudal ties derived from an earlier age. The arrangements ensured that the nobles obtained the services they needed while retainers benefited from their connections with the powerful men of the age.

There is plenty of evidence that great lords attracted large retinues of knights and others into their service. Wives undoubtedly contributed to the lordship exercised by their husbands when they intervened personally or by letter in their husbands' interests. Elizabeth, countess of Oxford wrote to John Paston I asking him to be a good friend to one of the de Vere dependants. In 1455 Eleanor, duchess of Norfolk wrote to ask him to support their nominees as knights of the shire for Norfolk, urging that her lord should have men connected with him in parliament.[10]

On the marriage of the heiress to a great estate her husband gained not only lands but also retainers and connections, as when Eleanor de Bohun married Thomas of Woodstock. The retinue rolls for her father Earl Humphrey for 1371 and 1372 included knights like Thomas Mandeville and Richard Waldegrave and esquires like John Gildesburgh and Thomas Coggeshale, all of whom went on to support and serve Thomas of Woodstock. John de Boys served in Thomas's military retinue and at the end of the fourteenth century was the steward of Eleanor's household; he was also one of her executors. The connection between the Mandeville family and the Bohuns can be traced back to the early fourteenth century. Such support, whether given in peace or war, at a time of stability or opposition crisis, was invaluable to Thomas, as it doubtless was to others in his position.[11]

The question remains, however, as to whether noblewomen were able to build up a retinue in their own right and whether

---

10 *Paston letters and papers of the fifteenth century* ed. N. Davis (2 vols) Oxford 1971–6 II 98–9, 117.

11 PRO E101/31/15; 32/20. A. Goodman *The loyal conspiracy* London 1971 13, 43, 92–104, 124, 126. J.C. Ward *The Essex gentry and the county community in the fourteenth century* Chelmsford 1991 18–19.

they could offer the sort of patronage which was attractive in the late medieval world. They were in a position to do this as widows but obviously they could not offer the prospect of military glory, profits and plunder. In spite of this, the evidence of livery lists, fees and annuities indicates that women did have their own retainers and therefore had an important part to play in strengthening the ties binding the upper ranks of society together. The lady's livery was given to a wide range of people, and her affinity included her stewards, councillors and top financial officials, some of her relatives, and men active in royal and county government. The categories cannot be regarded as distinct or self-contained; estate officials were often involved in local commissions for the Crown.

In addition to naming her yeomen, grooms and pages, Elizabeth de Burgh's livery list of 1343 contained the names of fifteen knights who headed the list, twenty-two clerks, and ninety-three esquires, some of whom had duties which centred on the household. Information for other noblewomen is derived from the giving of fees and annuities, and is probably not complete; the figures have to be regarded as the minimum number in the lady's affinity. Isabella Morley gave fees to six men outside her domestic household in 1463–4, and the same number of life annuities were entered in the account of the receiver-general of Alice, duchess of Suffolk ten years later. These figures can be compared with the twenty-four fees in the 1425–6 valor of Joan Beauchamp's English lands and three fees in the 1421 Welsh valor, given to councillors and men in Joan's service, and the fifteen annuitants named in Anne, countess of Stafford's valor of 1435–6.[12]

No noblewoman had an affinity as great as that of Thomas, earl of Lancaster or John of Gaunt but these were exceptional by the standards of the later Middle Ages. The ladies' affinities were, however, comparable with those of many noblemen. The livery roll of Edward Courtenay, earl of Devon in 1384–5 listed eight knights and forty-three esquires, and included some members of his family and possibly certain household officials.[13] His following was considerably smaller than Elizabeth de Burgh's

12 PRO E101/92/23; SC11/25, 816. BL Egerton Roll 8779; Additional MS 34122A. J.A. Bradney *A history of Monmouthshire* (4 vols) London 1904–32 II 4–5.

13 J.M.W. Bean *From lord to patron* Manchester 1989 159–60.

and reflected the fact that he was among the least wealthy of the earls. It is likely that the wealthiest noblewomen were able to attract a considerable affinity even though they could not exercise the charisma of military captains.

The amount spent on fees by noblewomen was not exorbitant, but it has to be borne in mind that these are minimum sums as a result of incomplete information. Isabella Morley's six fees amounted to £14 or 8 per cent of her income, which has been estimated at about £170 in the early 1460s.[14] The £137 spent by Joan Beauchamp on fees comprised 6 per cent of the value of her English lands. Anne Stafford's annuities in 1435–6 amounted to nearly £129 and the fees of stewards and other officers nearly £49; 8 per cent of the gross valuation of the lands (nearly £2,187) was spent in this way. The amounts paid to individuals varied widely; on Anne Stafford's valor sums ranged from £1. 6s. 8d. to £26. 13s. 4d. which was received by Sir Roger Aston.

The lady enjoyed a two-way relationship with all members of her affinity. They offered the skill and experience that the lady needed for the efficient running of her estates and the protection of her inheritance. They served as officials, feoffees, councillors and executors. In return all received fees and livery but the potential rewards were far greater, including land and benefices and the lady's backing in the prosecution of their affairs. A lady with powerful relations and contacts at court was in an excellent position to further the ambitions of her retinue.

All noblewomen retained royal officials and legal experts, although the practice of giving fees to royal justices came to an end in the late fourteenth century. The management of the estates often entailed litigation in the royal courts, negotiations with the exchequer, the purchase of writs and charters from chancery, and the petitioning of the Crown for favours. Constant vigilance was required to ensure that the lady's rights did not go by default. Elizabeth de Burgh spent £16 in 1330–1 on gifts and other expenses connected with the purchase of writs. A similar sum was spent seven years later, which included the cost of sealing two royal charters pardoning the debts of Roger Damory and the expenses of a professional pleader before the king's council in a case concerning the lady's lands at Wareham in Dorset. Legal expenses were on occasion considerably higher.

14 C. Richmond 'Thomas Lord Morley (d.1416) and the Morleys of Hingham' *Norfolk Archaeology* XXXIX (1984–6) 4.

When a judicial commission of oyer and terminer was issued in
1327 to try and punish persons who had entered Elizabeth's
chase at Cranborne, her councillors spent nearly £53, not only
on their own expenses in going to Cranborne but on gifts to
knights, serjeants and others.[15]

In view of the amount and cost of litigation, it was advantageous to have Crown officials and justices in the lady's affinity.
Even the widow of a knight found it advisable to do this.
Petronilla de Nerford of Norfolk had three local lawyers among
her councillors in 1320, two of them justices of the Common
Pleas. The professional pleader Gilbert de Thornton was on the
council of Isabella de Forz in 1274 and also received fees from
other lords; he became chief justice of the King's Bench in
1290.[16] According to Elizabeth de Burgh's livery roll, one of the
knights receiving livery was Sir John Shardlow, justice of the
Common Pleas, and the clerks included the chancery and
exchequer officials John de St Pol, William Everdon and William
Stowe. The two Williams were barons of the exchequer; John
often deputised for the chancellor between 1334 and 1340, and
subsequently became archbishop of Dublin and chancellor of
Ireland. In addition, Elizabeth's councillors included men who
had previously been in royal service, like the clerk Thomas de
Cheddeworth, who had been chamberlain of North Wales
between 1312 and 1315 and was one of those responsible for the
lands of the Contrariants in Wales in 1322. Nothing is known of
the actual services performed by the chancery and exchequer
officials for Elizabeth, but their generous livery allowances point
to the importance attached to them. Sir John Shardlow acted as
justice in two cases affecting her.[17]

These royal government officials were important to the lady
but only comprised a minority of her affinity. The majority were
clerks and gentry and it is when looking at these groups that it is

15 PRO E101/91/12 m. 3d; 91/24 m. 2; 92/7 m. 5. *Calendar of Patent Rolls 1324–7*
347.

16 J.R. Maddicott *Law and lordship: royal justices as retainers in thirteenth- and
fourteenth-century England Past and Present* supplement 4 (1978) 20–3. Denholm-
Young *Seignorial administration* 29.

17 PRO E101/92/23. T.F. Tout *Chapters in the administrative history of medieval
England* (6 vols) Manchester 1920–33 III 121, 124–5, 153, 159; VI 12–14, 21,
61. *Calendar of Fine Rolls 1307–19* 148, 162; ibid. *1319–27* 149. *Calendar of Patent
Rolls 1327–30* 207, 426; ibid. *1334–8* 135.

possible to see the attractions of her service and to get some idea of the extent of her influence. All members of the affinity received fees and livery, the livery being graded according to the recipient's importance. Among Elizabeth de Burgh's retainers Thomas de Cheddeworth received eleven and a half ells of cloth, three fur linings of Baltic squirrel and one and a half hoods of miniver, while the esquire Alexander Charman had six and a quarter ells of cloth and a fur lining of lamb. Fees doubtless provided a welcome increase of income, and many retainers received them from several members of the nobility.

Benefices provided additional reward for the clerks. Noblewomen exercised a considerable amount of ecclesiastical patronage. In the division of the Clare lands in 1317, Elizabeth de Burgh received the advowsons (the right to present the incumbents) of eleven churches in England, seven in Wales and two in Ireland, together with the patronage of seven religious houses in England and three in Wales. The great lady could also reward her clerks by petitioning the pope for favours. In 1352 Elizabeth de Burgh asked the pope for a canonry in St Paul's Cathedral, London, and the expectation of a prebend for John de Lenne who had been clerk of the wardrobe at the end of the 1330s; the request was granted.[18] Similar requests were made by other noblewomen, by wives as well as widows. Matilda, countess of Ulster and then married to Ralph de Ufford, was present at the papal court in 1343 and put in eight requests for benefices, including one for a kinsman, two for her clerks, three for members of her household, and one for Queen Philippa's almoner. The petitions by Marie de St Pol for benefices included men in France as well as England and also concerned pluralism and non-residence. She asked that her councillor William de Witlesey, archdeacon of Huntingdon, should be allowed to hold an additional benefice, and on three occasions obtained a privilege for certain of her clerks to enjoy the revenues of their benefices while being non-resident for three years and engaged in her service.[19]

Knights and esquires in the affinity sometimes received a

18 *Calendar of entries in the papal registers relating to Great Britain and Ireland. Petitions to the pope, 1342–1419* 230.

19 Ibid. 70, 74, 155–6, 209, 410, 502, 533. *Calendar of entries in the papal registers relating to Great Britain and Ireland. Papal letters, 1305–42* 381; ibid. *1342–62* 89, 261.

reward in land. John la Warre served as steward to Earl Warenne in 1261 before becoming the steward to Isabella de Forz between 1268 and 1274; he subsequently became sheriff of Herefordshire. Like Isabella he supported the baronial side in the mid-1260s, and he fought at Evesham and was besieged at Kenilworth. Isabella granted him the manor of Whitchurch.[20] Such grants of land were made by noblewomen from time to time but cannot be regarded as a common form of reward. The retainer was more likely to acquire land by inheritance, marriage or purchase.

Many men used their connections with noblewomen to further their careers. Taking office and receiving a fee from a great lady was simply one element in a man's advancement. This can be seen with John la Warre, and is also true of Geoffrey Russell who was steward of the abbey of Peterborough in the mid-thirteenth century before becoming steward to Isabella de Forz, the bishop of Durham and the honour of Wallingford. By the end of his life he was a royal justice and a considerable landowner.[21] Walter Kebell was a younger son and established himself in landed society as a result of his service to Joan Beauchamp. He was steward of the lordship of Abergavenny, probably from 1418 to Joan's death in 1435, was appointed one of her executors and received valuable bequests in her will. He acquired land in Leicestershire as a result of his marriage, which may have been facilitated by his connection with Joan.[22] In some cases a man spent much of his career with a particular family and his service to a noblewoman represented one stage in this; this did not preclude him from also serving on royal commissions and taking fees from other nobles. Others probably made use of the lady's friends and contacts to further their activities.

Many noblewomen inherited officials and advisers from their husbands and passed them on to their successors, and sometimes the connection spanned more than one generation. The link between the Bures family and the Clares goes back to the early part of Edward II's reign when Robert de Bures was steward of the honour of Clare, and he became the keeper of Roger

20 Denholm-Young *Seignorial administration* 75–6.

21 Ibid. 70. E. Miller and J. Hatcher *Medieval England – rural society and economic change 1086–1348* London 1978 172–3.

22 E.W. Ives *The common lawyers of pre-Reformation England. Thomas Kebell: a case study* Cambridge 1983 23–6.

Damory's lands after the battle of Boroughbridge. His son Andrew became prominent in Elizabeth de Burgh's service and was one of the knights receiving livery in 1343. Robert de Cheddeworth, the brother of Thomas de Cheddeworth, was steward of the honour of Clare under Roger Damory, received a pardon for adhering to the rebels in 1322, and served Elizabeth as councillor in the 1320s and 1330s, being much involved in the moves against the younger Despenser in 1325–6. Some of Elizabeth's officials passed into the service of Lionel, duke of Clarence, such as the clerk of the wardrobe William de Manton.

A similar pattern is apparent with the Stafford family.[23] Thomas Lawrence was receiver-general by Michaelmas 1399, and passed into the service of the dowager countess Anne after the death of her husband Edmund, earl of Stafford, in 1403. Roger Aston had been the earl's retainer and became Anne's steward by Michaelmas 1409. Nicholas Poyntz served both Anne and her son, the first duke of Buckingham; he received an annuity from Anne in 1435 and served as receiver for Gloucestershire, Hampshire and Wiltshire between 1438 and 1453. John Andrews was appointed attorney-general by Anne in 1431 to take charge of matters concerned with the Bohun inheritance; on her death he became a member of Duke Humphrey's household and held legal and financial responsibilities until at least 1457.

It is probable that men used their position with the lady to make new contacts and promote their interests and activities, but the evidence is suggestive rather than definite. Alexander Charman was one of Elizabeth de Burgh's esquires in 1343 and frequently acted as her attorney in Ireland. In that year he was also nominated in that capacity by Isabella de Ferrers and in the following year by Joan, Lady Fitzwalter for whom he acted on a number of occasions.[24] Whether Elizabeth recommended him to her daughter and her friend is unknown, but it remains a possibility.

Belonging to one or more affinities was a means of achieving upward social mobility. The noble household was the obvious centre of lordship in the locality and the lord or lady had the power to promote the fortunes of the ambitious, whether they

---

23 C. Rawcliffe *The Staffords, earls of Stafford and dukes of Buckingham 1394–1521* Cambridge 1978 70, 159–60, 196, 198, 201, 209, 219, 235.

24 *Calendar of Patent Rolls 1343–5* 2, 159, 224, 347, 349, 536; ibid. *1345–8* 154, 360; ibid. *1348–50* 151, 405, 422; ibid. *1350–4* 131, 223; ibid. *1358–61* 458.

were younger sons or established members of the gentry. Elizabeth de Burgh's relationships with the local gentry shows the importance attached to the noblewoman's patronage and influence. Nicholas Damory's advancement came about as a result of his association with Elizabeth, which lasted until her death; he was named as one of her executors. He may have been a nephew of Roger Damory and was mentioned as a king's scholar at Cambridge in 1318 and 1321. It is likely that he went on to higher studies because a book of civil law was bought for him in 1326. His acquisition of land came about as a result of marriage to the widow of Alan la Zouche, and he was one of the custodians of Alan's lands during his son's minority. It is possible that his chance to marry came about as a result of Elizabeth's influence; the fact that several members of her household attended Alan's funeral at Swavesey in Cambridgeshire points to a link between him and the lady. Nicholas's association with Elizabeth led to connections with her relations; he acted as feoffee to the earl of Athol, and was granted Holton in Oxfordshire by John Bardolf.[25]

It was more usual for an ambitious man to build up relationships with several lords, and John de Wauton's career is more typical of the later Middle Ages than Nicholas Damory's. John belonged to an Essex gentry family but was probably a younger son. He tapped most of the sources of lordship available in the north of the county in order to make his way in the world. He appears to have enjoyed military campaigning and therefore needed to join the affinity of a nobleman. He served in the retinue of Robert Fitzwalter on the Scottish expedition of 1322, and was with William de Bohun, earl of Northampton in the early years of the Hundred Years War; he was present at Crécy and died at the siege of Calais in 1347. In addition, he considered it advantageous to belong to the affinity of Elizabeth de Burgh and served as one of her auditors and councillors. His importance to Elizabeth is seen in the attendance of her councillors at his funeral. He held land of her in Steeple Bumpstead and Birdbrook but his main holding of Wimbish was granted to him by Robert Fitzwalter. John found that connections with both noblemen and women helped to further his standing and his career; he became

---

25 A.B. Emden *A biographical register of the university of Cambridge to 1500* Cambridge 1963 176. PRO E101/91/12 m. 1d; 92/30 m. 6. *Calendar of Close Rolls 1354–60* 16. *Calendar of Inquisitions post mortem* VIII no. 716; ibid. x no. 644; ibid. XII nos. 308, 327; ibid. XVII no. 452.

a prominent figure in the county, serving on royal commissions, as sheriff of Essex and Hertfordshire between 1330 and 1332, and as knight of the shire for Essex in 1330 and 1341.

Many of the men in the affinity were already established gentry but these also found that associations with the lady brought them advantages. Men like Andrew de Bures and Warin de Bassyngbourn, also Elizabeth's councillors, became prominent in the affairs of their counties of Suffolk and Cambridgeshire respectively, and their appointment to Crown office and commissions may have owed something to the lady's influence and contacts at court. Their nomination to commissions affecting Elizabeth's interests suggests that the lady may well have had a say in this, as when Andrew and Warin were appointed to a commission of oyer and terminer concerned with the taking away of the lady's goods at various demesne manors in the eastern counties. What is certain is that favours were obtained at the petition of the lady. In 1345 Edward III agreed to Elizabeth's request that both Andrew and Warin, who were occupied with Elizabeth's business, should not be compelled to go overseas on royal service for a year. Three years later, again at Elizabeth's request, the king pardoned Warin, then sheriff of Cambridgeshire, for the escape of prisoners from Cambridge castle.[26] It is probable that the lady made many more petitions for favours for her affinity and that these have gone unrecorded. From the point of view of the local gentry, the noblewoman's household was seen as the place for advancement as well as of service and reward. The noble lady's circle overlapped and enmeshed with many others, including the royal court.

The evidence of Elizabeth de Burgh's affinity shows that she played her part in attracting and providing for her following alongside other prominent local lords – the Bohuns, the Fitzwalters and the de Veres. She could not herself satisfy military aspirations, but there was much more to the relationship between noble and retainer than campaigning and battles. Elizabeth had wealth, prestige and contacts, and all three attracted ambitious clerks and gentry to her affinity. Her accounts show that the service she expected from her stewards, receivers and councillors was considerable and time-consuming, but it appears that they were ready to carry out the heavy duties demanded. In return they had the prospect of reward in the form of fees, benefices

---

26 *Calendar of Patent Rolls 1343–5* 77, 552; ibid. *1348–50* 96.

and land, together with the prospect of advancement in their careers. This appears to have been a sufficient inducement for men who were already established knights and gentry, and it says much for Elizabeth's power and reputation that she was able to draw men such as these into her following. Her retinue was comparable to that of other members of the nobility, not only in numbers but in the type of men it included.

The documentation for other noblewomen, although not as full, points to similar conclusions. Men found that it was advantageous to belong to their affinities and gravitated to their households, as well as joining the retinues of noblemen. Quite apart from the question of fees, they considered that the lady as well as the lord might help to further their interests and it was a good idea to belong to several affinities. In 1448–9 Sir Humphrey Stafford of Grafton held fees from the duke of Buckingham, the earl of Wiltshire, the duchess of Warwick and five others.[27] What is clear from this and other examples is that membership of the affinity of the noble lady held out strong attractions and that the lady had a definite and constructive role in strengthening social ties in the later Middle Ages.

27 K.B. McFarlane *The nobility of later medieval England* Oxford 1973 108–9.

Chapter 8

RELIGIOUS PRACTICE

Religious and charitable activities were regarded in the Middle Ages as fitting activities for women. In addition to attendance at Mass, hearing sermons and devoting time to prayer, as was expected of all members of noble society, Christine de Pisan emphasised the wise princess's duties of almsgiving and hearing petitions and the concern she ought to show for those worse off than herself.[1] Certain noblewomen were outstanding for their religious observance and the extent of their benefactions. Religious practice is, however, very much an individual matter and the depth of interest shown by noblewomen in making grants to the Church varied greatly, as was also true of their husbands and fathers. Sources such as wills and deeds are concerned with outward practices, and it is rare to obtain an insight into inner belief. Piety usually has to be seen through religious gifts, almsgiving and the preparations made for death.

Some noblewomen became nuns, entering religious houses either in childhood or as widows. In the later Middle Ages instances of noble abbesses were frequent, such as Matilda and Isabella de Montague at Barking in the mid-fourteenth century and Katherine de la Pole a hundred years later. The position of these women was comparable to that of noble widows running their household and estates. Several daughters of the Beauchamp earls of Warwick became nuns at the Gilbertine priory of Shouldham in Norfolk. Isabella, daughter of Thomas of Woodstock and Eleanor de Bohun, became a Minoress in the house outside Aldgate and subsequently abbess. Contemporaries were aware of the danger of children becoming nuns if they found as

---

1 Christine de Pisan *The treasure of the city of ladies or the book of the three virtues* trans. S. Lawson Penguin Classics Harmondsworth 1985 58–62, 71–2, 77–8.

they grew up that they lacked a vocation. This explains why Isabella, having entered the Minoresses as a child, was examined as to whether she wanted to make her profession.[2]

The decision to enter the religious life in widowhood was sometimes taken too precipitately, and the widow left the house and remarried. For some women, however, the decision was probably the result of genuine vocation. Matilda of Lancaster, the widow of William de Burgh, earl of Ulster and subsequently of Ralph de Ufford, became an Augustine canoness at Campsey Ash in 1347, but encountered too much disturbance from noble visitors and received papal permission in 1364 to transfer to the newly founded house of Minoresses at Bruisyard. She declared in her petition that she had intended to enter the order of Minoresses in childhood.[3]

Many widows decided to remain in the world and to combine the management of their affairs with some form of religious life, and the practice of taking a vow of chastity was widespread. This vow was taken before the bishop and if the vowess was married both husband and wife had to take the vow. Elizabeth de Burgh had taken such a vow by 1343, while Margaret Beaufort received permission from her third husband Thomas Stanley to live chastely.[4] Becoming a vowess was regarded as preparation for the next life and a few noblewomen virtually lived a religious life within their own households. Marie de St Pol's request in her will to be buried in the habit of a Minoress makes it likely that she adopted the religious life in her old age. Margaret, duchess of Clarence decided to live her celibate life as a widow near the Bridgettine monastery of Syon for the good of her soul, so as to be able to make her confession and receive the sacraments from the priests there.[5]

2 E. Power *Medieval English nunneries, c. 1275–1535* Cambridge 1922 7. *Calendar of entries in the papal registers relating to Great Britain and Ireland. Papal letters 1396–1404* 385. *Calendar of Patent Rolls 1416–22* 364.

3 *Papal letters 1362–1404* 37–8. *Petitions to the pope 1342–1419* 488. Bruisyard was founded by Matilda's son-in-law Lionel, duke of Clarence.

4 *Papal letters 1342–62* 113. A Crawford 'The piety of late medieval English queens' *The Church in pre-Reformation society* eds. C.M. Barron and C. Harper-Hill Woodbridge 1985 54.

5 H. Jenkinson 'Mary de Sancto Paulo, foundress of Pembroke college, Cambridge' *Archaeologia* LXXXVI (1915) 432. *Calendar of entries in the papal registers relating to Great Britain and Ireland. Papal letters 1417–31* 63–4, 149, 150, 170.

The growth of education and literacy led to increased lay involvement in religious observances in the later Middle Ages. Religious practice combined private prayer and devotion to the saints with participation in public services and ceremonies. The religious activities of the noblewoman were never completely divorced from those of her household and other communities, and she or her husband set the tone for the servants, officials and retainers. This can be seen in the household of Cicely Neville, duchess of York, the mother of Edward IV and Richard III, where a late fifteenth century household ordinance gives a description of daily life. Cicely was renowned for her piety and lived what amounted to a virtually monastic life. Although time had to be set aside for public business, her day was spent in public and private devotions. She owned several books on mysticism, and was particularly interested in the abbey of Syon and the cult of St Bridget of Sweden.[6]

Many noblewomen possessed psalters, books of hours and other devotional books which they bequeathed in their wills. Marie de St Pol referred to the journal in which she said her hours, and to two breviaries, one given her by the queen (possibly the queen of France), and the other by the sisters of St Marcel, who may have been the Minoresses of Lourcine-lez-Saint-Marcel near Paris. Elizabeth FitzHugh left two psalters, two primers and a prayer book to members of her family, and Eleanor Hulle possessed a great and a little breviary, a psalter and a Latin Bible.[7] Noblewomen also had their own relics, notably pieces of the true cross, which judging by their bequests they valued highly. Elizabeth de Burgh left a cross with a relic of the true cross in it to Henry of Grosmont, and Elizabeth, countess of Northampton was accustomed to carry a cross made of the wood of the true cross and containing a thorn from the crown of thorns.[8] These possessions throw light on the noble-

---

6 C.A.J. Armstrong 'The piety of Cicely, duchess of York: a study in late medieval culture' *England, France and Burgundy in the fifteenth century* London 1983 135–56.

7 Jenkinson 'Mary de Sancto Paulo' 420, 425–6, 432–3. *The register of Thomas Langley, bishop of Durham, 1406–37* ed. R.L. Storey (6 vols) Surtees Society CLXIX (1954) III 62–4. *The register of Thomas Bekynton, bishop of Bath and Wells, 1443–65* eds. H.C. Maxwell Lyte and M.C.B. Dawes (2 vols) Somerset Record Society XLIX (1934) I 352–3.

8 J. Nichols *A collection of all the wills of the kings and queens of England* London 1780 37. *Testaments Vetusta* ed. N.H. Nicolas (2 vols) London 1826 I 60–1.

woman's own religious attitudes and on her private prayers, which came to have a more prominent place in religious life in the later Middle Ages.

Noblewomen showed devotion to particular saints. Joan of Acre was said to have had a special devotion to St Vincent and built a chapel in his honour in the church of the Augustinian friars at Clare. This cult of a Spanish saint probably came from her mother Eleanor of Castile. Devotion to the Virgin Mary was widespread and Isabella Despenser, countess of Warwick appears to have had a special devotion to her, leaving precious bequests to her shrines at Tewkesbury, Caversham, Worcester and Walsingham.[9]

The cult of the saints often took the form of pilgrimage. Women visited shrines both with their husbands and on their own; in his will Nicholas Culpeper wanted his wife to carry out his promised pilgrimages to the shrine of the Virgin Mary at Walsingham and of St Thomas Becket at Canterbury.[10] Most pilgrimages took place to shrines in England. Elizabeth de Burgh visited Canterbury, Walsingham and the shrine of the Holy Rood at Bromholm, but in 1343 was dispensed from her vow to visit the Holy Land and the shrine of St James at Santiago de Compostella. She stated in her petition that she made the vow in her husband's lifetime, and at the age of forty (in fact she was forty-eight years old) she could not hope to fulfil it.[11] The offering that she would have made at Santiago was sent there, and in her will she left 100 marks for five men-at-arms to go to the Holy Land for the benefit of her own soul and those of her three husbands. Other noblewomen, however, travelled abroad on pilgrimage. Elizabeth Luttrell accompanied her husband to Santiago in 1361 and in 1310 Robert Fitzwalter was referred to as being about to set out for Jerusalem with his wife Alice.[12]

Charity and almsgiving were regarded by the Church as an

9 Sir William Dugdale *Monasticon Anglicanum* eds. J. Caley H. Ellis and B. Bandinel (6 vols) London 1817–30 VI part 3 1600. *The fifty earliest English wills* ed. F.J. Furnivall Early English Text Society original series LXXVIII (1882) 116–19.

10 *The register of Henry Chichele, archbishop of Canterbury, 1414–43* ed. E.F. Jacob (4 vols) Canterbury and York Society XLII (1937) II 539–40.

11 *Papal letters 1342–62* 112. *Petitions to the pope 1342–1419. 22–3.*

12 H.C. Maxwell Lyte *Dunster and its lords, 1066–1881* Exeter 1882 45. *Calendar of Patent Rolls 1307–13* 233.

essential part of religious practice and emphasis was put in teaching on the seven works of mercy. The relief of the poor was a major concern of the Lollards but is found among the orthodox as well. Noblewomen performed acts of charity to a varying degree throughout their lives by giving food and money to the poor. Certain days were singled out for special almsgiving; Elizabeth de Burgh made a special distribution of bread and herrings on the anniversary of the death of Roger Damory, and on Maundy Thursday, 1352, gave fifty poor people ninepence each. It is likely that noblewomen were encouraged to carry out these acts by their confessors, who were very often friars. It is known that some of Margaret de Brotherton's charitable activities, such as the repair of bridges and roads round Framlingham, stemmed from penances laid down by her confessor.[13] Almsgiving played a major part at funerals, when the nobility wanted the poor to be present and pray for the deceased. Some noblewomen, but by no means all, made a point of leaving money to hospitals or to particular groups of poor people. Eleanor Hulle wanted her executors to continue to support the poor whom she had relieved weekly, and her household bedding was to be distributed among the poor. On a more lavish scale, Joan Beauchamp left 100 marks to the poor at her funeral, 200 marks to her poor tenants in England, £100 to be distributed among the poor in her lordships in the form of clothing, bedding and livestock, £100 towards the marriage of poor maidens in her lordships, £100 for the repair of roads and bridges, and £40 for poor prisoners.[14]

Private devotions, pilgrimage and almsgiving only constituted a part of the noblewoman's religious observance. Her participation in public worship was a social activity undertaken in conjunction with her family, household and others. Knightly as well as baronial families had their own richly furnished chapels served by their chaplains or local clergy, and among the leading nobility wives and husbands often had separate chapels. The worship in the chapel tied in with the life of the household, the liturgical year determining the pattern of feasts and fasts. The

13 J. Catto 'Religion and the English nobility in the later fourteenth century' *History and Imagination. Essays in honour of H.R. Trevor-Roper* eds. H. Lloyd-Jones, V. Pearl and B. Worden London 1981 50.

14 *The register of Thomas Bekynton* Maxwell Lyte and Dawes I 352–3. *The register of Henry Chichele* Jacob II 535–6.

lady, her family, household and affinity formed a religious as well as an economic and social community.

Elizabeth de Burgh's chapel at Clare was served by the friars from the nearby priory. She and Roger Damory made an agreement with the priory that two friars should act as resident chaplains and sing mass daily at the castle; in return the priory was given ten quarters of wheat and ten quarters of malt a year.[15] Wherever Elizabeth was living, in addition to the regular yearly round of services sermons were preached at regular intervals by friars of all four orders, who received five shillings or half a mark for a sermon; the Dominican friar who preached at the feast of the Assumption of the Virgin Mary in 1352 was paid ten shillings. Elizabeth's chamber account of 1351–2 makes clear the concern shown for both present and past members of family and household and brings out the importance attached to prayers for the dead.[16] Offerings were made on behalf of the lady and her present household, as at the three masses on Christmas Day, and sometimes on behalf of the lady and her women and female relations who were making a visit. All members of the household who had died were commemorated on 22 October, and Elizabeth kept the individual anniversaries of her husbands, children, siblings and parents. A feeling of solidarity was shown on the death of a member of the affinity. This took the form of attendance at the funeral and offerings and prayers on behalf of his soul. Several of the household attended John de Wauton's funeral at Wimbish in 1347. When Thomas de Cheddeworth died in 1352, he was commemorated in Elizabeth's chapel and in two local parish churches at Finchingfield and Bardfield, and money was paid to several houses of friars to sing for his soul. Such prayers reinforced the strength of feeling of a community, both of the living and the dead.

The importance of the household as the centre of religious life was reinforced by papal indulgences which were eagerly sought by noblemen and women. They wished to have portable altars, to have the divine office privately celebrated in places under interdict, and to have the right to choose their own confessors who could give plenary remission of sins at the hour of death. Many of these privileges were given to husband and wife jointly,

15 *The cartulary of the Augustinian friars of Clare* ed. C. Harper-Bill Suffolk Records Society Suffolk Charters Woodbridge (1991) 32–3.

16 PRO E101/93/12.

but wives might themselves make the petition, as Elizabeth, countess of Northampton did in 1343. While at the papal court in the same year, Matilda of Lancaster, countess of Ulster presented petitions on behalf of herself, her husband, father, sister, and eight men seeking benefices.[17]

In licensing private chapels, bishops were concerned to stress obligations towards the parish church. The degree to which a noblewoman was involved with the parish church probably varied according to inclination and circumstances. It is possible that a lady who lived much of her life in the same place and who intended to be buried in the local church took a greater interest in it than one who was more constantly on the move around her estates. The interest shown in parish churches in the wills of many noblewomen was minimal; no reference is made to them at all by Marie de St Pol, while Elizabeth de Burgh singled out four only of the churches on her demesne manors for bequests – the churches of Clare, Bardfield, Standon and Bottisham – epitomising her residence in the eastern counties in her old age. In 1351–2 she occasionally attended the parish church where she was living; she was in Clare church on the feast of the Assumption of the Virgin Mary and gave five shillings to two children who were baptised in her presence. Prayers were sometimes said in the parish church as well as the chapel for the souls of her husbands and kinsmen, as was the case for her brother Gilbert, earl of Gloucester, who was commemorated in Clare church and in the household chapel on 23 June. This evidence for the parish church is, however, sparse compared with that for the private chapel, and it is probable that for Elizabeth and for other noblewomen the household constituted the real centre of their religious life.

Their religious patronage, however, took them well beyond the confines of the household. Underlying all the grants made by noblewomen to religious houses and colleges lay the desire for prayers, for their own souls and for the souls of members of their families. The belief in the efficacy of prayers was deep-rooted, and it was held that the soul's time in purgatory could be shortened as a result of prayers said on earth. The wish to be associated with those leading the monastic or mendicant life is mirrored in the papal indulgences giving noblemen and women the right to enter religious houses and to entertain the religious

17 *Petitions to the pope 1342–1419* 27, 31, 69–70, 74.

at their tables. Marie de St Pol received two indults in 1333–4 allowing her to enter nunneries once a year with a retinue of six matrons, or four matrons and four knights. Ten years later Elizabeth de Burgh was allowed to enter houses of the Minoresses, and in 1355 this licence was extended so that she might stay the night in a house of Minoresses with two honest women. Her confessor was given the right in 1346 to allow the religious to eat meat at her table, and Elizabeth is known to have entertained the Minoresses in her house in the outer precinct of their convent outside Aldgate.[18]

The attitudes of noblewomen towards religious benefactions varied markedly and not only because of different economic circumstances. There is a strong contrast between Elizabeth de Burgh and Marie de St Pol, who were exceptionally generous in their foundations, and Margaret de Brotherton, who showed little interest in education and religion.[19] The establishment of chantries and requiem masses was widespread except among Lollards, but it was rare for new religious houses to be founded.

In making their religious arrangements, many noblewomen showed the same sort of practical efficiency and drive which they displayed in their estate administration. In view of the amount to be done in securing the mortmain licence from the Crown, needed after 1279, acquiring rights to land and sometimes drawing up statutes, a businesslike approach was essential. Women were on occasion slow to make up their minds and their plans were subject to change, but in carrying through their final decisions they were both ruthless and high-handed. Margaret, Lady Hungerford showed these qualities when she decided to disendow the almshouse which her father had founded in Bath, determined the form that her husband's chantry should take in Salisbury Cathedral, and completed but modified her father-in-law's establishment of Heytesbury hospital.[20]

The importance of the chantry in saying prayers for the soul of the founder and other named souls is well attested in mortmain

18 *Papal letters 1305–42* 393, 413; ibid. *1342–62* 113, 190, 561, 586. *Petitions to the pope 1342–1419* 102, 300.

19 R.E. Archer 'The estates and finances of Margaret of Brotherton, *c.* 1320–1399' *Historical Research* LX (1987) 275–6.

20 M.A. Hicks 'Chantries, obits and almshouses: the Hungerford foundations 1325–1478' *The Church in pre-Reformation society* Barron and Harper-Bill 130–4.

licences and wills; alternatively, arrangements were made for a specific number of requiem masses. This type of benefaction was subject to immense variety but was made by the majority of noblewomen who outlived their husbands; it is only in a few cases of Lollards such as Sir Thomas Latimer and his wife Anne that it is not found.[21] Most noblewomen were included in their husband's chantry foundations, whether these were in parish or monastic churches or in cathedrals. It was considered, however, that further provision was advisable, and the wills of widows show that this was often done on a lavish scale. Joan Beauchamp lady of Abergavenny gave orders that she was to be buried by her husband in a new tomb in the Dominican church at Hereford. 5,000 masses were to be said for her soul as soon as possible after her death. She left 300 marks to the Dominicans at Hereford for two priests to celebrate masses for ever for the souls of her husband and herself, her parents, Sir Hugh Burnell, all her benefactors and all Christian souls. In addition, masses were to be celebrated by five honest priests for twenty years at Rochford in Essex and Kirby Bellars in Leicestershire for the souls of the same people and of her son Richard, earl of Worcester, who had died in 1422.[22]

Where a chantry was established in the widow's lifetime the arrangements were subject to successive modifications. Elizabeth de Burgh was closely involved with the Clare family priory of Anglesey, especially when she was living there for a considerable amount of time. She endowed a chantry in the priory in 1333 whereby two chaplains were to perform divine service daily for the salvation of Elizabeth, her ancestors and heirs and all the faithful departed, and at the same time she relinquished her rights of patronage over the priory. Three years later she added to the endowment and the chaplains were to say Mass in the Lady chapel which Elizabeth had built. Further adjustment was made in 1355.[23] Such a process of change was typical of many religious foundations in the Middle Ages.

It is rare to find a noblewoman, like Elizabeth FitzHugh,

21 M. Aston ' "Caim's castles": poverty, politics and disendowment' *The Church, politics and patronage in the fifteenth century* ed. R.B. Dobson Gloucester 1984 65.

22 *The register of Henry Chichele* Jacob II 535–6. Sir Hugh Burnell had conveyed all his property to Joan.

23 E. Hailstone *The history and antiquities of the parish of Bottisham and the priory of Anglesey in Cambridgeshire* Cambridge Antiquarian Society 1873 255–62.

specifying that the masses were to be said for her soul alone. The testator was more often concerned with her husband and children, sometimes her parents and ancestors, but only rarely with more distant relations. The emphasis was very much on the nuclear family, and the widow identified more with her husband or husbands than with her own kin. Servants were occasionally mentioned; in her will Elizabeth de Burgh left £140 for masses to be sung for the souls of her three husbands and herself, and of all her good and loyal servants who had died or would die in her service. More frequently prayers were to be said for all Christian souls, pointing to a social rather than an individual concern on the part of the testator.

The identification with the husband is also seen in the choice of place for the chantry. There is a link between William and Joan Beauchamp's burials in Hereford and Joan's establishment of the perpetual chantry there. Marie de St Pol's decision to set up a chantry in Westminster Abbey was determined by her husband's tomb there. Joan Hungerford's chantry was in the parish church of Farleigh Hungerford which her husband had rebuilt, and they were both buried there. It was only when the noblewoman was an heiress that she was likely to choose a place associated with her own family rather than her husband's. This applies to Elizabeth de Burgh and Anglesey, and also to Anne Stafford, who provided for prayers to be said for her every day for twenty years in the college of Pleshey founded by her father.[24]

The provision for chantries and requiem masses underlines the noblewoman's concern with her family, past and present, and points to a desire for their spiritual as well as their physical well-being. There was, however, more to the situation, since an examination of noblewomen's support of religious houses on their estates shows that they were influenced by considerations of tradition and family glorification. All these factors were intertwined. The nobility had monasteries on their honours which had long been associated with their ancestors or predecessors, and noblewomen maintained a connection with them and took on some responsibility for their fortunes. Again, wives usually identified with their husbands' interests, although heiresses retained a relationship with houses associated with their own families. In 1411 Lucia Visconti, countess of Kent petitioned the pope for a church to be appropriated to the abbey

24 Nichols *A collection of all the wills* 278–81.

of Bourne in Lincolnshire, which had been founded by her husband's ancestors and was his burial place. On her death she bequeathed 1,000 crowns to the abbey. Anne Stafford, however, maintained the Bohun family's link with the priory of Llanthony; she arranged to be buried there and left 100 marks to the church.[25]

Family glorification took the form of new buildings and elaborate tombs. Elizabeth de Burgh's work on the priory of the Augustinian friars at Clare reflected on the prestige of her family as well as herself. The priory had been founded by her grandfather in 1248 and endowed by her grandmother and mother. Elizabeth is credited with building the frater, dorter and chapterhouse, and her arms were included in the stained glass of the priory.[26] This work was eclipsed by that of her sister Eleanor at the abbey of Tewkesbury, which can still be seen today. Tewkesbury was the principal monastery of the honour of Gloucester which was allotted to Eleanor and Hugh le Despenser the younger in the partition of the Clare lands in 1317. It became the burial place of the Despensers as it had been of the thirteenth-century Clare earls of Gloucester. It was probably largely due to Eleanor that the east end of the church was rebuilt in the 1320s and 1330s as a burial chapel. Eleanor herself was possibly depicted as the naked donor figure in the east window, which had as its subject the Last Judgment and the coronation of the Virgin Mary. This is flanked by four windows depicting Old Testament prophets and kings, and the two westernmost windows have the lords of the honour, Robert Fitz Hamon and Robert, earl of Gloucester from the twelfth century, the four Clare earls of Gloucester, and Eleanor's two husbands.

Noblewomen were therefore not only maintaining a relationship with religious houses on their estates for reasons of tradition, but because these abbeys and priories, whether of monks or friars, served a present purpose. The main consideration in the mind of the lady was the provision of prayers, and these houses provided places for burial, for chantries and the saying of requiem masses. They provided chaplains and confessors for the lady's residence. On a more mundane level they provided

25 *Papal letters 1404–15* 294. *Testamenta Vetusta* ed. N.H. Nicolas (2 vols) London 1826 I 205–6. Nichols *A collection of all the wills* 278.

26 Dugdale, *Monasticon Anglicanum* VI part 3 1601.

entertainment and horses for the lady's journeys. Their well-being redounded to the lady's credit and reputation.

There is no sign of sentimental attachment, and the lady was not deterred from going ahead with religious benefactions by traditional associations. Elizabeth de Burgh's establishment of Franciscan friars at Walsingham in 1347 is a case in point. The priory of Augustinian canons with its popular pilgrimage shrine to the Virgin Mary had been associated with the Clare family since the twelfth century, and it was appalled at the prospect of the arrival of the friars. The canons argued that they would lose tithes and offerings and that their property would not suffice them for half the year unless they had the money brought in by the pilgrims. Their anxiety was partly due to the popularity of the friars as confessors and for saying masses for the dead. They also pointed out that for security reasons the priory gates were always closed at night and the pilgrims who arrived late were accustomed to make their offerings the next morning; they might no longer do so if they were intercepted by the friars. None of these arguments had any weight with Elizabeth and the establishment of the friars at Walsingham went ahead.[27]

The later Middle Ages was not a great period for the foundation of new religious houses. Among the monastic orders the establishment of a small number of Carthusian houses can be singled out, but noblewomen were not associated with these. Marie de St Pol's intention of making a Carthusian foundation did not materialise.[28] Judging by the number of bequests in wills the friars were popular but it is rare to find a noblewoman setting up a new house. There are, however, two areas in which noblewomen played a prominent part in foundations, namely the houses of the Franciscan nuns known as Minoresses, and the colleges in Oxford and Cambridge. It was in this work that the benefactions of Marie de St Pol and Elizabeth de Burgh were outstanding. Gifts of land alone were not enough to make a foundation, and without the noblewoman's skill and determination in negotiating with king, pope and interested parties, making statutes and regulations, and ensuring that necessary buildings were erected the new establishments would never have come into existence.

27 BL Cotton MS Nero E. vii fos 160–1. *Calendar of Patent Rolls 1345–8* 255; ibid. *1348–50* 7.

28 Jenkinson 'Mary de Sancto Paulo' 418.

The Minoresses followed the rule laid down by Isabella, the sister of Louis IX of France. Of the four houses in England, three were founded by women. The Minories outside Aldgate in London was particularly popular with noblewomen, having been founded in 1294 by Blanche of Navarre, the niece of Louis IX and wife of Edmund, earl of Lancaster. Waterbeach was founded in the same year by Denise de Montchensy, and Denny by Marie de St Pol in 1342. The foundation of Bruisyard in 1364 by Lionel, duke of Clarence may have come about at the instigation of his mother-in-law Matilda, countess of Ulster, who wished to move from Campsey Ash and become a Minoress.

The foundations at Waterbeach and Denny well illustrate the need for perseverance by their women founders and the length of time it took to get a house established. Denise de Montchensy secured royal permission in 1281 to grant Waterbeach to men of religion or to found a religious house. She was probably already thinking of a house of Minoresses, as in the same year she obtained a papal indulgence of remission of 100 days' penance for those who visited the sisters of London or Waterbeach. Yet it was only in the early 1290s that the buildings were prepared, and the sisters from Isabella's monastery of Longchamp near Paris arrived in 1294.[29]

That Waterbeach did not survive was due to the plans and ruthlessness of Marie de St Pol, who wanted to make her own foundation for Minoresses at Denny. She was granted the manor of Denny to her and her heirs by Edward III in 1336 and set about transforming what had been a house of the Knights Templar into a nunnery. The process took time. She received royal permission in 1339 to move the Minoresses from Waterbeach to Denny and the king approved the union of the two houses seven years later. It was not, however, until 1349 that the pope agreed to the compulsory removal of the sisters to Denny. Although an abbess and some nuns were at Denny by 1342, not surprisingly Marie's plans encountered opposition at Waterbeach, where a new abbess was chosen and more nuns received. However, most of the nuns moved to Denny within a couple of years of the papal decision of 1349. Marie was still securing papal privileges for Denny at the end of her life; in 1374 she

29 A.F.C. Bourdillon *The order of Minoresses in England* Manchester 1926 13–15. *Papal letters 1198–1304* 562, 566. *Liber memorandorum ecclesie de Bernewelle* ed. J.W. Clark Cambridge 1907 214–18.

gained an indulgence for the remission of penance for visitors to the church at the principal festivals. Her attachment to Denny is seen in her choice to be buried there in a sister's habit; she left £100 to the priory together with five marks for the abbess, ten shillings to each of the sisters, and half a mark to each of the brothers. During her life she remodelled the church, supplying it with a much larger chancel, and built a new cloister and hall.[30]

Whilst Denise and Marie were the principal benefactors of Waterbeach and Denny, the house of the Minories outside Aldgate attracted wider interest and a larger number of gifts. The house had a strong aristocratic element among the nuns and abbesses, was a favoured burial place for noblewomen, and had great ladies as visitors and tenants. Elizabeth de Burgh's example may well have encouraged other noblewomen to imitate her. She built her house in the outer precinct in 1352 and from then until her death spent part of the year there. The house was subsequently let to other noblewomen. Elizabeth and her council advised the sisters on business and gave them hospitality and entertainment. She chose the church for her burial and a chantry was established there. Her main gifts to the abbey appear in her will and comprised precious objects for the church, vestments and furnishings. She bequeathed £20 to the house, a further £20 to the abbess, one mark to each sister on the day of her funeral, and half a mark to each brother.

Noblewomen played an important part in the foundation of colleges at Oxford and Cambridge, and of the fifteen colleges established by 1400 they had a significant role in the setting up of three. They needed the same qualities of persistence and determination as they displayed in their other religious benefactions. Although the colleges were self-governing they needed a propertied endowment and this could only be provided by a wealthy and interested patron. The founder's motivation was probably threefold. One major concern was with the salvation of her and others' souls, and the college was seen as a chantry where prayers would be constantly offered. The college would contribute to the reputation and prestige of the founder and her

---

30 Bourdillon *The order of Minoresses in England* 19–22. Jenkinson 'Mary de Sancto Paulo' 421–2, 432. *Victoria county history of Cambridgeshire and the isle of Ely* (9 vols) Oxford 1989 IX 241. *Papal letters 1342–62* 285–6, 433; ibid. *1362–1404* 199. *Petitions to the pope 1342–1419* 160–1, 209. *Calendar of Patent Rolls 1327–30* 37; ibid. *1338–40* 242; ibid. *1340–3* 381; ibid. *1345–8* 119; ibid. *1350–4* 72–3. *Calendar of Close Rolls 1349–54* 237.

family. At the same time noblewomen were aware of the need for trained personnel both in the Church and in secular administration, and saw the colleges as a means of providing education. Elizabeth de Burgh made a point of training her clerks, and in 1331–2 four were receiving legal education in London, while two were studying under a master at Oxford. Their expenses for the year came to nearly £20.[31] Of the six, William de Oxwik went on to become clerk of the chamber, and Piers de Ereswell became her almoner and one of her executors. Early training in this case resulted in lifelong service.

All the women involved in founding colleges were widows but they can sometimes be seen as acting as agents for their husbands. This was especially the case with Dervorguilla of Galloway, the widow of John Balliol, who can be described as the second founder of Balliol College at Oxford. The foundation was imposed on John as a penance about 1257 by the bishop of Durham after the bishop had been attacked by John's men. John supported scholars until his death in 1269 but did not provide a permanent endowment. Dervorguilla was devoted to his memory (she carried his heart round with her for the rest of her life) and in 1284–5 bought property in Oxford for the scholars to live in and endowed them with land in Northumberland purchased with money set aside for this purpose in her husband's will. She made the grant for the salvation of the souls of herself and her husband, her parents and ancestors, children and successors, and her statutes laid down that three requiem masses were to be celebrated every year. The statutes also laid down some regulations concerning the students' studies and disputations, their attendance at services and sermons, and their communal life under a principal and two external proctors. How much say Dervorguilla had in the drafting of the statutes is not known, but she probably provided the dynamism necessary to put her husband's will into effect.[32]

The thirteenth-century history of Oxford University also shows that a medieval noblewoman could offer patronage to groups of scholars without establishing a new foundation. Ela

31 PRO E101/91/27 m. 4.

32 *The history of the university of Oxford* ed. T.H. Aston (in progress) 1 *The early Oxford schools* ed. J.I. Catto Oxford 1984 205, 240, 244–5, 283, 292–3. *The Oxford deeds of Balliol College* ed. H.E. Salter Oxford Historical Society LXIV (1913) 1–14, 277–83.

Longespee, countess of Warwick and her second husband Philip Basset granted Merton College the manor of Thorncroft in Leatherhead in 1266. Ela maintained her connection with Merton during her widowhood when she was living in Godstow nunnery; she made further grants and set up a requiem mass for her soul and the souls of all Christians, while the warden of the college gave her support and counsel. Her gifts were not limited to Merton. In 1293 she founded the Warwick chest, when she gave £80 to the university for the purpose of making loans to poor students. She also gave money for the establishment of Balliol's chapel.[33] Although she gained her connection with Oxford through her second husband, as a widow she seems to have been making her own decisions about benefactions.

In contrast to Dervorguilla and Ela, Elizabeth de Burgh's and Marie de St Pol's foundations at Cambridge appear to have owed nothing to their husbands' contacts or influence. It is, however, likely that the two of them influenced each other. Elizabeth took a practical and businesslike approach; she was ready to wait years to get the terms she wanted for her patronage. It was in 1326 that the chancellor of the university, Richard de Badew, founded University Hall, but the endowments were meagre and it is likely that Richard contributed to it financially over the next few years. In the face of mounting difficulties Elizabeth was asked to help the foundation and responded with the grant of the advowson of Litlington church in 1336. However, she insisted on taking over the foundation before giving further assistance, and, although Richard de Badew handed over his rights as founder and patron in 1338, he did not make a final quitclaim of his rights for another eight years. Once Elizabeth was fully patron she was ready to take action quickly; two royal licences were obtained in 1346, one for the transfer of the advowsons of Great Gransden and Duxford St John to Clare Hall, as it came to be called, and the other allowing the Hall to acquire possessions to the value of £40 a year. Elizabeth provided the Hall with an income of £60 a year.

33 *The history of the university of Oxford* ed. T.H. Aston (in progress) 1 *The early Oxford schools* ed. J.I. Catto Oxford 1984 240, 275–9, 282–3, 299. *The rolls and register of Bishop Oliver Sutton, 1280–99* ed. R.M.T. Hill (7 vols) Lincoln Record Society LII (1957) IV 83–5. *The early rolls of Merton College, Oxford* ed. J.R.L. Highfield Oxford Historical Society new series XVIII (1964) 27, 41, 258–9, 445–9. *Statuta antiqua universitatis Oxoniensis* ed. S. Gibson Oxford 1931 71, 76.

Elizabeth's concern went further than providing the endowment and monitoring the financial situation. Her statutes of 1359
provided for educational matters. There were to be twenty
fellows when the endowment was sufficient, of whom six were to
be priests; two were permitted to study civil law and one
medicine, while the rest studied arts or theology. At a lower level
some provision was made for the teaching of grammar. The
religious life of the college was also provided for and in 1348
Elizabeth secured a papal licence to build a chapel in the college;
however, this was not done until after her death. She left many
of the furnishings of her own chapel to the college, together with
plate and £40 in money.[34] That there were never probably more
than ten fellows should not detract from Elizabeth's generosity
and her determination to make a viable foundation.

Similarities exist between Clare Hall and Marie de St Pol's
foundation, which she named the Hall of Valence Marie but
which was soon known as Pembroke Hall. The college dates
from 1347, but Marie must have decided to make a foundation
five years earlier when she purchased part of the college site.
Like Elizabeth she continued to add to the college property and
left it 100 marks and relics and ornaments in her will. She was
concerned for the religious life of the foundation, and obtained a
series of papal bulls so that the college should have its own
chapel. The anniversaries of herself, her husband and her parents
were to be remembered. Her statutes show the same concern as
Elizabeth's for educational provision. There were to be twenty-
four major and six minor probationary scholars, all of whom
were to study arts and then theology except for two taking canon
law and one medicine. These numbers turned out to be over-
ambitious. She aimed to exercise authority over the college,
claiming the right to eject fellows. The points of contrast with
Elizabeth stem from Marie's French background and connections. Like Dervorguilla she wanted the college to have two
external rectors, but this did not materialise. Similarly, her
desire to have a fellow of French birth from Oxford or Cambridge
does not seem to have come about. Marie also planned to

---

34 A.C. Chibnall *Richard de Badew and the university of Cambridge 1315–40*
Cambridge 1963 16–17, 37–41. D.R. Leader *A history of the university of
Cambridge* I *The university to 1546* Cambridge 1988 82–3. *Calendar of Patent Rolls
1334–8* 237; ibid. *1345–8* 135–6; ibid. *1350–4* 510. *Papal letters 1342–62* 253,
269.

establish a college in the University of Paris in 1356 but this could not be carried out because of the Hundred Years War.[35]

Clearly only a few noblewomen were involved in these foundations of new religious houses and colleges. It took wealth, piety, generosity and acumen to bring them about successfully. However, the desire for prayers and the concern for the well-being and reputation of the family are factors which they have in common with the numerous less grandiose religious gifts made by the majority of noblewomen. All desired salvation after death and a shortening of the time in purgatory for themselves and their relations.

The burial of the noblewoman may be viewed as her last public appearance and one which she often appeared eager to make the most of and prepared for carefully. The sources have little to say about the deathbed where the noblewoman made her last confession and received the sacrament of extreme unction; provided that the appropriate papal indulgence had been obtained, her confessor could give her plenary remission. The body of the dead noblewoman was received into church the day before the funeral, placed on a platform and surrounded with candles. The service of *dirige* was conducted. It was usual to keep a vigil all night, and the requiem mass was said the next day, to be followed by further masses as prescribed in the will to ease the passage of the soul through purgatory. At some later date a tomb was erected as a memorial.

Attitudes towards display at the time of death were polarised in the later Middle Ages. On the one hand the nobility enjoyed pomp and ceremony and a magnificent funeral was a fitting conclusion to the splendour of the noblewoman's public life. On the other hand the idea that the body was wretched and subject to corruption was widespread. It was possible to resolve the contradiction by compromise. Joan Beauchamp spoke in the preamble of her will of her simple and wretched body and of this wretched and unstable life on earth. Yet her funeral was not to take place until her household was clothed in black, and she wanted everything to be done as was fitting for a woman of her rank so that her soul would be remembered by kinsmen, friends and servants. Quite apart from her provision for requiem masses

35 Leader I *The university to 1546* 83–4. Jenkinson 'Mary de Sancto Paulo' 422–4, 433. *Papal letters 1342–62* 306; ibid. *1362–1404* 58, 88–9, 167, 171–2. *Petitions to the pope 1342–1419* 155–6, 410, 533. *Calendar of Patent Rolls 1345–8* 61, 444.

and the gifts to be made to churches where her body rested on its way to burial at Hereford, she left 1,000 marks for the cost of her funeral.[36]

Most noblewomen wanted to be buried with one of their husbands and sometimes with other members of their family as well. Elizabeth Despenser wanted to be buried at Tewkesbury between her husband Edward, who died in 1376, and her son Thomas who was put to death in 1400 after the unsuccessful rising to restore Richard II.[37] In a few cases, the pull of the woman's own family was stronger than that of her husband's. Anne Stafford chose to be buried at Llanthony, and Isabella Despenser, countess of Warwick at Tewkesbury. In other instances a close connection with a religious house led to its choice as place of burial, as with Marie de St Pol at Denny and Elizabeth de Burgh in the church at the Minories.

As the noblewoman was taken to her burial the cortège was impressive. Elizabeth, countess of Ulster, the wife of Lionel of Clarence, died in Ireland early in 1364 while her husband was viceroy. Nicholas de Fladbury, her former chaplain, and another of Lionel's officials brought her body back for burial at Bruisyard. The journey took them from Ireland to Neston in the Wirral, and then via Chester and Coventry to Bruisyard. The coffin was covered with a linen pall on which was a cross of red silk, and the funeral was taken by the bishop of Norwich.[38] Presumably on its journey the body rested overnight in churches. Elizabeth, countess of Salisbury, who died in 1415, asked for *dirige* in the evening and a requiem mass on the morrow at each stopping-place on her way to burial at the Montague priory of Bisham, reckoning on about £20 being spent on the journey, the same sum as that allowed to Nicholas de Fladbury.[39]

Provisions for the funeral itself were often lavish and expensive. When the countess of Salisbury's body arrived at Bisham twenty-four poor men in gowns and hoods of russet were to carry torches at *dirige* and at the requiem mass at her burial. The 'herse' was to be covered with black cloth and five great candles

36 *The register of Henry Chichele* Jacob (1937) II 535.

37 *Testamenta Vetusta* Nicolas I 174.

38 PRO E101/394/19. *Chaucer Life-Records* eds. M.M. Crowe and C.C. Olson Oxford 1966 17.

39 *The register of Henry Chichele* Jacob 14–18.

CONCLUSION

Throughout her life the noblewoman had an important part to play in late medieval society in the context of her family, her household and affinity, her estates, and her religious practice. Through her marriage or marriages she helped to forge family alliances and strengthened ties of kinship among the nobility. As an heiress she transmitted estates to a new family, enabling them to increase their power and status. The birth of a male heir, or preferably heirs, was regarded as ensuring the future security of the inheritance. The noblewoman was vitally important within the family as wife and mother, but her role was by no means limited to this. In addition she had a number of public roles to play, both in conjunction with her husband and on her own.

Many of the sources focus attention on the widow, and this is understandable in view of her legal position as *femme sole*, under the control of neither father nor husband, and in view of her economic independence. Yet the importance of the wife's activities also has to be taken into consideration. Wives with an extensive inheritance, dower and jointure were likely to take a prominent part in their household and on their estates. Much doubtless depended on the personalities involved and probably also on the relative wealth of husband and wife. Wives are known to have defended their rights to land, as when Elizabeth Berkeley appeared before the royal council to present her plaint against James Berkeley.[1] Moreover, the absences of the lord on royal service meant that considerable responsibilities devolved on the

---

1 C.D. Ross 'The household accounts of Elizabeth Berkeley, countess of Warwick, 1420–1' *Transactions of the Bristol and Gloucestershire Archaeological Society* LXX (1951) 83. *Proceedings and ordinances of the privy council of England* ed. N. H. Nicolas (7 vols) Record Commission London 1834–7 II 287, 289, 295–6.

lady, and in an age of war these absences might well be frequent. Even if the husband was in England, the life lived by the nobility often entailed the separation of husband and wife, who had their own households and travelled independently. In these circumstances the wife again had duties apart from her immediate family. Her husband's trust in her practical abilities is seen in the number of times she was appointed to be executrix of his will.

As head of the household the wife or widow was in charge of a business enterprise which was often run on a large scale, and she was responsible for its spiritual as well as its physical well-being. The smooth running of the household was essential not only for the benefit of the lady herself, and the officials, servants and visitors, but for the family's reputation in the region and for the attraction of the affinity. The organisation and provisioning of the household, and arrangements for residence and travel were carried out by officials but were ultimately the lady's responsibility. In the case of widows, the same was true of the estates which provided the family's wealth and needed careful management. Although the lady had a well-structured estates' administration from her councillors down to her bailiffs, reeves and parkers, she needed to show an alert interest and on occasion take the initiative. The same qualities were called for in the arrangements over her religious benefactions.

Did the lady's responsibilities extend further into the realm of politics and government? On the face of it this appears a ridiculous notion as women were not numbered among the king's councillors, war-captains and officials. Yet as landowners women had judicial and military responsibilities towards the Crown, the fulfilment of which was essential for the good ordering of the realm. Even after the *quo warranto* pleas of Edward I's reign many noblewomen exercised leet jurisdiction on their estates and had private hundreds. At the court leet they held the view of frankpledge for their tenants, ensuring that every man belonged to a tithing as a guarantee of his good behaviour, and dealt with petty criminal business. These franchises were exercised with a view to financial profit, but the fact remains that the lady had a duty to preserve the peace in the locality. The privilege of return of writs, enabling the lady to carry out the king's orders on her estates and so to exclude the sheriff, was less widespread than leet jurisdiction. The most extensive liberties were those exercised by the nobility in the Marches, where Edward I's policy of subjecting Marcher custom to the Crown achieved only a short-lived success.

The military responsibilities which the noblewoman was expected to meet varied from the provision of troops to undertaking defence. In the thirteenth century and on a few occasions in the fourteenth she was expected to produce her quota of knights for the feudal host. Noblewomen with Marcher lordships were expected to levy Welsh infantry for the royal army. In 1347 Joan, countess of March was ordered to array forty Welshmen from her lordship of Ewyas Lacy and eighty from Wigmore for overseas service, Elizabeth de Burgh one hundred from Usk, and Mary, countess of Norfolk 150 from Strigoil and Netherwent.[2] Royal orders for the provisioning and defence of Marcher castles were sent to noblewomen just as they were to lords.[3]

Noblewomen were expected to play their part in the defence of the realm against invasion during the Hundred Years War, but here clashes occurred with the sheriffs and royal commissioners who wanted to take the final responsibility. In 1339 Edward III arranged for the isle of Portland to be defended by men chosen by the sheriff of Dorset, who were to be provisioned by the lady of Portland, Elizabeth de Burgh. Elizabeth, however, informed the king that she wanted to provide for the defence herself and complained that although she had stationed men-at-arms on Portland the sheriff was hindering her. Thirty-one years later, at the end of her life, the commissioners of array in Essex and Suffolk were ordered not to array men-at-arms and archers from Elizabeth's demesne manors nor to insist that they should be stationed on the seashore. Elizabeth had informed the king that she was staying at Clare castle during the invasion threat with all her household and with armed men who were ready to march whenever and wherever invasion occurred. She asserted that the castle was near the coast; in fact, Clare is about forty miles from the sea.[4]

Noblewomen were summoned to send deputies to councils which considered defence matters, whether these concerned the French war or Ireland. In 1335 Margaret, widow of Edmund, earl of Kent, Marie de St Pol and Joan de Botetourt were

2 *Register of Edward the Black Prince* I 55–6.

3 *Calendar of Close Rolls 1337–9* 543.

4 *Calendar of Close Rolls 1339–41* 12; ibid. *1360–4* 19–20.

ordered to send trusted members of their households to London to the council which was to discuss the defence of the realm; they were also commanded to have their men ready to serve in the event of an invasion.[5] The nearest women came to fighting was when they acted as castellans, responsible for a castle's defence. Often they acted for their husbands. Eleanor de Montfort held Dover castle in the summer of 1265. It was Margaret, the wife of Bartholomew de Badelesmere, who refused Queen Isabella admittance to Leeds castle in 1321 and had to face a siege from Edward II's army; she capitulated after a few days.

In addition to their duties as landowners noblewomen carried out miscellaneous services for the Crown. Marie de St Pol served as lady to Queen Philippa in 1328, and ten years later acted as guardian to her daughter Joan. She was described as being overseas on the king's business in 1331 immediately after Edward had done homage to Philip VI. Her interests and connections in France made her a possible messenger or intermediary with the French Crown. Her bequest to the king of France of a sword without a point symbolises her desire for peace.[6] Noblewomen maintained their families' claims to perform personal services for the Crown. Margaret de Brotherton gave herself the title of countess marshal and asserted the right to perform the office by deputy at Richard II's coronation, but this was refused.[7]

Provided that the lady was in favour with the king she enjoyed the fruits of royal patronage. It is significant that Edward II only granted Elizabeth de Burgh's requests in the spring and summer of 1317 immediately after her marriage to Roger Damory. In contrast she received many marks of favour from Edward III. Not only were her lands fully restored to her soon after the accession, but she received favourable treatment over Roger's debts to the Crown; in 1337 it was arranged that they should not be levied until after Elizabeth's death. Wardships were a popular form of patronage and were granted to both men and women. The grant

5 *Calendar of Patent Rolls 1334–8* 517. T. Rymer *Foedera, Conventiones, Litterae et Acta Publica* eds. A. Clarke, J. Caley, J. Bayley, F. Holbrooke and J.W. Clarke (4 vols) Record Commission London 1816–69 II part 2 916.

6 H. Jenkinson 'Mary de Sancto Paulo, foundress of Pembroke college, Cambridge' *Archaeologia* LXXXVI (1915) 410, 427, 434. *Calendar of Patent Rolls 1330–4* 105; ibid. *1338–40* 53. *Calendar of Close Rolls 1337–9* 94.

7 R.E. Archer 'The estates and finances of Margaret of Brotherton, c. 1320–1399' *Historical Research* LX (1987) 271.

to Elizabeth of the Welsh lands of the earldom of Pembroke was designed to meet the debts which Damory was owed by the Crown.[8] Elizabeth was an inveterate petitioner for what she wanted, but she would not have received the favours unless she had been close to the king.

In only one instance was a title conferred on a noblewoman in her own right. Among his creations of 1397 Richard II gave the title of duchess of Norfolk to Margaret de Brotherton for life. He wanted to honour her and enhance her status, just as was the case with the men who received the title of duke at the same time.[9] Margaret was not present when this occurred. There is no doubt that she had the wealth and land to support her title. She was related to Richard, but it is significant of the importance attached to landowning and local power that she was included among those who had contributed to the honour of the king and the realm.

It was the wealth and authority of some of the most prominent noblewomen that enabled them to play some part in political events. At times of crisis their loyalties were divided. The countess of Oxford, mother of Richard II's favourite Robert de Vere, kept her loyalty to Richard after his deposition, and had made and distributed gold and silver harts, Richard's badge. Her servants spread the report that Richard was alive and would be restored to the throne.[10] Joan de Bohun, dowager countess of Hereford and mother-in-law of Henry IV, had a hand in the punishment of John Holland, earl of Huntingdon, one of those who had hoped to seize Henry at Windsor in early January 1400. John was captured in Essex, condemned by the commons, but taken by Joan to her castle at Pleshey. It was intended to send him to London under guard, but the commons threatened to attack the castle and the earl was handed over to them and executed. It is likely that Joan was hostile to him as being involved in 1397 in the attack on the Appellants, the deaths of her son-in-law Thomas of Woodstock and her brother the earl of

---

8 *Calendar of Close Rolls 1327–30* 501; ibid. *1330–3* 192; ibid. *1339–41* 209–10. *Calendar of Patent Rolls 1330–4* 551; ibid. *1334–8* 475–6. *Calendar of Fine Rolls 1327–37* 288–9.

9 *Rotuli Parliamentorum* (6 vols) London 1703 III 355a.

10 *Thomae Walsingham quondam monachi Sancti Albani Historia Anglicana* ed. H.T. Riley (2 vols) London 1863–4 II 262. *The chronicle of England by John Capgrave* ed. F.C. Hingeston London 1858 285–6.

Arundel, and the exile of another brother, Thomas Arundel, Archbishop of Canterbury.[11]

The support of noblewomen on one side or the other during civil war was valued. Isabella de Forz favoured Simon de Montfort in the mid-1260s, while her mother supported Henry III. In view of Isabella's extensive dower lands and her succession to the earldom of Devon she was an important adherent of the baronial party, and her bailiffs in Holderness and the Isle of Wight were active on the baronial side.[12] Noblewomen played their part on both sides during Queen Isabella's invasion of 1326. Eleanor Despenser was then in the Tower of London and was subsequently accused of taking royal jewels and treasure. The fine demanded by Edward III for her pardon was not paid off in her lifetime.[13] On the other side, Marie de St Pol twice visited the queen while she was in France in September 1325. Elizabeth de Burgh took steps to support the queen as soon as she landed, although she also remained in touch with the king; she was probably mindful of the fate of the rebels five years earlier. Her councillors were notified of the news, and William de la Beche, Robert de Cheddeworth and others were soon on their way to Wales in pursuit of Hugh le Despenser with every intention of joining the queen.[14]

It was taken for granted in the later Middle Ages that war and politics were the concern of men, and this was usually the case. Yet the involvement of women cannot be overlooked, and there were occasions when the part they played was of importance. The circumstances of medieval life and landholding meant that many women had considerable wealth and authority. They enjoyed luxury and magnificence, and participated fully in the lifestyle, entertainments and ideas of their time. For much of their lives they were subject to fathers and husbands, but even during their marriages they had family and public responsibilities to fulfil. These increased during widowhood and women

11 A. Goodman 'The countess and the rebels: Essex and a crisis in English society' *Transactions of the Essex Archaeological Society* third series II part 3 (1970) 267–9.

12 F.M. Powicke *Henry III and the Lord Edward* (2 vols) Oxford 1947 II 707–8.

13 *Calendar of Close Rolls 1327–30* 590; ibid. *1330–33* 179, 182, 333, 553, 563; ibid. *1337–9* 302, 573. *Calendar of Fine Rolls 1327–37* 308, 344.

14 Jenkinson 'Mary de Sancto Paulo' 411. PRO E101/91/11 m. 1; 91/12 m. 1d, 2d, 3, 3d.

showed then that they had the ability and determination to carry
out their duties successfully. Despite the sparse references to
noblewomen in the chronicles they had an important part to
play in the society of late medieval England.

GLOSSARY OF TERMS

advowson The right of patronage over parish churches and certain religious houses; the right to appoint the incumbent of the parish church, and to approve the appointment of the head of the religious house.

affinity The group of men who received fees and liveries from a lord was known as his affinity.

aids The vassal owed money payments to his lord, as laid down in Magna Carta in 1215, for the knighting of the lord's eldest son, the first marriage of his eldest daughter, and the ransoming of the lord's person.

alienation of lands The granting of lands to another family.

attainder and forfeiture Forfeiture involved the loss of lands by rebels to the Crown; in the fifteenth century acts of attainder against rebels were passed by parliament and included provisions for forfeiture.

commission of oyer and terminer One of the judicial commissions issued by the Crown to hear and determine criminal cases.

dower The land to which the noblewoman was entitled after the death of her husband according to feudal custom; it amounted to one-third of his land.

enfeoffment The grant of land by a lord to his vassal in return for the vassal's service. The grants made after the Norman Conquest were usually in return for the service of a certain number of knights in the lord's contingent sent to the king's army. This is why the vassal's land is usually referred to in terms of a number of knights' fees.

entail   The grant of land to a named person and a specified line of heirs. This contrasts with the **fee simple** where inheritance was based on primogeniture.

escheator   The royal official responsible for lands which came into the king's hands. He was responsible for taking the inquisitions *post mortem* which contained descriptions of the lands held by a lord on the day of his death and which also named the heir or heirs.

essoin   An excuse for not appearing in court to defend an action on the day appointed.

feodary   An official in charge of the feudal business concerning the vassals of an **honour** (a group of demesne manors and knights' fees held by a particular lord).

feoffee   Many lords conveyed parts of their estates to feoffees who held them for a named beneficiary. This device was used to prevent lands falling into the hands of the Crown if an heir succeeded who was under the age of twenty-one.

homage and fealty   The ceremony which bound the vassal to his lord; the vassal knelt before the lord and swore to be loyal to him.

honour court   All vassals owed suit to their lord's honour court; they were supposed to attend its meetings, usually every three weeks. In fact, few did so in the later Middle Ages.

hundred   The hundred was a subdivision of the county and had its own court. Some hundreds were held by lords rather than by the king and are known as **private hundreds**.

jointure   Land settled jointly on husband and wife which the wife would continue to hold after the death of her husband.

leet jurisdiction   The right of the lord to hold the court leet which held the **view of frankpledge** and dealt with petty offences. (All men had to belong to groups known as tithings, which were responsible for their members' good behaviour, and the tithings were checked at the view of frankpledge.)

probate   The proving of a will before ecclesiastical officials.

quitclaim   The release of a title or claim to an estate.

quo warranto pleas Pleas initiated by Edward I to establish whether lords had a right to the judicial privileges which they claimed.

relief Payment made by a vassal on succeeding to land at the rate laid down by Magna Carta in 1215 of £5 per knight's fee.

return of writs Some lords had the right of carrying out the king's orders, as contained in his writs, on their estates. This privilege enabled them to exclude the sheriff from their lands.

valor The document recording the valuation of estates.

Welshries In Welsh lordships, the areas, mostly in the uplands, which only had Welsh tenants were known as Welshries. These areas were often in the charge of officials known as **bedels**; hence they were also called **bedelries**.

GENERAL BIBLIOGRAPHY

Introduction

Work on the late medieval nobility owes much to K.B. McFarlane *The nobility of later medieval England* Oxford 1973. A more recent study is C. Given-Wilson *The English nobility in the late Middle Ages: the fourteenth-century political community* London 1987. Books and articles on individual families include information on noblewomen, e.g. M. Altschul *A baronial family in medieval England: the Clares, 1217–1314* Baltimore 1965; M. Aston *Thomas Arundel. A study of church life in the reign of Richard II* Oxford 1967; F.R. Fairbank 'The last earl of Warenne and Surrey and the distribution of his possessions' *Yorkshire Archaeological Journal* XIX *(1907) 193–264*; J.S. Hamilton *Piers Gaveston earl of Cornwall, 1307–12* Detroit 1988; M.W. Labarge *Simon de Montfort* London 1962; J.R. Maddicott *Thomas of Lancaster, 1307–22* Oxford 1970; J.R.S. Phillips *Aymer de Valence, earl of Pembroke, 1307–24. Baronial politics in the reign of Edward II* Oxford 1972; C. Rawcliffe *The Staffords, earls of Stafford and dukes of Buckingham 1394–1521* Cambridge 1978; C. Richmond 'Thomas Lord Morley (d. 1416) and the Morleys of Hingham' *Norfolk Archaeology* XXXIX (1984–6) 1–12; R. Somerville *History of the duchy of Lancaster* (2 vols) I *1265–1603* London 1953.

A number of works on the gentry include consideration of wives and widows: H.S. Bennett *The Pastons and their England: studies in an age of transition* Cambridge 2nd edn. 1932; C. Carpenter 'The fifteenth-century English gentry and their estates' *Gentry and lesser nobility in late medieval Europe* ed. M. Jones Gloucester 1986 36–60; C. Richmond *The Paston family in the fifteenth century. The first phase* Cambridge 1990; S.M. Wright *The Derbyshire gentry in the fifteenth century* Derbyshire Record Society VIII (1983).

Articles on particular noblewomen cover many aspects of their lives: R.E. Archer 'The estates and finances of Margaret of Brotherton, *c.* 1320–1399' *Historical Research* LX (1987) 264–80; H. Jenkinson 'Mary de Sancto Paulo, foundress of Pembroke College, Cambridge' *Archaeologia* LXXXVI (1915) 401–46; M. Jones and M. Underwood 'Lady Margaret Beaufort, 1443–1509' *History Today* XXXV (August 1985) 23–30.

Research into women's history has burgeoned in recent years. For a general survey, see S. Shahar *The fourth estate. A history of women in the Middle Ages* trans. C. Galai London 1983. E. Ennen *The medieval woman* trans. E. Jephcott Oxford 1989 concentrates on women in European towns but there is some information on the nobility. There have been several volumes of essays dealing with particular aspects of women's history, e.g. *Medieval women* ed. D. Baker Studies in Church History Subsidia 1 Oxford 1978; *Medieval women and the sources of medieval history* ed. J.T. Rosenthal Athens Georgia 1990; *The role of women in the Middle Ages* ed. R.T. Morewedge London 1975; *Women of the medieval world. Essays in honour of J.H. Mundy* eds. J. Kirshner and S.F. Wemple Oxford 1985.

Of the sources, the Nelson Medieval Classics and Oxford Medieval Texts issue chronicles with the Latin text and English translation, e.g. *Vita Edwardi Secundi* ed. N. Denholm-Young London 1957; *The Westminster Chronicle* eds. L.C. Hector and B.F. Harvey Oxford 1982. For collections of letters, see *The Stonor letters and papers, 1290–1483* (2 vols) ed. C.L. Kingsford Camden Society third series XXIX, XXX (1919); and *Paston letters and papers of the fifteenth century* ed. N. Davis (2 vols) Oxford 1971–6. Christine de Pisan *The treasure of the city of ladies or the book of the three virtues* trans. S. Lawson is issued by Penguin Classics Harmondsworth 1985.

Chapter 1: Marriage

The best recent surveys on medieval marriage are C.N.L. Brooke *The medieval idea of marriage* Oxford 1989; J.A. Brundage *Law, sex and Christian society in medieval Europe* Chicago 1987; G. Duby *The knight, the lady and the priest. The making of modern marriage in medieval France* trans. B. Bray Harmondsworth 1983. Useful articles include: K. Dockray 'Why did fifteenth-century English gentry marry?: the Pastons, Plumptons and Stonors reconsidered' *Gentry and lesser nobility in late medieval Europe* ed. M. Jones Gloucester 1986 61–80; A.S. Haskell 'The Paston women on marriage in fifteenth-century England' *Viator* IV (1973) 459–71; J.R. Lander

'Marriage and politics in the fifteenth century: the Nevilles and the Wydevilles' *Bulletin of the Institute of Historical Research* xxxvi (1963) 119–52; R.C. Palmer 'Contexts of marriage in medieval England: evidence from the king's court circa 1300' *Speculum* LIX (1984) 42–67; J.T. Rosenthal 'Aristocratic marriage and the English peerage, 1350–1500: social institution and personal bond' *Journal of Medieval History* x (1984) 181–94; M.M. Sheehan 'The influence of canon law on the property rights of married women in England' *Medieval Studies* xxv (1963) 109–24; M.M. Sheehan 'Choice of marriage partner in the Middle Ages: development and mode of application of a theory of marriage' *Studies in Medieval and Renaissance History* new series i (1978) 1–33; J.A.F. Thomson ' "The well of grace": Englishmen and Rome in the fifteenth century' *The Church, politics and patronage in the fifteenth century* ed. R.B. Dobson Gloucester 1984 99–114; K.P. Wentersdorf 'The clandestine marriages of the Fair Maid of Kent' *Journal of Medieval History* v (1979) 203–31.

Chapter 2: The widow and her lands

The role of the executrix is examined by R. Archer and B. Ferme 'Testamentary procedure with special reference to the executrix' *Reading Medieval Studies* xv (1989) 3–34.

Dowagers are discussed by R.E. Archer 'Rich old ladies: the problem of late medieval dowagers' *Property and politics: essays in later medieval English history* ed. A. Pollard Gloucester 1984 15–35.

For treason and its effects see: J.G. Bellamy *The law of treason in the later Middle Ages* Cambridge 1970; J.R. Lander 'Attainder and forfeiture, 1453–1509' *Historical Journal* iv (1961) 119–51; C.D. Ross 'Forfeiture for treason in the reign of Richard ii' *English Historical Review* LXXI (1956) 560–75. For the activities of the younger Despenser in the 1320s see: N. Fryde *The tyranny and fall of Edward ii, 1321–6* Cambridge 1979; G.A. Holmes 'A protest against the Despensers, 1326' *Speculum* xxx (1955) 207–12.

Chapter 3: The household

The most recent general discussion of the subject is by K. Mertes *The English noble household, 1250–1600. Good governance and politic rule* Oxford 1988. There is a useful introduction to household accounts by J.M. Thurgood in *The account of the great household of Humphrey, first duke of Buckingham, for the year 1452–3* ed. M. Harris Camden Miscellany xxviii Camden Society fourth series xxix (1984). See also M.W. Labarge *A baronial household of the thirteenth century*

London 1965; C.D. Ross 'The household accounts of Elizabeth Berkeley, countess of Warwick, 1420–1' *Transactions of the Bristol and Gloucestershire Archaeological Society* LXX (1951) 81–105, and C.D. Ross *The estates and finances of Richard Beauchamp earl of Warwick (1382–1439)* Dugdale Society Occasional Papers 12 (1956).

Chapter 4: Lifestyle and travel

On lifestyle: R. Barber and J. Barker *Tournaments, jousts, chivalry and pageants in the Middle Ages* Woodbridge 1989; C. Dyer *Standards of living in the later Middle Ages. Social change in England c. 1200–1520* Cambridge 1989; *English court culture in the later Middle Ages* eds. V.J. Scattergood and J.W. Sherborne London 1983; M. Girouard *Life in the English country house* New Haven 1978; B.A. Henisch *Fast and feast. Food in medieval society* Pennsylvania and London 1976; W.E. Mead *The English medieval feast* London 1931; S.M. Newton *Fashion in the age of the Black Prince. A study of the years 1340–1365* Woodbridge 1980; J.T. Rosenthal *Nobles and the noble life, 1295–1500* London 1976; J. Vale *Edward III and chivalry. Chivalric society and its context, 1270–1350* Woodbridge 1982; E.M. Veale *The English fur trade in the later Middle Ages* Oxford 1966; M. Wood *The English medieval house* London 1965.

On travel: J.J. Jusserand *English wayfaring life in the Middle Ages* trans. L. Toulmin Smith 8th edn London 1891. N. Ohler *The medieval traveller* trans. C. Hillier Woodbridge 1989 discusses conditions of travel and gives various descriptions of journeys. For roads see: B.P. Hindle 'The road network of medieval England and Wales' *Journal of Historical Geography* II (1976) 207–21; F.M. Stenton 'The road system of medieval England' *Economic History Review* VII (1936) 1–21 and *Preparatory to Anglo-Saxon England* ed. D.M. Stenton Oxford 1970 234–52. The household on the move is discussed by G. Stretton 'The travelling household in the later Middle Ages' *Journal of the British Archaeological Association* new series XL (1935) 75–103.

Chapter 5: Children, kinsmen and friends

The position and training of children are examined by P. Ariès *Centuries of childhood* trans. R. Baldick London 1962; N. Orme *From childhood to chivalry. The education of the English kings and aristocracy 1066–1530* London 1984; S. Shahar *Childhood in the Middle Ages* London 1990; R.V. Turner 'Eleanor of Aquitaine and her children: an inquiry into medieval family attachment' *Journal of Medieval History* XIV (1988) 321–35.

Chapter 6: Estates and revenue

For general background: J.L. Bolton *The medieval English economy 1150–1500* London 1980; J. Hatcher *Plague, population and the English economy 1348–1530* London 1977; E. Miller and J. Hatcher *Medieval England – rural society and economic change 1086–1348* London 1978.

The estates of Isabella de Forz are examined in N. Denholm-Young 'The Yorkshire estates of Isabella de Fortibus' *Yorkshire Archaeological Journal* XXXI (1934) 388–420; N. Denholm-Young *Seignorial administration in England* Oxford 1937; M. Mate 'Profit and productivity of the estates of Isabella de Forz (1260–92)' *Economic History Review* second series XXXIII (1980) 326–34. The estates of Elizabeth de Burgh are discussed by G.A. Holmes *The estates of the higher nobility in fourteenth-century England* Cambridge 1957; information about Irish estates is given by T.E. McNeill *Anglo-Norman Ulster. The history and archaeology of an Irish barony, 1177–1400* Edinburgh 1980, and R. Frame *English lordship in Ireland 1318–61* Oxford 1982. For further information on other Welsh and Irish estates see R.R. Davies *Lordship and society in the March of Wales, 1282–1400* Oxford 1978 and R. Frame *English lordship in Ireland, 1318–61* Oxford 1982.

For consideration of baronial incomes see: R.R. Davies 'Baronial accounts, incomes and arrears in the later Middle Ages' *Economic History Review* second series XXI (1968) 211–29; H. L. Gray 'Incomes from land in England in 1436' *English Historical Review* XLIX (1934) 607–39; T.B. Pugh and C.D. Ross 'The English baronage and the income tax of 1436' *Bulletin of the Institute of Historical Research* XXVI (1953) 1–28; C.D. Ross and T.B. Pugh 'Materials for the study of baronial incomes in fifteenth-century England' *Economic History Review* second series VI (1953–4) 185–94.

Chapter 7: Lordship and patronage

The most recent studies on the developments in lordship are J. M.W. Bean *From lord to patron: lordship in late medieval England* Manchester 1989; P.R. Coss 'Bastard feudalism revised' *Past and Present* no. 125 (1989) 27–64; S.L. Waugh 'Tenure to contract: lordship and clientage in thirteenth-century England' *English Historical Review* CI (1986) 811–39. A study of the men and women of the Paston family has been made by P. Maddern 'Honour among the Pastons: gender and integrity in fifteenth-century English provincial society' *Journal of Medieval History* XIV (1988) 357–71.

Chapter 8: Religious practice

For general background, J. Catto 'Religion and the English nobility in the later fourteenth century' *History and Imagination. Essays in honour of H.R. Trevor-Roper* eds. H. Lloyd-Jones, V. Pearl and B. Worden London 1981.

On private devotion and the possession of books see C.A.J. Armstrong 'The piety of Cicely, duchess of York: a study in late medieval culture' *England, France and Burgundy in the fifteenth century* London 1983 135–56; J. Backhouse *Books of hours* The British Library London 1985; C. Richmond 'Religion and the fifteenth-century English gentleman' *The Church, politics and patronage in the fifteenth century* ed. R.B. Dobson Gloucester 1984 193–208; J. Sumption *Pilgrimage. An image of medieval religion* London 1975.

The implications of the ideas on purgatory and the foundation of chantries have been studied by J. Le Goff *The birth of purgatory* trans. A. Goldhammer Aldershot 1984; J.T. Rosenthal *The purchase of paradise. Gift giving and the aristocracy, 1307–1485* London 1972; M. Rubin *Charity and community in medieval Cambridge* Cambridge 1987; K.L. Wood-Legh *Perpetual chantries in Britain* Cambridge 1965.

On religious houses for women see: A.F.C. Bourdillon *The order of Minoresses in England* Manchester 1926; E. Power *Medieval English nunneries c. 1275–1535* Cambridge 1922; S. Raban *Mortmain legislation and the English Church, 1279–1500* Cambridge 1982.

The patronage of the men and women of a particular noble family has been examined by M. A. Hicks 'Piety and lineage in the Wars of the Roses: the Hungerford experience' *Kings and nobles in the later Middle Ages. A tribute to Charles Ross* eds. R.A. Griffiths and J. Sherborne Gloucester 1986 90–108; M.A. Hicks 'The piety of Margaret, Lady Hungerford (d. 1478)' *Journal of Ecclesiastical History* xxxviii (1987) 19–38.

There have been a number of recent studies on the medieval colleges at Oxford and Cambridge: A.B. Cobban *The medieval English universities: Oxford and Cambridge to c. 1500* Aldershot 1988; D.R. Leader *A history of the university of Cambridge* I *The university to 1546* Cambridge 1988; *The history of the university of Oxford* ed. T.H. Aston (in progress) I *The early Oxford schools* ed. J.I. Catto Oxford 1984.

For death and funerals see P. Ariès *The hour of our death* trans. H. Weaver Harmondsworth 1981; T.S.R. Boase *Death in the Middle Ages* London 1972.

INDEX

The following abbreviations have been used: css = countess; ct = count; d = died (dates of death are only given to distinguish members of a family with the same Christian name and title); dk = duke; dr = daughter; dss = duchess; e = earl; k = king; pr = prince; s = son; sr = sister; w = wife.

INDEX

57, 74, 77, 104, 116, 124, 141,
155, 166, 167, 169
Edward IV k of England, 18, 145
Edward pr of Wales (Black Prince),
15, 36–7, 74, 78, 104, 105
Eleanor of Castile w of Edward I, 146
Ereswell, Piers de, 55, 157
Essex, 18, 21, 35, 91, 105, 106, 108,
112, 119, 122, 123, 130, 131, 140,
141, 166, 168
earls of, 18
Everdon, William, 136
Ewelme, Oxon, 163
Eynesham, Robert de, 63, 64

Farleigh, Hungerford Somerset, 152
Fastolf, John, 18
Fauconberg, Joan, 22
Felstede, Richard de, 84
Ferrers
Robert e of Derby, 43
Thomas, 21
Ferrers of Groby
Henry de, 18, 48, 99
Isabella de Verdun w of Henry de,
18, 42, 48, 99–100, 139
Margaret Ufford w of William de,
18, 100
William de, 18, 100
Fife, Joan de Clare w of (1) Duncan e
of, (2) Gervase Avenel, 41
Finchingfield, Essex, 148
Fitz Alan
Alice dr of e Richard d 1376, 29
Eleanor of Lancaster second w of e
Richard d 1376, 31
Isabella Despenser first w of e
Richard d 1376, 31
John e of Arundel, 116
Margaret dr of e Richard d 1376,
26
Richard e of Arundel d 1376, 12,
26, 29, 31, 36
Richard e of Arundel d 1397,
168–9
FitzHugh, Elizabeth Grey w of
Henry, 80, 101, 145, 151–2, 162
Fitz Ralph, William, 131
Fitz Simond, Richard, 131
Fitzwalter

Alice w of (1) Warin del Isle (2)
Robert d 1326, 146
family, 141
Joan de Multon w of Robert d
1328, 105, 105n, 139
John, 35
Robert d 1326, 140, 146
Fladbury, Nicholas de, 161
Forde, John atte, 64
Fobbing, Essex, 61
Forz
Isabella de, css of Devon and lady
of Isle of Wight w of William ct
of Aumale, 43, 97, 102–3, 109,
110–11, 112, 114, 116–17, 120,
129, 136, 138, 169
William de, ct of Aumale, 109
Foulsham, Norfolk, 125
Framlingham, Suffolk, 60, 122, 147
Freville, Margaret, 37

Gaveston, Piers e of Cornwall, 4, 19,
42, 94, 96
Joan dr of Piers, 94, 96
see also Audley
Gildesburgh, John, 133
Glemsford, Suffolk, 55
Gloucester, 61
abbey, 89
abbot, 89, 90, 94
earl Robert, 153
honour of, 132, 153
Gloucestershire, 61, 86, 87, 112, 122,
123, 132, 139
Godstow abbey, 158
Goldyngham, John, 106
Goodrich, Herefs, 46, 71, 85–6, 87,
88, 89, 90
Gough, John, 55, 59
Gransden, Great, Hunts, 158
Gravesend, Kent, 86
Grey of Rotherfield, John de, 41

Halstead, Stansted in, Essex, 18
Hampshire, 123, 139
Harling, Guy, 60–1
Harwich Essex, 121–2
Hastings
John, 46
John, 65

John de, e of Surrey d 1347, 3, 23,
32, 36–7
Warre, John la, 138
Warwickshire, 37, 112, 123
Waterbeach, Cambs, 86, 107
abbey, 155, 156
Watton, Norfolk, 90
Waverley, abbot of, 104
Wauton, John de, 115, 140–1, 148
Wenlock, Giles de, 55
Westacre, Norfolk, 90
Westminster, 87
abbey, 34, 94, 152
Wexford, 17
Wigmore abbey, 5, 94
Willoughby, Hugh, 37
Wiltshire, 123, 139
Wimbish, Essex, 140, 148
Winchelsea, Sussex, 78, 89
Windsor, 74, 105
Wingfield, Suffolk, 35, 96

Wintney priory, 104
Wisbech, Cambs, 55, 59, 102
Witlesey, William de archdeacon of
Huntingdon, 137
Worcester, 62, 86, 146
Wotton, Gloucs, 75, 87
Writtle, Essex, 60
Wynterton, John de, 63–4

Yarmouth, Norfolk, 61
York, 47, 114
York
Cicely Neville w of dk Richard, 17,
72, 145
Edward dk of, 124
family, 22
Richard dk of, 17, 21

Zouche
William de la, 41, 153
Alan la, 140